The German Question
since 1919

The German Question since 1919

An Analysis with Key Documents

STEFAN WOLFF

PERSPECTIVES ON THE TWENTIETH CENTURY
Edward R. Beauchamp, Series Adviser

Westport, Connecticut
London

943.087
W85g

Cau

Library of Congress Cataloging-in-Publication Data

Wolff, Stefan, 1969–
    The German question since 1919 : an analysis with key documents / Stefan Wolff.
        p. cm.—(Perspectives on the twentieth century, ISSN 1538–9626)
    Includes bibliographical references and index.
    ISBN 0–275–97269–0 (alk. paper)
        1. Germany—Politics and government—20th century—Sources. 2. Germany—Foreign
    relations—1918—Sources. 3. Political culture—Germany—History—20th
    century—Sources. I. Title. II. Series.
    DD232.5.W65   2003
    943.087—dc21   2002032974

British Library Cataloguing in Publication Data is available.

Library of Congress Catalog Card Number: 2002032974
ISBN: 0–275–97269–0
ISSN: 1538–9626

First published in 2003

Praeger Publishers, 88 Post Road West, Westport, CT 06881
An imprint of Greenwood Publishing Group, Inc.
www.praeger.com

Printed in the United States of America

The paper used in this book complies with the
Permanent Paper Standard issued by the National
Information Standards Organization (Z39.48–1984).

10 9 8 7 6 5 4 3 2 1

Contents

Series Foreword

Whoever first coined the phrase "When the siécle hit the fin" described the twentieth century perfectly! The past century was arguably a century of intellectual, physical, and emotional violence unparalleled in world history. As Haynes Johnson of *The Washington Post* has pointed out in his *The Best of Times* (2001), "since the first century, 149 million people have died in major wars; 111 million of those deaths occurred in the twentieth century. War deaths per population soared from 3.2 deaths per 1,000 in the sixteenth century to 44.4 per 1,000 in the twentieth."[1] Giving parameters to the twentieth century, however, is no easy task. Did it begin in 1900 or 1901? Was it, as in historian Eric Hobsbawm's words, a "short twentieth century" that did not begin until 1917 and end in 1991?[2] Or was it more accurately the "long twentieth century," as Giovanni Arrighi argued in *The Long Twentieth Century: Money, Power, and the Origins of Our Times?*[3] Strong cases can be made for all of these constructs, and it is each reader's prerogative to come to his or her own conclusion.

Whatever the conclusion, however, there is a short list of people, events, and intellectual currents found in the period between the nineteenth and twenty-first centuries that is, indeed, impressive in scope.

There is little doubt that the hopes represented by the Paris Exhibition of 1900 represented the mood of the time—a time of optimism, even utopian expectations, in much of the so-called civilized world (which was the only world that counted in those days). Many saw the fruits of the Industrial Revolution, the application of science and technology to everyday life, as having the potential to greatly enhance life, at least in the West.

In addition to the theme of progress, the power of nationalism in conflicts—not only over territory, but also over economic advantage and intellectual dominance—came to characterize the last century. It was truly a century of war, from the "little" wars of the Balkans and colonial conflicts of the early 1900s to the "Great" War of 1914–1918 that resulted in unprecedented conflict over the remainder of the century.

Every century has its "great" as well as "infamous" individuals, most often men, although that too would begin to change as the century drew to a close. Great political figures such as Lenin, Trotsky, Stalin, Hitler, Mussolini, Churchill, the two Roosevelts, de Gaulle, Adenauer, Mahatma Gandhi, Mao Tse-tung, Ho Chi Minh, and others were joined in the last part of the century by tough competent women like Golda Meir, Indira Gandhi, Margaret Thatcher, and scores of others who took the reigns of power for the first time.

A quick listing of some major events of the century includes World War I, the Russian Revolution, the rise of fascism, the Great Depression of the 1930s, the abdication of Edward VIII, Pearl Harbor and World War II, the unleashing of atomic bombs on Hiroshima and Nagasaki, the long Indochina War, the Cold War, the rise of nationalism (with an increase in nation-states from about fifty to almost two hundred), the establishment of Israel, the triumph of the free market, an increasingly strident battle between religious fanaticism and secular preferences, and on and on. At the same time that these events occurred, there was a great creative flourishing of mass entertainment (especially television and the Internet), not to mention important literary, dramatic, cinematic, and musical contributions of all kinds.

These elements incorporate some of the subject matter of this new series focusing on "Perspectives on the Twentieth Century," which strives to illuminate the last century. The editor actively seeks out manuscripts that deal with virtually any subject and with any part of our planet, bringing a better understanding of the twentieth century to readers. He is especially interested in subjects on "small" as well as "large" events and trends, including the role of sports in various societies, the impact of popular music on the social fabric, the contribution of film studies to our understanding of the twentieth century, and so on. The success of this series is largely dependent on the creativity and imagination of its authors.

Edward R. Beauchamp

NOTES

1. Haynes, Johnson, *The Best of Times: The Boom and Bust Years of America before and after Everything Changed* (New York: Harcourt, 2001), p. 3.

2. Eric Hobsbawm, *The Age of Extremes: A History of the World, 1917–1991* (New York: Pantheon, 1994).

3. Giovanni Arrighi, *The Long Twentieth Century: Money, Power, and the Origins of Our Times* (London: Verso, 1994).

Acknowledgments

In the following, I draw freely on my previous published and unpublished work on the subject matter, in particular *German Minorities in Europe: Ethnic Identity and Cultural Belonging* and on *Coming Home to Germany? The Integration of Ethnic Germans from Central and Eastern Europe in the Federal Republic*, the latter of which I coedited with my colleague David Rock at Keele University. I am also relying on research, parts of which were published in *Disputed Territories: The Transnational Dynamics of Ethnic Conflict Settlement*. All three volumes were published between 2000 and 2002 by Berghahn Books in New York and Oxford.

I am indebted for insightful comments on earlier versions of this book to my friend and colleague Karl Cordell at the University of Plymouth, with whom I share a long-standing interest in the German question in the twentieth century and beyond. Thanks are also due to my colleagues at the University of Bath, for providing an enjoyable and stimulating working atmosphere over the past three years—in particular to Ingolfur Blühdorn and to Mark Gilbert, who is now at the University of Trento. For facilitating the publication of this book and including it in this series, I am also grateful to Edward Beauchamp and Heather Staines.

Finally, the book would not have been possible without the constant support and encouragement of Lucy Marcus. She knows how much I owe and appreciate her.

Chapter 1

The Nature of the German Question and Its Historical Origins

The distinction of the German from all other European nations
is founded in nature. Based in a common language and in a common national character, which unite the Germans, the latter are
separated from the former.

—Johann Gottlieb Fichte (1834)

The history of Europe from about the time of the French Revolution
in the late eighteenth century onward to the present could be told as
a history of different larger and smaller national questions, many of
them linked to one another, most of them at some point causing conflicts and not seldom wars, and all of them, in one way or another,
related to questions of nationhood and territory. In this sense, the German question is not very different from, say, the Russian or Albanian
question. However, what distinguishes it from any other national question in European history is the sheer extremes to which the German
question has driven the continent, and on two occasions ultimately
the entire world. This alone makes it a worthwhile subject of study
for a variety of scholarly disciplines ranging from history to anthro-
pology and from psychology to political science, the latter of which

will be the predominant focus of this volume. Adopting a political-science perspective is not to claim that this approach is in any way superior to that of other disciplines in the social sciences or humanities. Rather, it is to set out the obvious limits and potential strengths of the subsequent examination.

What follows is not a social, cultural, or economic history; and it is not an in-depth analysis of psychological aspects or an anthropological study, either. It is first and foremost an analysis of the behavior of politically relevant elites, of the decisions they made, and of the consequences that these decisions had. Such a focus may seem narrow and one-sided, even limiting. But the great advantage that it offers is that it allows concentrating on the very currency of politics—power and the use and pursuit of it—that is essential in understanding the complex national and international dynamics involved in the German question. It also provides a good starting point from which to tackle the subject matter—namely, to identify the elites that were politically relevant for the many developments related to the German question. In other words, before it can be analyzed, the German question has to be defined—and this is where things begin to get complicated. For a single German question as such has never existed; rather, a multitude of issues have arisen from a fundamental problem in European history, namely, the fact that the territory of any German state or states never included the entirety of all members of the ethnically defined German nation. A unified German state came into existence only in the second half of the nineteenth century, stretching from Alsace and Lorraine in today's France all the way across Central Europe to East Prussia—known today as District Kaliningrad, and as such part of the Russian Federation. Although this German state included some sixty million Germans at the time, large groups remained outside.

This was most obviously the case with the Germans in the Austro-Hungarian Empire, who, although not a majority in numerical terms and widely dispersed outside the territory of today's Republic of Austria as well, played a dominant role in the empire. A third group of Germans, who hardly ever figured in the national or territorial calculations of German nationalists, were the Germans of Switzerland. They had joined in a confederal state with three, significantly smaller, other ethnic groups (of French, Italian, and Romansch origin) several hundred years earlier. Following a short civil war–like conflict in 1848, the Swiss federation as it exists today was formed. The only significant group of ethnic Germans living outside the confines of these three states were those Germans who had emigrated to Russia since the middle of the eighteenth century and lived there as colonists, enjoying specific privileges granted by imperial decree.

Quite clearly, the German situation, or rather the situation of Germans, is no exception in this respect. The demarcation of borders in Europe, and particularly in Central and Eastern Europe, happened according to the interests of the Great Powers rather than according to the settlement patterns of ethnic groups. The gradual withdrawal from Europe of the Ottoman Empire since the late nineteenth century and the dissolution of the Austro-Hungarian Empire in the early twentieth century created a series of new states, hardly any of which either was homogenous or contained within its boundaries all members of the ethnic group for which it was named. The settlement patterns of diverse ethnic groups that had grown over centuries of imperial hegemony in Central and Eastern Europe would, at best, have made it extremely difficult to create states in which political and ethnic boundaries coincided. The fact that borders were established in accordance with the interests of the Great Powers rendered any such attempt impossible. In addition, even though a Romantic version of nationalism had become a powerful ideology in the region, not all ethnic groups had well-established national identities in the sense of expressing a preference for their own or any specific state at all; instead, many of them had developed strong regional identities that were, in the first instance, not focused on ethnicity. Nevertheless, nationalism had made a tremendous impact on interethnic relations in the region, and the three waves of state "creation"—at the Congress of Berlin in 1878, after the first and second Balkan wars in 1912–13, and after the First World War—left their mark in Central and Eastern Europe by establishing ethnically plural states whose constituent ethnic groups were ill at ease with each other.

The Romantic conception of the nation throughout Central and Eastern Europe additionally complicated matters as it defined the nation as based on shared cultural, linguistic, and customary traits within a geographic and demographic context in which migration, colonization, and conquest had shaped the ethnic composition of the four empires dominating the region more than anything else. The Russian, German, Ottoman, and Austro-Hungarian Empires were truly multi-national entities. The German Empire stood out among them as a late-comer, in the sense of building a state for its dominant national group. By the time the first German nation-state was founded in 1871, an understanding of what the German nation was had long existed. This leads us to a "first set" of German questions.

WHERE AND WHAT IS GERMANY?

This common way to paraphrase the German question is primarily about the nature and content of a German national identity, and thus a question that is primarily directed at the Germans and mostly asked by themselves. Yet at the same time, it also gives rise to broader considerations about Germany's place and role in European and world politics—considerations that have been made by Germany's neighbors, and that have, more often than not in the twentieth century, amounted to serious concerns for the security and stability of the European and international orders. From that perspective, the German question is also about how Germany can fit into any system of states without threatening, or being perceived as threatening by, its neighbors. Many answers have been given to this particular dimension of the German question—a loose confederation of states was the answer of the Congress of Vienna in 1815, a German nation-state excluding Austria that of 1871, a state truncated territorially and burdened by reparations that of the Peace Treaty of Versailles, an enlarged Germany that of the Munich Agreement of 1938, an occupied and subsequently divided state that of the Potsdam Agreement of 1945, and a unified Germany firmly integrated in NATO and the EU of 1990. With the exception of the latter (one hopes), none of these proposed solutions to the German question was stable, or even viable, in the long term, although the reasons for the eventual collapses of such settlements varied considerably over time. What the settlements all had in common was that they only partially addressed the complexity of the German question.

This complexity arises from the fact that the German question is a multidimensional phenomenon. It has been, and to some extent still is, foremost a political problem. As such, the German question has been about whether there should be one German nation-state or more, what the borders and internal political structures of such a state (or states) should be, with which methods it should be achieved, and what consequences this would have for Europe and the world (Geiss 1990: 22). At the same time, the German question is also a cultural problem— or more precisely, a problem of defining German culture and, related to this, of defining a German identity and thus determining who is German. Obviously, the cultural and the political dimensions of the German question have been inextricably linked, although in different ways through time. For example, while Austrians today have a distinctly Austrian (national) identity—one that is at least politically not a German identity—this was not the case at the time when the German Empire

Germany, 1871–1919

was founded in 1871, and even less so before, when a German national identity, in a political sense, as such hardly existed.

For several hundred years, "Germanness" had been defined, if at all, primarily in cultural terms. A German identity, inasmuch as it existed, had been one of an ethnocultural nature relying on language, custom, religion, and traditions to set it apart from other identities. Ironically, Germanness became politically significant only after the collapse of the Holy Roman Empire of the German Nation in 1806, but it proved a powerful tool of mobilizing "Germans" in the Napoleonic Wars. This "political nationalization" of Germans was one manifestation of a wider European development. While for hundreds of years ethnocultural differences between people(s) had been neither a problem nor a source of mobilization, it was with the arrival of nationalism as a political ideology and the emergence of the nation-state as the primary principle of organizing people into political units and regulating the relations between these units that ethnicity began to matter as a factor in domestic and international politics. Naturally, nationalist ideologies clashed with each other as demands for the creation of nation-states resulted in the same territories being claimed by different aspiring nations. This is where many of the roots of the various national questions in Central and Eastern Europe lie, and consequently that of the German question, too.

The question "What and where is Germany?" is also a question about who is German. For most of the twentieth century, German citizenship was determined according to descent. The 1913 *Reichs- und Staatsangehörigkeitsgesetz* (Citizenship Act) determined that only descendants of Germans could be German citizens. This was a deliberately chosen adoption of the principle of *ius sanguinis* in order to promote and preserve the ethnic tradition of the German nation-state and to maintain links with ethnic Germans outside the political boundaries of the German nation-state. The complexity of this issue is reflected in the difficulty that exists in finding proper English terms for the three key concepts of German legal and political thought in this respect: *Staatsangehörigkeit* (defined as the formal legal relationship between citizen and state), *Staatsbürgerschaft* (defined as the participatory membership in a polity or commonwealth), and *Volkszugehörigkeit* (defined in terms of ethnocultural identity) (Brubaker 1992: 50f.). Until the changes in German citizenship law at the end of the twentieth century, this meant that a German ethnocultural identity normally was an essential condition for full political participation. In turn, the link established between *Volkszugehörigkeit*, on the one hand, and *Staatsbürgerschaft* and *Staatsangehörigkeit*, on the other, was problematic inasmuch as it gave rise to issues of potentially conflicting loyalties for ethnic Germans who lived outside any German nation-state.

The period between the two world wars is probably the best-documented example of how such conflicting loyalties were instrumentalized and how their alleged implications eventually became self-fulfilling prophecies. The rise of the Nazis in Germany and the way in, and purpose for, which they established links with ethnic Germans across Europe was perceived as a threat by many governments in Europe. Their response was to curtail German minorities in their rights. This in turn encouraged ever larger sections within the minorities to put their hopes in Hitler, as was most obviously the case with the Sudeten Germans, but to a lesser extent also with German minorities elsewhere in Central and Eastern Europe. Prior to the expulsions of most members of these minorities after the Second World War in 1945–50, this had the worst consequences for the German minority in Russia, whose members were collectively deported to Siberia and Central Asia. Even though the ethnonational foundations of *Staatsangehörigkeit* and

Staatsbürgerschaft had indirectly had such disastrous consequences, it was precisely some of these consequences (namely, the expulsions and the discrimination against the remaining members of German minorities in Central and Eastern Europe) that made it apparently impossible and politically undesirable to change German law in this respect, as it would have deprived the ethnic Germans emigrating to the Federal Republic from Central and Eastern Europe after 1950 of their entitlement to German citizenship.

Thus, talking about the complexity and multidimensionality of the German question also means to acknowledge the (long-term) link between domestic and international dimensions and between political and ethnic aspects. In different ways, this link has persisted throughout the existence of the German question, particularly during the interwar period and since the end of the Second World War. Yet post-1945 developments can be understood properly only on the basis of the historical developments that "created" ethnic Germans outside Germany.

Thus, before turning to an examination of the German question in the second half of the twentieth century, it is necessary to take a further step back and explore the origins of ethnic German minorities in Central and Eastern Europe and to trace the multiple developments to which their settlement across this part of the continent gave rise.

THE ORIGINS OF ETHNIC GERMANS IN CENTRAL AND EASTERN EUROPE

The fact that a large number of ethnic Germans lived, and still live, in many countries in Central and Eastern Europe has its reasons in three distinct, but often interrelated, processes—conquest and colonization, migration, and border changes. The latter is primarily a phenomenon of the twentieth century, connected most obviously with the peace settlements of Versailles and St. Germain in 1919 and, to a lesser extent, Trianon in 1920, and with the territorial and political reordering of Europe after 1945. The former two processes, in contrast, reach back into the twelfth century. In the Carpathian Mountains of today's Slovak Republic, for example, the first German settlers arrived in the middle of the twelfth century, invited by the Hungarian king Bela IV and local aristocrats because of their expertise as miners and vine farmers. As in the Banat region and Transylvania in today's Romania, where the first ethnic Germans arrived around the middle of the thirteenth century, the colonists enjoyed significant tax and other privileges, such as elected local officers and councils, market rights, and the right to property transactions (Marcus 2000). Similar processes happened in the twelfth and thirteenth centuries in Pommerania, East Brandenburg, Bohemia and Moravia, and Silesia, where local aristocrats were keen to have their vast lands colonized and developed. In the thirteenth century too, the Teutonic Order (Deutscher Ritterorden) conquered most of today's Baltic states—that is, Lithuania, Estonia, and Latvia, and East and West Prussia. Like the German colonists in other parts of Central and Eastern Europe, the Teutonic knights had been invited by local aristocrats, in this case the Polish prince Konrad of Masowia in 1225. They were charged with the task of subduing the non-Christian Baltic tribes, converting them and colonizing their lands; they were promised sovereignty in return for their services. Thus, parallel to the process of conquest between 1231 and 1283, the colonization of the conquered territories began with the settlement of German farmers, craftsmen, and merchants.

This first stage of colonization and conquest had come to an end in Central and Eastern Europe in the fifteenth century; relatively little happened for the next several hundred years. In southeastern Europe, this was mostly due to the fact that large parts of Hungary and almost all of the Balkans had been conquered by the Ottoman Empire by the middle of the sixteenth century. Yet with the withdrawal of the Ottomans from Hungary and some parts of the Balkans since the late seventeenth century, new opportunities for colonization arose; German settlers were recruited to settle in the Banat, in Slavonia, and in Hungary. The three so-called Swabian Tracks of 1722–26, 1763–73, and 1782–87 brought tens of thousands of Germans to areas that belong to today's Romania and Hungary and to the successor states of the former Yugoslavia. Toward the end of the eighteenth century, Germans also migrated to the Bukovina and in the early nineteenth century to Bessarabia and to the Dobrudja. As all these areas were part of the Habsburg Empire (since 1867, the Austro-Hungarian dual monarchy), German settlers were, and were perceived as, acting on behalf of the emperor. Alongside the colonization of undeveloped regions of the empire, they were also to represent the central power and ensure the preservation of the (multiethnic) empire.

The final stage of German settlements in Eastern Europe began in the middle of the eighteenth century in Russia. In 1762 and 1763, the Russian empress Catherine II issued two decrees that granted significant privileges to German settlers willing to colonize areas on the lower Volga River. By the end of the 1760s, more than twenty thousand colonists had settled in these areas as free farmers. They were exempted from tax for several years, were not drafted for military service, could use German as an administrative language, were allowed to establish German schools, and enjoyed religious freedom (Stricker 2000). A second wave of settlers arrived in the first half of the nineteenth century, settling on the coast of the Black Sea and in the Caucasus.

Thus, by the end of the nineteenth century ethnic Germans could be found in settlements across the German and Austro-Hungarian Empires as well as in Russia; however, in all the areas where they had arrived as colonists and were numerically in a minority position, their privileged status began to decline, and relations between them and other ethnic groups and nations began to become more tense. The reasons for these increasing tensions were many, and they differed across Central and Eastern Europe. Among the most prominent ones were the rise of competing doctrines of nationalism among different ethnic groups (which resulted, among other things, in demands for an end to political privileges based on membership in particular ethnic groups) and in the increasing appeal of the concept of popular sovereignty. To some extent, there was also growing competition for scarce economic resources.

With the exception of Russia, where ethnic Germans always had been in a minority position, their status of being members of the dominant ethnic group in the German and Austro-Hungarian Empires was revoked only at the end of the First World War. The peace settlements of Versailles and St. Germain resulted in significant changes in the political geography of Central and Eastern Europe. The breakup of the Austro-Hungarian Empire was confirmed, and with it the creation of several new states, all of which became host states of a number of ethnic minorities, including Germans. The size and political significance of these minorities differed vastly, and so did the treatment that they received at the hands of their new rulers. In post-Trianon Hungary and in the newly established Kingdom of Serbs, Croats, and Slovenes, there were only a few hundred thousand ethnic Germans, but in Romania they numbered almost a million. In Czechoslovakia there were more than three million ethnic Germans in 1919, a figure that made them the second-largest ethnic group in the country, after the Czechs but before the Slovaks and Hungarians. The German Empire too lost territories in Central and Eastern Europe. The so-called Polish Corridor, which gave Poland access to the Baltic Sea, separated East Prussia from the rest of the territory of the Weimar Republic and contained large numbers of Germans who had been nationals of the Second Empire before 1919. Upper Silesia was divided between Poland and Germany, leaving another significant ethnic German minority in Poland. In all, the territorial changes in Central and Eastern Europe after the end of World War I left approximately five million ethnic Germans in countries outside Germany and Austria, while another almost two million lived in various parts of the emerging Soviet Empire.

Thus, the settlement at the end of World War I had, in a typical fashion, addressed some aspects of the German question, ignored others, and created new ones. In the west the emphasis had been on securing territorial changes that would increase the defense capabilities of France and Italy. Placing Germany under unprecedented reparation payments and curtailing its industrial and military capacities was meant to prevent it from reemerging as a, if not the, major economic, political, and military power in Europe. In Central and Eastern Europe, the intentions were somewhat different. Here, the peace conference sought to establish a new order that would satisfy the demands of the multiple national movements for the creation of independent nation-states, while establishing a regime under the auspices of the League of Nations that could ensure that ethnic groups that were either not granted their own nation-state or would not live on its territory would be sufficiently protected. In addition, considerations about the "economic viability" of Poland and Czechoslovakia led to the territories of these new states being rather ill defined in terms of their ethnic composition. Thus, not only was a situation created in which any stable political and economic development in Germany was precluded almost from the outset, but revisionist politicians in Germany were also given plenty of ammunition to stir up domestic (and, for example, in 1938 even international) political support for their goals, while some members of the increasingly dissatisfied German minorities in many of the states in Central and Eastern Europe served as willing agents of destabilization in the region. The rise of Nazism in the Weimar Republic was one of the first signs, albeit hardly a direct consequence, that the settlement of 1919 had, if anything, exacerbated the German question as a problem of European and international security. From this perspective, the Second World War was nothing but the culmination of a development that had arisen from a badly conceived strategy to deal with a problem that, by then, had obviously not been understood in its entirety.

LESSONS LEARNED? POST-1945 APPROACHES TO THE GERMAN QUESTION AND THE FATE OF THE ETHNIC GERMANS IN CENTRAL AND EASTERN EUROPE

The failure of the peace settlement after the First World War, and the (partial) recognition of this failure, heavily influenced the approach to the German question during and after the 1940s. Equally important, however, were individual aspirations of the Allied powers, their conception of what precisely the German question was, and the relationship that they had with each other and with Germany.

Thus, the lessons learned from the interwar period were only one among many factors. Most crucially, the learning process had been highly selective. The occupation of Germany and the strict control of its political and economic processes by the Allies were two components of this learning process. Over the course of few years, their consequence was the division of Germany into two states, the development of very different political regimes in each of them, and their integration in the two opposing world systems during the ensuing Cold War. This revived an aspect of the German question in the twentieth century that politicians in Germany and Europe had not had to confront since the second half of the nineteenth century—German unification. The geopolitical reality of superpower dominance during the Cold War made the German question as a whole to some extent more easily manageable, if only by marginalizing it in the struggle for global dominance and the defense of spheres of interest.

Yet the most dramatic way in which lessons had been drawn from the failure to solve the German question in 1919 was the expulsion of more than ten million Germans from Central and Eastern Europe. This included some three million from Czechoslovakia, approximately seven million from territories that were annexed to Poland and the Soviet Union, and the rest from other countries in Central and Eastern Europe, primarily from Yugoslavia, Hungary, and Romania. It was the most dramatic episode of the learning process, because of the sheer magnitude of the migration it implied and because of the brutality with which it was carried out, particularly in the early months after the end of the war before the Allies reached a formal consensus on the "orderly and humane" transfer of ethnic Germans in the Potsdam Agreement of August 1945. Obviously, the expulsions have to be seen in the context of the Second World War. German warfare and occupation policy in Central and Eastern Europe had been excessively brutal, and many members of ethnic German minorities in the countries affected had played an active role in it. In addition, the forced migration of ethnic Germans had begun much earlier than 1945, although under a different pretext. From the late 1930s onward the Nazis had initiated a massive resettlement program aimed at consolidating ethnic Germans in a German core territory consisting of Germany as it had existed since the Munich Agreement of 1938 (thus already including Austria and the Sudetenland) plus parts of occupied western Poland, which were systematically cleansed of any non-German population. This so-called *Heim-ins-Reich* policy affected approximately one million ethnic Germans before the end of the war, people who were resettled in western Poland on the basis of bilateral agreements with some states in Central and Eastern Europe and on the basis of unilateral decisions taken by Germany in occupied countries.

A third aspect that is worth mentioning is that the expulsion of ethnic Germans from Central and Eastern Europe did not only have a westward direction, toward occupied Germany. Many ethnic Germans were also deported to forced labor camps either within their host states or to the Soviet Union. Finally, forced migration also had an internal dimension. In the Soviet Union, ethnic Germans had been deported from the European territories of the country to Siberia and Central Asia at the beginning of the war in 1941, and they were not allowed to return to their traditional settlements after the end of the war. To a smaller degree, this also affected ethnic Germans who were allowed to remain in Czechoslovakia.

The forced migration of more than ten million Germans to occupied Germany at the end of the Second World War added an entirely new dimension to the German question. The integration of ethnic Germans who, whatever their individual degrees of guilt, had experienced a traumatic uprooting into the economic, social, and political process(es) of a collapsed country occupied by powers whose relationship toward one another evolved very quickly into a Cold War, was by no means an easy task, let alone one for which any comparable historical precedent existed. This task was accomplished relatively successfully within the course of less than two decades. What it did not, and probably could not, accomplish was a coming to terms with the expulsion as part of German and European history. Despite the politicized rhetoric of the expellee organizations and their opponents inside and outside Germany, German society as a whole has never fully acknowledged the suffering of the expellees, nor has it been able to embrace the history and cultural traditions of former and still existing German minorities as part of a German cultural identity. This failure to acknowledge history for what it is—something that cannot be reversed but needs to be appreciated in order to prevent its repetition—has extended beyond Germany into Central and Eastern Europe, where the issue of the expulsions at the end of the Second World War could now threaten, or at least delay, the enlargement of the European Union. The inability of German postwar and postunification society to deal with the expulsions from the perspective of their impact (or lack thereof) on German identity has also meant that some of the expellees and their descendants persist in their own selective views of history, which almost completely shut out any events predating the expulsions. As such the expulsions and their aftermath constitute an almost classic example of the multidimensionality of the German question.

This is also true from the point of view that they, of course, did not solve the German question, perhaps did not even contribute to a solution. On the one hand, the expulsions created a small, and perhaps decreasing, but nevertheless vocal political group in Germany that has let no opportunity pass to call for a return to the Federal Republic of the former *Ostgebiete,* German territories that were annexed by Poland and the Soviet Union in 1945. The official representatives of the German expellees have since 1990 denounced these demands on various occasions, and support for this extreme position is less even than marginal. A larger segment, but again by no means a majority even among the expellees, has always insisted on the right to their homelands—that is, the right to return to the areas from which they were expelled after the Second World War. The problem here is not so much how serious these demands are or how many people support them but the perception that they created, and still create, in Poland and the Czech Republic, particularly, and that they can be used as welcome "proof" of German revisionism by nationalists and Euro-skeptics alike. From that perspective, too, the German question has not lost anything of its European and international relevance.

It is quite important to note that the expulsions, although occurring in unprecedented magnitude, were in fact selective. First, there were exceptions for those who had actively fought against the Nazis. These people were very few, and not even all of them were, or could be, protected from expulsion, nor were all of those who could have claimed exemption keen on staying behind. Second, some of those ethnic Germans who had intermarried were allowed to remain in their homeland, but again, many of them chose to emigrate either during the period of actual expulsions or in later years. Third, in Poland, a distinction was made between ethnic Germans who had had the citizenship of Germany before the war—that is, those who had lived in the territories placed under Polish control by the Soviet Union in 1945 (and confirmed at the Potsdam Conference of the Allies in July and August 1945) and so-called autochthonous Germans (those who had had Polish citizenship before the war). Ironically, together with some other distinctions, the decision about who was to be expelled from Poland was thus based on a Polish equivalent of the so-called *Volkslisten* of the Nazis, which had determined the degree of Germanness of ethnic Germans in Central and Eastern Europe. The fourth exception made was in many cases only a temporary one but explains why the expulsions were not completed before the end of the 1940s. Particularly for Poland and Czechoslovakia it was essential to guarantee the continued functioning of their economies. Germans had not only owned a number of factories, mines, etc., but were also needed as specialists to oversee the proper running of these enterprises. While farmers could be replaced relatively easily, although again not without causing disruptions, this was less the case with skilled workers, foremen, and engineers. Apart from such specialists, a number of ethnic Germans were also prevented from leaving but were sent to forced labor camps in their host countries as well as in the Soviet Union. Many of them spent up to five years in these camps and were released and expelled only in 1949.

The fact that the expulsions did not solve the German question is also illustrated by the fact that the "problem" of German minorities in Central and Eastern Europe persisted after 1950 and became an integral part of German foreign policy toward this region. Post-1950 emigration of ethnic Germans from Central and Eastern Europe had primarily to do with the continued discrimination that ethnic Germans were facing because of their ethnic identity, but partly also because of the general political and economic conditions in the Eastern Bloc. Consequently, over the course of half a century, German policy priorities in this respect have changed—from consistent attempts throughout the Cold War to arrange for as many ethnic Germans as possible to be allowed to emigrate to the Federal Republic of Germany, to more recent policies that aim at securing minority rights and decent living conditions for members of German minorities who still live in Central and Eastern Europe. Neither policy approach has been without difficulties. Until 1993, when changes in German legislation occurred, approximately 3.5 million ethnic Germans had resettled in the Federal Republic. About half of them had arrived between 1950 and 1987, mostly from Poland and Romania. Their integration had been as successful as that of the expellees. The other half arrived in the six-year period after 1987. Since the changes in German law in 1993, another half a million ethnic Germans have emigrated to the Federal Republic. Of them, almost two-thirds came from the successor states of the former Soviet Union. For the period since 1995, their share is a staggering 97 percent. Their integration has been far less successful, for a variety of reasons, including poor knowledge of German, occupational profiles that no longer fit the needs of the German economy, and the increasing xenophobia in German society. As with the expellees, this dimension of the German question is both a domestic and international one, and it raises political as well as cultural questions about what and where Germany is.

A RESOLUTION OF THE GERMAN QUESTION?

A glance at the annual immigration figures of ethnic Germans over recent years reveals that their numbers have constantly declined from a peak of almost four hundred thousand in 1989 and 1990 to just above one hundred thousand ten years later. It is equally important to note that in their overwhelming majority these ethnic Germans come from the successor states of the former Soviet Union. There are two implications of this. One is that the German policy approach aiming to restrict ethnic German immigration by means of changing the law and simultaneously making financial aid available to the still-existing settlement areas of ethnic Germans in Central and Eastern Europe has worked. The other is that the situation in the host countries has improved sufficiently to make staying an acceptable alternative to emigration. This suggests that the German question as a problem of ethnic German minorities in Central and Eastern Europe seems close to resolution.

Other dimensions of the German question have been resolved as well. In 1990 the unification of the Federal Republic with the German Democratic Republic was achieved by peaceful means, and a treaty was signed between the unified Germany and Poland guaranteeing the border between the two countries as it had been de facto established in 1945. Relations between Germany and Poland, between the German expellees and Poland, and between the German minority in Poland and Poles and the Polish government have significantly improved. Thus, the German question as a territorial and bilateral problem between Germany and Poland also seems largely to be resolved. Germany's relationship with the Czech Republic has also significantly improved, although a number of problems remain. The German-Czech Declaration of 1997 and various initiatives following on from it have made a positive impact on German-Czech relations. However, they have not been able to resolve all outstanding issues. Many expellees remain disappointed at the refusal of the Czech government to rescind the so-called Beneš Decrees of 1945 and 1946 that legalized the collective victimization of the Sudeten Germans and gave amnesty to anyone who committed a crime in the course of their expulsion. More recently, initiatives have been started in the Czech Republic to address many of these unresolved issues at local level—that is, in the towns and villages where the expulsions actually happened. This has been welcomed, but the situation has not yet fundamentally improved, and it is unlikely that this will occur as long as hard-liners on both sides give each other pretexts to sabotage a comprehensive process of reconciliation. With other countries, such as Romania, Hungary, or the successor states of the former Yugoslavia, relations have for a long time been conducted in effective isolation from the German question. This is the case also for the countries of the former Soviet Union, from where emigration of ethnic Germans still continues, albeit no longer to the same extent as it did in the early 1990s. In all of these countries, Germany is no longer seen as a political, economic, or military threat but as a valuable partner that can pave the way toward closer integration and cooperation with the West. And in this process, German minorities are seen as an asset rather than as a liability.

In Germany itself, the integration of ethnic Germans into political, social, and economic life remains a complicated process. As such, it is part of the continued quest for a German national identity. The arrival of more than sixteen million ethnic Germans in the country since the end of the Second World War has been a major contributory factor to a process that has, so far, not been completed satisfactorily. Thus, while the international dimensions of the century-old German question may finally near resolution at the beginning of the twenty-first century, the German question as a question about German national identity still awaits an answer. Likewise, the traditional interconnectedness of political and cultural and of domestic and international dimensions of the German question persists. This means that an answer to the question about German national identity can be given only if the Federal Republic and the states and nations of Central and Eastern Europe come to terms with the legacy of the expulsions and emigration of ethnic Germans since World War II.

DIMENSIONS OF THE GERMAN QUESTION

Following this broad outline of the nature and origins of the German question, it is now possible to return to my starting point, namely, who the politically relevant elites were and are whose decisions need to be examined in order to provide a comprehensive political analysis of the German question. Broadly speaking, it will be necessary to consider four different levels—the German domestic elites; those in other European countries and in the United States; wherever they were significant as independent political actors, the leaderships of German minorities abroad; and especially in the post–Second World War period, international governmental organizations. As will become clear in the course of the following chapters, none of these elites acted in isolation. While they may not always have considered each other's interests and opportunity structures, no decision taken by any of them in regard of the German question occurred in a vacuum but had concrete consequences that affected other elites and their constituencies and prompted reactions among them. Similarly, none of the individual dimensions of the German question was autonomous, and decisions made with an eye to any one of them have always had intended and unintended consequences for others.

These essential characteristics of the German question are traced throughout the following study. Chapter 2 considers developments in the German question from the Treaty of Versailles to the Munich Agreement. Starting with a summary of the relevant provisions of the Treaty of Versailles, it details the developments relating to the German question in the interwar period, including the border changes and their impact on Germany, the policy of border consolidation (in Western Europe) and revisionism (in Eastern Europe) during the Weimar Republic, the rise to power of Nazism and the continuities and changes in Germany's policies in relation to borders and ethnic German minorities in Europe, and the way in which other European states responded to these policies throughout the period.

The third chapter assesses the impact of the Second World War on Germany. Outlining the major developments of the German question during the war both in terms of German policies and in relation to Allied plans for the territorial reorganization of Europe after the end of the war, I examine the *Heim-ins-Reich* resettlement program of ethnic Germans from Central and Eastern Europe, the consequences of German occupation policies, and the gradual shaping of an Allied strategy for a new European order from the Atlantic Charter of 1941 to the Yalta Conference of 1945. This is followed by a discussion of the Potsdam Agreement and its implementation, including territorial changes, the expulsion and deportation of ethnic Germans from Central and Eastern Europe, and the post-Potsdam policies of the Allies that led eventually to the founding of two German states in 1949.

In chapter 4, I look at the German question as a demographic problem and examine the integration of ethnic German refugees and expellees in the two German states, including an overview of the legal framework of the integration process, an analysis of the political and economic impact of the refugees and expellees on the Federal Republic and the German Democratic Republic, and an examination of the social changes that occurred in both states as a consequence.

The fifth chapter considers a dimension of the German question that is in many ways unique in the nation's history. With the founding of the two German states in 1949, the German question as a whole began to be dominated by the relationship between the Federal Republic of Germany and the German Democratic Republic. Given the geopolitical realities of the Cold War, this relationship was not between two sovereign states but between two member states of hostile military alliances. Thus, I document how the inter-German relationship developed over the forty years of the existence of the two states against the international background of bloc confrontation. This includes an analysis of the Berlin Crisis in the late 1950s, the building of the Berlin Wall in 1961, and the impact of the *neue Ostpolitik* from the middle to late 1960s onward. Ultimately, I outline the major developments that preceded German reunification of 1990. The German-German dimension was not the only territorial aspect of the German question in the post-1945 period. The former *Ostgebiete*—German territories to the east of the Oder-Neisse line that had remained part of Germany after the Treaty of Versailles and were placed under provisional Polish administration in the Potsdam Agreement—were a major bone of contention in West German–Polish relations until Germany and Poland signed the so-called Border Treaty in 1990 that recognized the Oder-Neisse line as their mutual border. The other, often forgotten, territorial dimension of the German question after 1945 was the conflict between France and

Germany over the Saar. With its origins having been examined in chapter 3, the discussion of the territorial aspects of the German question after 1945 offers an opportunity to examine the conditions that made Germany's "little reunification" in 1957 possible, setting an important precedent for inter-German developments in 1989–90.

Despite the expulsions between 1945 and 1950 and the subsequent emigration of ethnic Germans, there are still significant minority populations of ethnic Germans living in their traditional homelands in other countries in Europe, and in the areas to which they were deported in the former Soviet Union. Given the significance that these minority groups have had as an essential factor in the development of the German question, their situation after the end of the Second World War warrants separate treatment. In this context, I also examine the role that the Federal Republic has played as a kin-state for the minorities in Central and Eastern Europe and assess similarities and differences of external minority politics in the different historical periods of the development of the German question in the twentieth century.

Finally, an assessment of the German question would be incomplete without revisiting my original premise—that the essence of the German question is the incompatibility between (the borders of) its territory and (the perceived size of) its nation, and the way in which Germany and European and/or world powers have responded to this problem. I thus examine in the sixth chapter whether this definition still holds true more than ten years after the collapse of communism. While it is obvious that significant changes in the post–Cold War period have contributed to a fundamental transformation of the German question, it equally cannot be denied that certain dimensions of it are still haunting Germany and its neighbors, particularly in Central and Eastern Europe. Looking at the negotiations on the accession of Poland and the Czech Republic to the European Union, I illustrate that not all is forgiven and forgotten, and that the German question is still an issue in Central and Eastern Europe.

Chapter 2

From Versailles to Munich, 1919–1938

If, just as before 1870, German unification (inasmuch as Germans and Austrians aspire to it) is prevented; if apart from Alsace ... Germany is to lose further territories in the West, let alone in the East; if, apart from the compensation of Belgium, Germany is to pay reparations under the pretence of damages caused by war and thus by actions of both parties, then every last working man in Germany, who is aware of this, will become a revisionist.[1] Hatred between peoples is permanent and German irredentism with all the usual revolutionary means of self-determination will arise.

—Max Weber (1919)

VERSAILLES AND ITS CONSEQUENCES

The Treaty of Versailles in 1919, together with the treaties concluded in St. Germain in the same year and in Trianon in 1920, meant a fundamental change of the old European order; in fact, the end of the First World War brought with it the end of the old European order as well.[2] The most obvious dimension of the beginning of a new era was territorial—not only had new states been created on the ruins of empires, but the size of those previously existing had been changed as well. Given the effects that the treaties of Versailles and St. Germain had on Germany and Austria, it is little exaggeration to say that the origins of the German question in the twentieth century can be found in the peace settlements of 1919. This is not to say that all subsequent developments were caused by them, but it is to acknowledge that in particular the territorial arrangements put in place in 1919 were much less than favorable for the external security and internal stability of most European states. The terms of the Treaty of Versailles were imposed in a way that left its mark on the collective identity of the Germans, who, encouraged by domestic political and economic crises and extremist propaganda from the left and right, increasingly came to see Versailles as unfair and discriminatory.

To begin with, Germany lost a significant number of territories: Alsace and Lorraine, which it had acquired only after the Franco-German war of 1870–71, were given to France; Prussian Moresnet, Eupen, and Malmedy had to be ceded to Belgium; a sizable stretch of German territory was given to Poland to allow the country access to the Baltic Sea (this also meant the separation of East Prussia from the rest of Germany); the Baltic port city of Danzig was made an extraterritorial Free City; a small part of Silesia was assigned to the new Czechoslovak state; referenda in Schleswig and Upper Silesia changed the borders with Denmark and Poland to ones that corresponded more closely with ethnic lines; for fifteen years, the Saar became a trustee territory under the authority of a five-member governing commission appointed by the League of Nations; and the left bank of the Rhine was occupied by France and Belgium between 1923 and 1930 in an attempt to enforce German reparations payments. In addition, Germany lost all her overseas colonies, and unification with Austria was expressly forbidden under the terms of the peace treaties.

Furthermore, Germany was prohibited from rebuilding its military power, and conscription was banned. Finally, the country was required to pay a large sum of reparations to the victorious powers, especially to France and Belgium, on the basis of the so-called war guilt article (Article 231) of the Versailles treaty, which stated that the "Allied and Associated Governments affirm and Germany accepts the responsibility of Germany and her allies for causing all the loss and damage to which the Allied and Associated Governments and their nationals have been subjected as a consequence of the war imposed upon them by the aggression of Germany and her allies." The treaty specified in its Article 235 and Annex II that Germany had to pay—in gold, commodities, ships, securities, or otherwise—by April 1920 the equivalent of twenty billion gold marks and to deposit bonds worth another twenty billion marks payable no later than 1 May 1921 and not bearing any interest; a further forty billion marks' worth of bonds bearing an annual interest of 2.5 percent for the period of 1921 to 1926 and 5 percent thereafter; and finally, Germany was to be prepared to issue another forty billion marks' worth of bonds bearing 5 percent interest at a time to be specified by the reparations commission. As part of the reparations, Germany had to deliver livestock, parts of its merchant and naval fleets, coal, reconstruction materials, and various agricultural and industrial machinery to the Allied and Associated Powers in order to help them rebuild their countries.

Despite the unprecedented magnitude of these reparations claims, despite the significant loss of territory and despite severe postwar revolutionary unrest in the early 1920s, characterized by several communist uprisings and politically motivated assassinations conducted by right-wing groups, the situation in Germany had stabilized by the middle of the 1920s, and it became clear that Germany had remained a European power to be reckoned with. This was as much a result of Germany's own recovery as one of the weakness of its neighbors. The states created in Central and Eastern Europe were too weak internally and not united enough externally to be matches for Germany; the Soviet Union remained isolated from the rest of Europe and was shunned and feared by almost all other states in the region, except Germany, with which it concluded the Treaty of Rapallo in 1922 and the Treaty of Berlin in 1926. Consequently, a power vacuum existed in those areas that had belonged to or been under the influence of the tsarist and Habsburg empires. This power vacuum was to become one of the crucial determinants of German foreign policy in the interwar period.

FIRST- AND SECOND-CLASS BORDERS: EXTERNAL MINORITIES AND THE POLICY OF BORDER REVISIONS, 1919–1939

The substantial loss of territory and population and the enormous amount of reparations Germany had to pay to the Allied and Associated Powers formed a considerable part of the background against which German foreign policy was formulated throughout the 1920s and 1930s, when the revision of the Versailles treaty assumed highest priority. Border revisions, rearmament, and an end to the reparation payments were the three distinct, yet closely connected, key objectives. With the exception of the border revisions, they were all accomplished before the Nazis came to power: the occupation of the Rhineland ended in June 1930, the end of reparation payments was achieved at the Lausanne Conference of July 1932, and Germany was allowed military parity at the Geneva Conference in December 1932. Two more border changes were accomplished without war: the Saar was reincorporated into Germany after a referendum in 1935, and the Munich Agreement of 1938 forced Czechoslovakia to cede the German-populated Sudetenland. Key for these "accomplishments" was the goodwill of the Western powers, which meant that Germany's western borders with France, Belgium, and, after 1938, Italy as well as the German-speaking populations in Western and Central and Eastern Europe assumed an instrumental role in German foreign policy making.

I now turn to a discussion of the "western" cases before comparing and contrasting them with German policy toward Poland and Czechoslovakia. Initially, however, it is important to examine the Treaty of Locarno, which in many ways was the embodiment of this twin strategy of border consolidation in the West and border revisions in the East, and thus also exemplifies a trend in the development of the German question in its international dimensions after 1919, a trend that highlights the importance of Germany's relationship with Central and Eastern Europe while simultaneously underlining the significance of this relationship for the German question as a whole.

Locarno

Representatives of Britain, France, Germany, Italy, Czechoslovakia, and Poland came together at Locarno in Switzerland in 1925 and negotiated several treaties that were meant to stabilize and further guarantee the settlement reached at Versailles six years earlier. The main treaty, guaranteed by Britain and Italy, was concluded among Germany, France, and Belgium, who accepted one another's borders as they had been defined by the Treaty of Versailles. As a reward for its recognition of the permanence of its western borders, Germany was allowed to join the League of Nations in 1926. In line with German foreign policy, this included the promise not to send German troops into the demilitarized Rhineland and to accept that Alsace and Lorraine were permanently parts of France. There could have been hardly any more striking revelation of Germany's long-term aspirations

Germany, 1919–1938

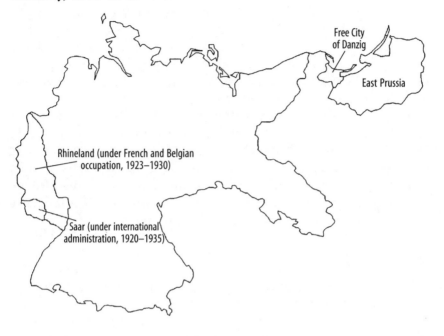

Free City
of Danzig

East Prussia

Rhineland (under French and Belgian
occupation, 1923–1930)

Saar (under international
administration, 1920–1935)

to revise its eastern borders than its refusal to include Poland and Czechoslovakia in this treaty or to sign a similar treaty with them. As a result, France sought to provide some degree of security for these two countries by signing with each of them separate treaties that provided for French assistance should Germany attack either Poland or Czechoslovakia. The Treaty of Locarno, initially hailed as a major achievement of diplomacy (not least by resulting in a Nobel Peace Price for the French and German foreign ministers in 1926), remained in force until 1936, when the redeployment of the German army to the Rhineland invalidated it. The Franco-Czechoslovak treaty survived only a few years more; it was essentially weakened by the Munich Agreement of 1938 and eventually not invoked when in 1939 Hitler set out to destroy the rest of Czechoslovakia. The only one of the three treaties concluded in Locarno in 1925 not to be scrapped was the Franco-Polish treaty: Following Hitler's invasion of Poland in 1939, France declared war on Germany.

The implication of the Treaty of Locarno was clear—Weimar Germany had little intention of going to war with either France or Belgium over the borders established between the three countries in

1919. By the same token, it would be mistaken to assume that the noninclusion of Poland and Czechoslovakia was an implicit declaration of war, either. By the end of the interwar period, a revision of the German-Czech border had been accomplished, without violence albeit with threat of force, through the Munich Agreement of 1938. However, Hitler's larger territorial and other ambitions required him to plunge the world into another war.

Although Locarno had failed by 1936, for more than ten years it provided an important framework for Germany's foreign policy in Europe, especially as far as relations with German minorities abroad were concerned. The system of first- and second-class borders created in Locarno was replicated in the different strategies pursued by the German Foreign Office in relation to the German minorities in France and Italy and those in Poland and Czechoslovakia.

Germany and Alsace

The relationship between Alsace and Germany in the interwar period was complex and has to be analyzed from two different angles— Alsace as an object of German foreign policy considerations, and the commitment of the two Alsatian émigré organizations in Germany— the *Hilfsbund der Elsaß-Lothringer* (aid organization of refugees from Alsace and Lorraine) and the *Alt-Elsaß-Lothringische Vereinigung* (association of former residents of Alsace and Lorraine)—to the preservation of German culture in Alsace (Grünewald 1984).

Between 1919 and 1922, Germany had tried to turn the question of Alsace and Lorraine into a precedent for the right to self-determination to which not only defeated states but also the victorious powers had to bow. This was seen in terms of wider considerations of the situation of German minorities living, in particular, in states in Eastern Europe, parts of which had previously belonged to the German Empire. This was not a very successful policy; however, it did not change the German determination to utilize Alsace for its revisionist policy in Eastern Europe. After this rather firm pro-self-determination stance of 1919, the German Foreign Office soon came to realize that the difficulties existing in Alsace were an internal affair of the French Republic. Consequently, a 1922 analysis of the situation by German diplomats acknowledged that Alsace did not qualify as a minority problem in the strict sense of the concept, since the population did not insist on its different ethnicity (*Fremdständigkeit*), let alone on its German origin (Rothenberger 1975: 74). Although this assessment was accurate for the early 1920s, it had to be changed later, when Alsatians began to see themselves as a minority, in the way the League of Nations defined the term, and increasingly insisted on their distinctiveness in terms of culture, language, and tradition. The rediscovery of their German roots and the recognition of the German element in Alsatian culture, in turn, led the Foreign Office to support cultural efforts in Alsace in addition to more serious political considerations and a policy of funding political parties there. The political calculations began with the assessment that border revisions were only possible in the East and only with the consent of the Western powers. The role that Alsace came to play in this respect was twofold. While regaining the former *Reichsland* was impossible, a formal abandoning of all territorial claims could assure the French government of the security of its borders with Germany. At the same time, continuing problems in Alsace would weaken French resistance to desired border changes in the "German East." While the former was achieved with the Treaty of Locarno in 1925, the latter policy was pursued from the second half of the 1920s onward, mostly through funding of cultural activities and, especially between 1927 and 1929, political propaganda. In 1930–31 cultural funding continued at a reduced level, and even after Hitler's takeover in 1933 it was not immediately abandoned. The aim of German support, thus, was not to encourage Alsatian secessionism but rather to make France more willing to concede border revisions in the East. In this context, the organizations of the *Reichsland* émigrés played a central part, as they were to channel financial support to Alsace and bear responsibility for its uses. While activists in both organizations were generally less willing to accept that there would be no border revision, the two émigré organizations' and the Foreign Office's aims met in one crucial point—the attempt to minimize the impact of French assimilation policies in Alsace.

Germany and South Tyrol

The Treaty of St. Germain in 1919 was signed by a democratic Italian government, the representatives of which gave a number of assurances for the well-being of the German-speaking minority in South Tyrol, a formerly Austrian area south of the Alpine Brenner mountain range, which had been annexed to Italy in 1919 following a secret deal between Italy and the Entente in 1915 (according to which Italy would be rewarded with South Tyrol if it entered the war against Germany, Austria, and their allies). For a brief period of time thereafter it seemed as if the ethnic Germans in the area could become politically integrated into the Italian polity. However, a program of rapid Italianization was introduced immediately after Mussolini's takeover on 29 October 1922. The fascists' assimilation program extended into three main areas: culture, the economy, and the political and administrative sectors, and it aimed at the systematic destruction of the linguistic, religious, and demographic foundations of the ethnic German identity of the German-speaking South Tyrolese population.

Opposition to assimilation came not only from the German South Tyrolese themselves but initially also from Austria. In contrast to the loss of other territories, Austria had never accepted that of South Tyrol. Austrian resistance to the separation of South Tyrol, however, weakened under the pressures of international developments. Successive Austrian chancellors recognized the importance of an alliance with Italy against German annexation plans and acted accordingly. In 1928 Chancellor Ignaz Seipel declared that South Tyrol was an internal Italian affair, and in 1930 a friendship treaty was signed between Italy and Austria. Thus, it cannot come as a huge surprise that the South Tyrolese Germans vested their hopes primarily in Hitler and his pan-German aspirations. However, in the light of political developments in Italy and the importance of the country as an ally for Germany, Hitler had made it very clear that he was not willing to sacrifice his global interests for the fate of three hundred thousand German-speaking South Tyrolese, stating in 1922 that "Germany has to join forces with Italy, which experiences a time of national rebirth and has a great future ahead of itself. In order to accomplish this, a clear and final renunciation of all claims to South Tyrol is necessary" (quoted in Gruber 1974: 171).

While this foreshadowed the long-term future of South Tyrol in Nazi foreign policy goals, it did not have immediate effect on the South Tyrol policy of the Weimar Republic. Given Italy's treatment of the German minority, official and private institutions in Germany saw it as their duty to support the South Tyrolese German speakers in their efforts to fight off assimilation, and they did so by contributing financially and materially to the preservation of German culture in the region. The policy change after 1933 happened gradually. Initially, the new coordinating institution for the affairs of ethnic Germans living abroad, the so-called *Volksdeutsche Mittelstelle*, which by July 1938 had become the lead institution in the Reich for liaison with ethnic Germans abroad (Lumans 1993: 63), tolerated the continuation of these efforts by such organizations as the *Verband für das Deutschtum im Ausland*. However, from 1937 onward this began to change, and following the annexation of Austria and the Sudetenland in 1938 there was an ever-increasing need to appease Mussolini and solidify the German-Italian relationship. In the course of Germany's expansion in 1938, hopes among the Sudeten Germans for unification with the now enlarged German Reich had been raised considerably, and this very much threatened relations between Rome and Berlin. Consequently, in an attempt to resolve the South Tyrol problem once and for all, the "Option" was designed. In 1939, the German-speaking population in South Tyrol had to choose between remaining in Italy and being subjected to further Italianization or relocating to the German Reich. Of the 268,000 German-speaking South Tyrolese eligible for participation, forty-four thousand abstained. Of the 224,000 participants in the plebiscite, 183,000 voted to leave and thirty-eight thousand to stay (Cole and Wolf 1974: 57; also Alcock 1970: 45ff.). However, only about seventy thousand, or less than 40 percent, of those who had opted for resettlement actually left.

Germany and the Saar

The Saar presents a somewhat different case in the context of Germany's western policy in the interwar period, as the Versailles treaty stipulated holding a referendum on its status after a fifteen-year period of international trusteeship. Nevertheless, it provides interesting insights into some aspects of the German question in this period.

On 24 January 1919, France placed the Saar under military government and pursued a policy of separating it from Germany, of promoting union with France, and of long-term integration into the French Republic. As a first sign of the integration efforts, the military government introduced French as a compulsory subject in Saar schools on 15 February 1919 (Hirsch 1954: 25), despite the strong resistance of the Saar population, official protests from the German National Assembly in Weimar, and opposition from the French socialists. Similarly, the industrial sector was subjected to strict regulation by the French military authorities, and economic links between the Saar and France were established. Nevertheless, France had to settle for a provisional status of fifteen years' international administration of the Saar, the final status of which was to be subject to a referendum at the end of this period.

The implementation of this Saar statute was supervised by a commission appointed by the League of Nations. With the appointment of this commission the Saar was given a government that had exceptionally strong powers and was not accountable to an elected parliament. This and the fact that the commission was strongly pro-French did not increase the willingness of the Saar population to cooperate (Cowan 1950: 120). From 1922 onward, a so-called Advisory Council, or *Landesrat*, existed. Its thirty members were elected by universal suffrage for three-year terms, but they had no power; their responsibilities were limited to advising the commission on matters of legislation. With the introduction of the French franc as the only valid currency in the Saar on 1 June 1923, economic ties between France and the Saar were considerably strengthened and the territory became an important market for French goods. This was part of a more general French policy in the Saar that sought to strengthen French influence and develop Saar autonomy. Until 1926–27, both of these goals were balanced against one another. Afterward, however, greater emphasis was placed on the realization of French interests in the Saar. Consequently, tensions between the population and the government of the Saar grew, and a movement began to form that demanded the reunion of the Saar with Germany before the 1935 referendum (Pohlmann 1992: 25).

In the meantime, the *Saarverein*, which had been founded in Germany in the early 1920s, coordinated the efforts of the Saar emigrants in Germany to achieve a speedy return of the district. Although economic integration into France made some progress, the political situation in the Saar became increasingly anti-French and pro-German. The Nazis, while rising to political power in Germany, competed for the first time in elections to the Saar *Landesrat* in 1932 but gained only two seats. The Advisory Council was dominated by the Catholic Center Party (fourteen seats), the communists (eight), and the Social Democrats (three), all of which were opposed to a pro-German plebiscite. This constellation began to change in the course of 1933. In July, the smaller right-wing pro-German parties (German National People's Party, Peasant's Party, Saar German People's Party, Saar Economic Party) formed the German Front, to coordinate their efforts in support of a pro-German referendum. The Catholic Center joined the Front in October 1933 and the Nazis in March 1934. The two parties opposing this development—the Social Democrats and communists—aligned their forces with the Saar Economic Association and a small number of Catholics, led by Johannes Hoffmann, who did not support the Catholic Center's policy and formed the Saar Freedom Front, later renamed the Antifascist Unity Front. However, they were less well organized and far less powerful than the alliance of the Catholic Center and the Nazi party. Religion being an important part of the Saar population's identity, and the Catholic clergy thus playing a major role in the social and political life of the Saar, the chances for the opponents of reunification with Germany to gain a significant part of the vote were shattered when the bishop of Trier encouraged the population to vote for the return to Germany.

Despite the fact that the Nazi paramilitary organizations had been banned in the Saar since 1928, clashes between the German Front and the Antifascist Unity Front increased significantly throughout 1933 and 1934. The Saar commission faced the problem that the administration in the Saar was, at least numerically, dominated by Germans. Although they did not occupy the top positions in ministries and departments, their influence on the day-to-day running of Saar affairs could not be underestimated, as their generally pro-German attitude did not support the commission's efforts to secure fair conditions for the plebiscite (Kraus 1988: 37). The commission called in 3,300 foreign troops from Britain, Ireland, the Netherlands, and Sweden to supervise and secure the referendum, which took place on 13 January 1935. Of the 528,000 votes cast, 477,000 were in favor of a return of the Saar to Germany, forty-six thousand for the status quo, and only two thousand for union with France.

* * *

There are some obvious similarities in the above three cases—Alsace, Saar, and South Tyrol—that shed some light on the development of the German question in the interwar period. For both the Weimar Republic as well as the Nazis, minority as well as border issues in Western Europe played primarily an instrumental role in the accomplishment of very different foreign policy goals. The Weimar Republic used them as bargaining chips to reestablish German credibility on the international stage and to achieve, in the longer term, Western blessing for border revisions in the East and an easing of the reparations payments. For Hitler, the issue was similar. Since his long-term goals stretched well beyond the comparatively minor minority and border issues in the West, Alsace lost most of its former importance in foreign policy making, while South Tyrol and the German-speaking population there were used as trade-offs for Mussolini's cooperation in the annexation of Austria and the Sudetenland, and to solidify the relationship between Germany and Italy. Other developments in relation to the Saar and Alsace show the importance of émigré organizations in the pursuit of a foreign policy concerned with ethnic kin groups abroad. Their incorporation into official and secret policies in the interwar period foreshadowed some of the roles that the expellees and their organizations were to play in the period after 1945. The key difference between Weimar and the Third Reich is thus primarily one of scale and motivation. The Weimar foreign policy elite was as much geared toward revising the territorial settlement of Versailles as were the Nazis, but they did not risk another war over it, nor were they driven by racist motivations. In a sense, the failure of the Versailles treaty was therefore not just one of contributing to the creation of conditions that were conducive to the rise of Hitler but also one of enabling Germany within a few years to become once again the dominant power on the European continent, based on its economic might and the size of its population. Versailles had been too harsh as a conciliatory peace, and too accommodating as a Carthaginian peace (Martin 1992: 191).

Germany and Poland

German policy toward Poland in the interwar period was guided by the basic premise that only a numerically strong and culturally and politically visible German minority in Poland would provide the justification for German revisionism and legitimize the "recovery" of the territories lost to Poland in the peace settlement at Versailles. Two distinct policies were employed to achieve this goal—a pattern in many ways characteristic of developments after the Second World War. On the one hand, official negotiations with Poland at a bilateral level and through the institutions of the League of Nations had the objective of improving the legal position of the German minority in Poland and easing relations between the two countries; on the other hand, financial and material aid channeled through various institutions and organizations were to secure the political and cultural survival of the German population in Poland (Krekeler 1973: 149).

As for the first part of this strategy, the Polish Minority Treaty, the first such treaty concluded under the auspices of the League of Nations, which subsequently assumed a model character for similar agreements across Central and Eastern Europe and for a variety of ethnic minorities in other countries, was to guarantee the rights of the German minority in Poland. Accounting for less than 4 percent of the population, Germans in Poland lived mostly in territories acquired from Germany at Versailles—the "Polish Corridor" and Upper Silesia—while a smaller number also resided in central Poland and Volhynia. Regardless of its small size and international protection, the German minority population was perceived by Poland as a potential threat, primarily because of its location in the strategically important borderlands of the Polish Corridor. Embarking on a course of assimilation and oppression, the Polish government had managed to make some eight hundred thousand ethnic Germans leave Poland by 1923. On the other hand, Polish policy also contributed to resentment and the partial radicalization among some of the remaining Germans and their political and cultural organizations, including their political parties and press. One case in point is the Volksbund, an umbrella organization of some three hundred local branches serving Poland's German minority. Supported and encouraged by institutions in Germany, it filed almost ten thousand complaints with the League of Nations against the Polish government alleging violation of the minority treaty (Komjathy and Stockwell 1980: 68). Even though the League only looked into about forty of these, the generally perceived disloyalty of ethnic Germans contributed to tensions between minority and majority and between minority and state, both of which further complicated German-Polish relations. While the Weimar Republic had refused to guarantee Poland's borders in the Treaty of Locarno in 1925, Hitler, at least initially and temporarily, seemed interested in peaceful relations with Poland, signing a nonaggression pact in 1934 and seeking to limit the involvement of Reich-based organizations with the German minority in Poland.

In 1934, Poland withdrew from the minority treaty. Together with Germany's leaving the League of Nations, this could have meant an end of any attempts to deal with the status of the German minority in Poland by legal means. However, it was in both countries' interests, for the time being, not to let their relations deteriorate further over the minority question. After prolonged negotiations, they issued in 1937 a minority declaration that also guaranteed Polish rights in the Free City of Danzig, which had come under increasing threat from the activities of Nazi groups there. Seemingly addressing concerns of the German minority in the areas of education, culture, and the economy, the declaration raised some hopes for real improvement in the situation of the minority. However, these were short-lived, as Polish policy continued almost unchanged. The fact that Germany, although its role as patron of the German minority in Poland had been officially recognized in the declaration, did little in 1938 to exercise pressure on the Polish government had its basis in Hitler's wider strategy of territorial revisions, in which Poland did not yet figure prominently. Rather, the minority declaration and German guarantees for the status of Danzig and assurances that Poland would receive its share from the envisaged dismemberment of Czechoslovakia had secured Polish acquiescence to the annexation of Austria and the Sudetenland (Komjathy and Stockwell 1980: 86).

The other element of Germany's twin strategy in relation to Poland was that of financial and other material support for the German minority there. Especially during the years of the Weimar Republic, millions of Reichsmarks were poured into Silesia and the territories of West Prussia and Posen, which formed the Polish Corridor, to secure the cultural, economic, and political survival of the German population there. Various organizations were set up within Germany to channel funds as direct aid or as loans, and in either case political calculations outweighed economic considerations (Krekeler 1973; Komjathy and Stockwell 1980: 65–101). The aid measures implemented may have alleviated some of the hardship that the German minority, just like many other ethnic groups in Poland and elsewhere in Europe, suffered as a consequence of heightening international tensions. However, they proved insufficient to protect the members of the German minority from Polish assimilation policies and from the increasing violence directed at them by Polish nationalists in the second half of the 1930s, and particularly in 1939, when the German-inspired crisis over Danzig approached its climax.

Germany and Czechoslovakia

The relationship between Germany and Czechoslovakia in the interwar period is often thought to be symbolized by the events surrounding the Munich Agreement of 1938—that is, the forced cession of the mostly German-inhabited Sudetenland to the German Reich and the subsequent destruction of the Czechoslovak Republic in 1939. While these events in many ways epitomize the aggressiveness with which Hitler pursued his foreign policy and the failure of major European powers to respond adequately to the threat he posed, the relationship between Germany and Czechoslovakia cannot be reduced to the events of the second half of the 1930s.

As a state, Czechoslovakia was a new creation in 1919, born out of the old Austro-Hungarian Empire. Historically, the Czech lands of Bohemia and Moravia had been inhabited by Germans and Czechs

The Annexation of the Sudentenland in 1938

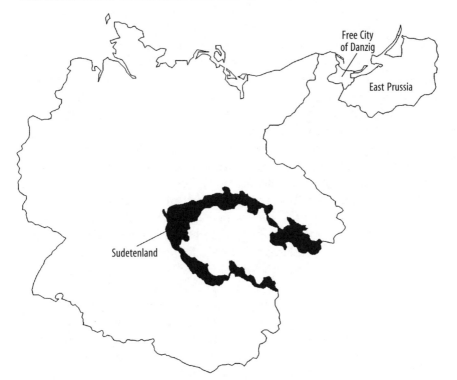

alike, who had lived there together peacefully for centuries, with social dividing lines running not along ethnic lines but rather along those of religion and class. It was only with the advent of nationalism in its Romantic form in the late eighteenth and early nineteenth century that the relationship between the two population groups, and in fact most of their common history, was redefined and reinterpreted along ethnic lines. Interethnic tensions grew, especially in Bohemia, as elsewhere in the Habsburg Empire, and centered mostly on issues of language parity. By the beginning of the First World War in 1914, all strata of the population—from the working class to the aristocracy—had fallen in line behind the ethnic divisions that had emerged over the previous century. Not surprisingly, the borders of the new Czechoslovak state that were drawn up at the Paris peace conference were not very popular with the majority of Germans suddenly finding themselves in a newly, if not artificially, created nation-state in which they were, if the second-largest population group (after the Czechs, but before the Slovaks and Hungarians), nevertheless a minority and no longer, as they had been in the Austro-Hungarian Empire, the state-bearing nation. Initially, protests against the perceived injustice of their separation from Austria were frequent and often escalated into violent clashes with Czechs and the Czech military, leading to a number of casualties. However, once the treaties of St. Germain and Trianon in 1919 and 1920 had officially recognized the new Czechoslovak state, the Sudeten Germans (temporarily) came to accept their situation.

It would, therefore, be wrong to assume that the Sudeten Germans in their majority sought secession from Czechoslovakia from the very beginning. It would be equally untrue to accuse the Czechoslovak state of not honoring the commitments it had subscribed to in a minority treaty, quite similar to the one signed by Poland. Although relations between the two population groups and their political elites were not always easy, both recognized the needs for, and benefits of, cooperation. So-called activist parties, which favored constructive engagement in and with the Czechoslovak state, regularly polled the highest percentage of votes among Germans right until 1935, and even then one-third of German voters continued to support them despite pressure and intimidation not to do so. The generally cooperative atmosphere also manifested itself in the participation of two of the activist German parties, the German Agrarian Party and the Catholic German Christian Social Party, in a coalition with Czechoslovak middle-class and conservative parties. In 1929, following the electoral success of the Czechoslovak and the German Social Democratic Parties, the latter joined the new center-left coalition government. While this cooperation at an elite level is indicative of some positive tendencies in interethnic relations from the mid-1920s onward, it must not be mistaken as evidence for problem-free relations between Czechs and Germans. Germans never formally declared their loyalty to the Czechoslovak state; Czechs and Slovaks never accepted them as equal partners or as a third state-bearing nation. Nevertheless, the prudence of political elites produced relative stability in Czechoslovakia in the 1920s.

Yet this was not to last in the following decade, once the world economic crisis reached the country. The depression hit particularly the Germans. The country's industries depended heavily on the ability to export to foreign markets, and the Czechoslovak state, like many other countries in Europe, was unprepared for, and unable to cope with, rising unemployment and social unrest. The old ethnic divisions quickly came to the fore again, polarizing and radicalizing Czechs as well as Germans, and eventually led to the breakup of the country. This was neither an automatic nor an inevitable process. On the German side, the driving force of the repoliticization of ethnicity, or at least of the intensification of this process, was Konrad Henlein's Sudeten German Party. In contrast to other organizations among ethnic Germans in Europe, Henlein's first movement and later party was homegrown and initially developed rather independently of the Nazi Party and, after 1933, the state in Germany, which meant that although support was forthcoming, the Nazis initially kept their distance from Henlein (Jaworski 1986: 43). However, with the Sudeten German Party's platform built around ethnic issues, it was relatively easy for Henlein to incorporate most of the smaller nationalist German parties, and when the party polled over 60 percent in the parliamentary elections of 1935, the Nazis began to engage more actively with it. Soon after this, the strongly pro-Nazi and secessionist wing in the party took over, and interethnic tensions intensified.

The success of the Sudeten German Party is best understood against the background of the strong links, if not identity, between social and national issues in the eyes of many Sudeten Germans and the ability of the party to play on this and present itself as the champion of the German population in Czechoslovakia. The continuing and partially increasing social and economic problems, coupled with anti-German policies of the Czechoslovak state and widespread anti-German sentiments among the Czech population (Jaworski 1986: 34), experienced by the majority of Germans in Czechoslovakia contrasted sharply with the economic recovery Germany had experienced since the takeover by Hitler. This explains why national and social issues became so interlinked for the Sudeten Germans. While the Czechoslovak state made a number of (albeit belated) efforts to address social and economic grievances of the Sudeten Germans in the run-up to the Munich Agreement, these were not sufficient to convince a majority of the German population that their continued existence in a Czechoslovak state was preferable to secession and unification with the German Reich. It must also be stated very clearly in this context that these Czechoslovak policies in the second half of the 1930s were not a matter of "too little, too late"; regardless of what the state did or could have done, the minds of most Germans in the country and above all of the dominant political elites in the Sudetenland and the Reich were firmly geared toward the destruction of the Czechoslovak state.

While the relations between Czechoslovakia and the Weimar Republic had never been particularly stable, they also never acquired the same explosive status that those between Czechoslovakia and the Third Reich would assume after 1933. Following the failure of the Western powers to resist the annexation of Austria, a clear breach of the Versailles treaty, Hitler's interest turned to Czechoslovakia, which, in the larger scheme of his expansionist plans, figured prominently on the one hand as a potentially uncomfortable military ally of France, and on the other hand as a rich resource of armaments production and pool of a skilled labor force. Using, and contributing to, the escalation of Czech-German tensions in Czechoslovakia, Hitler managed to convince both France and Britain that a cession of the Sudetenland to Germany was the last item on his "wish list" of revisions of the Versailles treaty.[3] Thus, severe diplomatic pressure from Britain and France and the threat of military force from Germany made Czechoslovakia concede and sign what has become known as the Munich Agreement in November 1938, effectively giving up large parts of its territory and valuable economic assets located there. The Western miscalculation to have thus achieved "peace in our time" became obvious only a few months later when, under the pretext of a Slovak drive for independent statehood (carefully honed and encouraged by Hitler), Czechoslovakia eventually ceased to exist as an independent state, being replaced by an "independent" Slovakia and the so-called German protectorate of Bohemia and Moravia.

Although the German minority in Czechoslovakia, compared to that in Poland, had played an evidently more crucial role in the course of these events and reaped some economic benefits, albeit fewer than expected, from the complicity of its leadership and significant numbers of its members in the destruction of Czechoslovakia, Hitler's policy was not one driven by the concern for the well-being of a kin group in a neighboring state. Rather, the extinction of Czechoslovakia as a sovereign state was an important piece in the puzzle of nationalist expansion. Western policy in Munich failed to recognize this: what Britain and France achieved was at best a delay of the inevitable—that is, the destruction of the Czechoslovak state. At worst, it allowed Hitler to achieve his aims at a much reduced cost.

Within less than one year after Munich, Hitler would not only seek the ultimate revision of the Versailles treaty by beginning another world war but also abandon the principles of Locarno: first- and second-class borders alike would be overrun, and Poland, France, and Belgium would all become German-occupied territories.

THE "OTHER" GERMAN QUESTION IN THE INTERWAR PERIOD: WHO IS A GERMAN?

Even though international developments between 1919 and 1939 often take precedence in analyses of the German question in the interwar period, often to an exclusionary extent, it would be wrong to neglect important developments in the way in which Germanness was defined during that period.

Being German is both a question of ethnic identity and citizenship. In many ways, the two are linked to one another, but contrary to common perceptions, neither today nor in the past has German ethnicity been the sole criterion for German citizenship. The link between ethnic origin and the modern concept of citizenship, as opposed to being the subject of a monarchical ruler, was established in Germany for the first time in 1848 by the Frankfurt National Assembly, which declared in Article 1 of its charter of basic rights that "every German has the citizenship of the Reich." However, the failure of German unification at this time also meant that the idea of a German citizenship had to be abandoned for the time being. The diet of the North German Union revived the concept in 1866 in its Law on the Acquisition and the Loss of Federal and State Citizenship. After the southern German states joined the North German Union in 1871, leading to the creation of the German Reich, this law was extended across the entire Reich, thus laying the foundations of German citizenship in its modern sense. However, it was more limited in that it did not create a single German citizenship; rather, German citizenship was acquired through citizenship in one of the federal states. Thus, for example Prussian citizens of Polish extraction held German (Reich) citizenship despite the fact that they were not German in an ethnic sense. By the same token, ethnic Germans living outside the borders of the Reich and thus not having citizenship in one of the federal states did not qualify for German citizenship under this law. The 1913 *Reichs- und Staatsangehörigkeitsgesetz* relaxed some of the rules on the loss of citizenship (especially after prolonged periods of residence abroad, an issue that became relevant because of Germany's expanding colonial empire), but it did not change one fundamental provision, that of *ius sanguinis*, law of the blood, according to which a descendant of

German parents is German. Again, this was not at all an exclusively ethnic provision—it simply meant that children of German citizens were German citizens as well. By the same token, the link between citizenship of a federal state and Reich citizenship had clear implications after the Versailles treaty. German citizens living in areas that the Weimar Republic had had to cede to the victorious powers of the First World War lost their German citizenship. On the other hand, in a way quite similar to developments after 1945, they could regain it by moving to the remaining territory of the Reich if they could prove having held it prior to the cession of territories.

There is no doubt that the citizenship issue alone does not provide a satisfactory answer to the question who is a German, especially if this question is asked with specific reference to ethnic characteristics. As demonstrated above, there was little interest among Foreign Office officials and activists in the various cultural and political organizations concerned with Germanness abroad to extend their activities to the Germans into Poland and Czechoslovakia. They remained committed to their more traditional clientele farther away in Eastern and Southeastern Europe, most of whom identified themselves as Germans on the basis of criteria such as language, customs, and traditions as well as the origin of their forefathers, sometimes centuries before. This approach did principally not change after Hitler acceded to power in 1933, but it became significantly "refined" over the years, and careful distinctions were made between different classes of Germans abroad on the basis of so-called *Volkslisten,* which determined the degree to which ethnic Germans had retained their German characteristics. While most of these policies could be implemented only after the beginning of the war, an internal redefinition of Germanness, based on both racial and ideological criteria took place much earlier. The liquidation of enemies of the Reich, including their physical elimination, incarceration, and forced emigration, first affected left-wing opponents to the Nazi regime but soon also extended to liberal intellectuals. These policies of redefining Germanness reached a first peak in the Nuremberg Race Laws, limiting Reich citizenship to citizens of German or related extraction who were loyal to the German Reich. They specifically excluded Jews from citizenship rights and banned marriage or premarital affairs between Jews and German citizens. The Nazis' obsession with a racial redefinition of Germanness finally culminated in the Holocaust against Jews, Sinti, and Roma, and the euthanasia programs conducted against the mentally ill and physically disabled.

This qualitatively new dimension of racially determined domestic as well as foreign policies distinguishes the development of the German question under the Nazis from all other periods in German history. Racism has always existed in Germany, but never before had it come to be a key factor in formulating policy (cf. Calleo 1980: 176). This, together with the aggressive territorial expansion of Germany, the brutal occupation policies in the conquered territories, and the expulsion and resettlement programs affecting Germans and non-Germans alike meant that the German question and the answers given to it from the German political elite were about to reach a grueling climax under the Nazis.

NOTES

1. My translation. In the original, Weber uses the term "chauvinist" rather than revisionist.

2. In this context, it should also be noted that apart from the changes in Central Europe, the Balkans were also affected by similar developments. Following territorial and demographic revisions after the Balkan Wars in 1912–13, further treaties and conventions were concluded after the end of the First World War in the Balkans that also resulted in losses and gains of territory and a number of forced population transfers. Of these, the Treaty of Lausanne of 1923 between Greece and Turkey is the most significant.

3. In a speech given in Birmingham on 17 March 1939 (one day after the final destruction of Czechoslovakia by Hitler), British prime minister Neville Chamberlain admitted that "in view of . . . repeated assurances, given voluntarily to me [by Hitler], I considered myself justified in founding a hope upon them that once this Czecho-Slovakian question was settled, as it seemed at Munich it would be, it would be possible to carry further that policy of appeasement."

Chapter 3

The Impact of the Second World War: Potsdam, Its Origins and Consequences

[A] German question cannot be solved without Germany. . . .
Fate and history have placed the German people in the midst of
Europe. It cannot be the meaning of history that we, the Ger-
mans, should constitute the line of division in Europe, its main
point of dispute, an arena of terrible strife between East and West.
—Hans Ehard (1947)

When Germany attacked Poland on 1 September 1939, the German
question reached an entirely new and chilling quality in its development in the twentieth century. Six years later, tens of millions of people
would be dead, injured, or displaced. In addition, large parts of, especially, Central and Eastern Europe would be economically and
infrastructurally devastated. From these ruins of Europe a new order
would emerge that would divide the world and Germany into two antagonistic systems, an order that would be overcome only after 1989
as a consequence of the collapse of communism.

The communiqué issued by the United States, the Soviet Union,
and the United Kingdom at the end of the Potsdam Conference in
August 1945 (subsequently France acceded to it as well) is often seen

as the embodiment of a new resolve, stronger than ever, to deal with the German question once and for all. As a singular historical document it certainly is impressive in its scope and ambition, but at closer examination it is more accurately described as one element in a much longer and more complex set of developments that started at least as early as the Atlantic Charter of 1941 and ended, preliminarily, with the foundation of two German states in 1949. For the period after 1939, what the policies of both the Allies and successive political elites in Germany have in common is that, in one way or another, they sought to address what they perceived to be the root causes of the German question. Looking at various different dimensions of these policies—the Holocaust; the German occupation regime; the resettlement of ethnic Germans in Central and Eastern Europe; their subsequent flight, deportation, and expulsion; and the territorial changes imposed after 1945—reveals that neither the nature of the German question nor its perception in Germany and abroad had fundamentally changed. It was still a problem of incompatibility between nation and state territory that Germany was "required" to rectify by means of a war of aggression and that led the Allies to look for ways in which the obvious security threat posed by a strong German state in the heart of Europe could be eliminated in the future. From this perspective, the war and postwar policies formulated and implemented by all the elites in Bonn, Berlin, Moscow, London, and Washington were the driving forces behind the dynamics of the German question throughout the 1940s.

ASPECTS OF GERMAN POLICY DURING THE SECOND WORLD WAR

This is not the place to recount the history of the Second World War. While it is true that this war in itself symbolizes the extremes to which the German question, or more precisely certain attempts to answer it, could go, histories of the period between 1939 and 1945 exist in abundance, and there is no need for replication. Rather, I shall highlight some of the processes and events that are more closely connected to the German question as defined in this book.

As examined in the previous chapter, Hitler's rise to power did not mean a fundamental reorientation of German policy in relation to territory and nation compared to the Weimar Republic. It did, however, mean that this and other areas of policy making became increasingly race determined—that is, the Nazis' obsession with the alleged superiority and necessary purity of the German nation began to drive domestic as well as foreign policy making and led, among other excesses, to the Holocaust. While the case of the attempted annihilation of European Jews is one of the best documented and most abhorrent events of the twentieth century, it must not be forgotten that there were other victims of the Nazis' genocidal policies, too. Roma became a prime target for extermination across Europe, as did the mentally and physically disabled, especially in Germany, where large-scale euthanasia programs were put in place. Yet policies to create a "pure" German nation did not stop there. They affected just as much, albeit differently, German minorities in other European countries, people who had always thought of themselves as German, had been backed politically and financially by successive governments in the Weimar Republic and the Third Reich, and in many cases had put their hopes in Hitler and supported his aggressive foreign policy. This, however, did not automatically qualify them as Germans in the eyes of the Nazis, who had scientifically dubious, but nevertheless clearly defined, categories of Germanness according to which they sought to establish the degree of "suitability" of these various communities of ethnic Germans for integration into the German nation.

Deployment in Alsace illustrates this point quite well. Here, the German-speaking population had already not been very enthusiastic in 1870–71 about integration into the then emerging German nation-state. Its desire to be integrated in the German Reich was even lower in 1940, not least because Alsatians had watched the developments in Nazi Germany carefully before the outbreak of the war. Despite the attraction national socialism had exercised for a small proportion of the population, the political loyalty of the overwhelming majority of Alsatians lay with France. After the German victory over France in 1940, Hitler initially promised to respect French territory but subsequently annexed Alsace and Lorraine and began an immediate integration and assimilation process; French civilians and especially civil servants were expelled, and the latter were replaced with Nazi officials from the neighboring *Gau* (district) of Baden, into which Alsace and Lorraine were integrated. German laws were introduced, and many Alsatians received German citizenship and initially benefited from preferential treatment. Although prominent Alsatian autonomists from the interwar period in France were given important posts in the administration, hopes for real autonomy, similar to that achieved under the 1911 German constitution, disappeared quickly. Instead, brutal Germanization and repression of any kind of particularism were what the Nazis offered the Alsatians. The introduction of an obligatory six-month labor service in May 1941 and of conscription in August 1942, the separation of church and state, the banning of religious education in school, and plans for the dissolution of abbeys were just some examples of this. Integration policy was multifaceted and occasionally bizarre. Not only did German become the only permitted language, so that street, place, and family names had to be Germanized, but the occupation authorities prohibited the wearing of "French" berets (Kettenacker 1973: 163–74). Although Alsatian resistance was predominantly of a passive nature, it soon became obvious to the Nazis that cultural assimilation through "education" had not borne the expected fruit. The Nazi administration then turned to increasingly violent means to enforce Germanization in Alsace, including deportations, concentration camps, and death sentences, but this approach only reinforced the Alsatians' awareness of their cultural distinctiveness from Germany and their unwillingness to be part of the German nation.

Elsewhere such reluctance was rare. The majority of ethnic Germans in Poland and the Czech parts of the former Czechoslovakia welcomed German troops, as did later in the war the Germans who lived farther away from the Reich—for example, in Hungary, Romania, and various parts of the Balkans. Those less enthusiastic were always in a minority. In the Sudetenland, for example, some thirty thousand German communists and Social Democrats and about the same number of people who the Nuremberg race laws would have identified as Jews escaped to rump Czechoslovakia, many of them only to be rounded up by the authorities there and sent back to Germany.

Especially in Poland and the Sudetenland, the reasons why ethnic Germans welcomed their incorporation into the Reich were not so much unequivocal support for the Nazis' racist ideology and policies— although supporters of those policies existed—as the belief that becoming part of Germany would end their status as disadvantaged, maltreated, and unwanted minorities. No matter how exaggerated such perceptions might have been, there was genuine hope among many that their situation would quickly and dramatically improve. For several reasons, these hopes hardly ever materialized. First, Nazi Germany was a highly centralized totalitarian state in which state and party had become virtually indistinguishable. Nazi rule not only left no room for any kind of dissent but also did not tolerate difference, a harshness that soon began to manifest itself in the extension of German laws and regulations to the incorporated territories and their implementation by Nazi officials from the Reich. This, however, is not to say that ethnic Germans in these areas did not play a part in the realization of Nazi policies, especially when it came to "dealing with" the non-German population. In addition, ethnic Germans too would soon feel the consequences of the Nazis' racially determined policies, as most of them would be subjected to classification under the *Volkslisten* (which distinguished between four groups: racially above average, average, below average, and unsuitable). Second, while there was some initial economic and material improvement, especially in the Sudetenland and later also in the predominantly German parts of Western Silesia, this was short-lived, and conditions began seriously to deteriorate as the war wore on. Third, the war itself took its toll. While the introduction of labor service may have been merely unpleasant, conscription and Allied bombing raids soon began to result in loss of life.

Before turning to the effects of German occupation policy on the non-German population groups, another aspect of the Nazi approach to the German question needs to be discussed—the resettlement program aimed at ethnic Germans outside what was considered German *Lebensraum* (living space). This *Lebensraum* doctrine, a central element of Nazi ideology, claimed that the German nation needed, and was in fact entitled to, a large area of contiguous territory for the realization of its full potential. Yet the *Lebensraum* question was not only a territorial issue; it also required large-scale resettlement of ethnic Germans from outside the designated territories of Greater Germany— Germany proper, Austria, the Czech lands, Alsace and Lorraine, and large parts of Western Poland occupied in 1939 and incorporated into the Reich. This, in turn, "necessitated" the deportation or otherwise elimination of most of the non-German population from these areas. The resettlement program of ethnic Germans was poignantly called *Heim-ins-Reich* (home to the Reich), and Heinrich Himmler, the head of the SS, was put in charge of it. With few exceptions in the case of Luxembourg and Alsace and Lorraine, the resettlement program affected almost exclusively the ethnic Germans of Southern and Eastern Europe. It was selective in that not all German minority groups were "eligible" for resettlement; those that could serve valuable purposes in projecting the image of the superior German and in strengthening relations with Hitler's allies in the region were to remain in their traditional settlement areas. Others that could become sources of tension—for example, with Italy in the case of South Tyrol, or with the Soviet Union in the case of the Baltic Germans—were resettled to the Reich. However, resettlement also depended on racial suitability according to the criteria established by the *Volkslisten*. Ethnic Germans in its first two categories (racially above average and average) were deemed useful for colonizing the new *Lebensraum;* in exceptional cases, some from the third category (racially below average) were included in this group as well. Germans in the last two categories (below average and unsuitable) and non-Germans in categories one and two were to undergo Germanization in parts of the so-called old Reich (i.e., Germany in the borders of 1938), while non-Germans found to be racially below average or even unsuitable were simply excluded from the resettlement program, or, if they had somehow slipped through the net of the initial screening, sent back to where they had come from.

The Destruction of Czechoslovakia in 1939

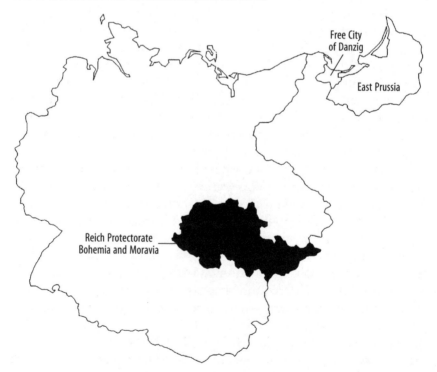

Germany after the Occupation and Annexation of Western Poland, 1939

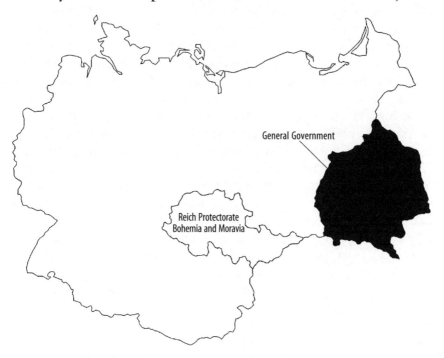

On the surface, Hitler's announcement of the resettlement program on 6 October 1939 marked a departure from what had appeared to be his policy toward ethnic German minorities, at least in Central and Eastern Europe, namely, their incorporation into the Reich by way of territorial aggrandizement. Yet this interpretation of events overlooks the primarily instrumental role Hitler had assigned to them at this stage. With further acquisitions and conquests temporarily ruled out for strategic reasons after the victory over Poland, resettlement served two purposes: the elimination of minorities as potential threats to friendly relations with Germany's allies at the time (in particular Mussolini and Stalin), and the beginning of the building of a new racially pure nation in Germany's enlarged *Lebensraum*.

A first wave of resettlement affected, apart from South Tyrol, the three Baltic republics and eastern Poland, all of which had become part of the Soviet zone of influence according to the August 1939 Molotov-Ribbentrop pact and its amendment at the end of September. From

Volhynia and Galicia in eastern Poland, some 135,000 ethnic Germans
were evacuated to the Reich, followed in the summer of 1940 by about
thirty thousand ethnic Germans from areas of Poland that had not been
annexed to the Reich—the so-called *Generalgouvernement*. In contrast
to the latter, which was the first unilateral resettlement action taken by
the Nazis, the former resembled very much earlier Balkan cases, such
as the Bulgarian-Turkish population exchange of 1919 and the Greco-
Turkish exchange of 1923, in that it was based on the principle of reciprocity. According to a German-Soviet Treaty of November 1939, the
Germans from eastern Poland were to be "exchanged" with Russians,
Ukrainians, and Belorussians from the parts of Poland that had been
assigned to the German zone of influence. Resettlement from the Baltic
states occurred in two steps. About sixty thousand ethnic Germans from
Latvia and Estonia had moved to the Reich by the end of 1939, only
about three-quarters of the estimated total in both states. However,
when the Soviet Union invaded the three states and subsequently formally incorporated them as union republics, people who had initially
declined resettlement quickly changed their minds. The Soviet invasion
also raised the issue of ethnic Germans in Lithuania and created a territorial dispute between the two supposed allies over a small strip of
Lithuanian territory "belonging" to the German zone of influence according to the Molotov-Ribbentrop pact. After negotiations that were
drawn out into the autumn of 1940, a deal was struck according to
which the remaining almost twenty thousand ethnic Germans from
Latvia and Estonia were allowed to leave, alongside some fifty thousand
from Lithuania, in exchange for Germany's surrendering its claim to a
stretch of Lithuanian borderland.

A second wave of resettlement began in the autumn of 1940. The
first two resettlement operations, from the Romanian territories of
Bessarabia and northern Bukovina, also occurred primarily in order
to avoid tensions with the Soviet Union. In striking similarity to the
second stage of resettlement from the Baltic states, the principle of
territory in exchange for people was applied. Hitler conceded to Stalin
that in addition to what had been agreed in the Molotov-Ribbentrop
pact, he would not object to the Soviet annexation of northern
Bukovina. In return, the Soviets agreed to the resettlement of over
ninety thousand ethnic Germans from Bessarabia and of more than
forty thousand from northern Bukovina. Another agreement was then
concluded with Romania to resettle two further groups of ethnic
Germans—those living in the Romanian part of Dobrudja and in the
southern Bukovina, in total almost seventy thousand people.

Other resettlement operations in Eastern Europe were primarily determined by the course of the war. After the invasion of Yugoslavia in April, ethnic Germans had to be removed from those parts that were awarded to Italy, based on the same considerations that had prompted the 1939 option agreement between Hitler and Mussolini on South Tyrol. Larger groups of ethnic Germans were also evacuated from Croatia and Serbia, where they had come under increasing partisan attack. The German community of Bulgaria was resettled almost in its entirety, as was that of Greece. The proportionately smallest number of ethnic Germans was evacuated from the Soviet Union. Following Hitler's attack in June 1941, Stalin had reacted immediately and deported almost all ethnic Germans from the European part of the Soviet Union, including those from the centuries-old Volga Republic, to Central Asia, leaving behind only a few women, children, and elderly people, most of whom had been sent to the Reich by German occupation forces by the summer of 1942.

Most important for developing a comprehensive understanding of the Nazi approach to the German question is its broader context. Resettlement was only one element in the Nazis' strategy for solving the German question their way. One day after his announcement of the resettlement program to the Reichstag in October 1939, Hitler signed a formal decree with far wider implications—not just to resettle ethnic Germans in the Reich but to remove all racially or otherwise undesirable elements from the German nation and its *Lebensraum* and to colonize those of the occupied territories assigned for resettlement. The latter two policies affected initially above all Jews and Poles, but later also most other peoples living under German occupation. Polish losses amount to almost one-quarter of the entire prewar population— six million people, half of them Jews. Their elimination was part of a deliberate strategy—the *Generalplan Ost,* drafted in 1941—to create a large contiguous area suitable for the building of a racially pure German nation in its exclusive *Lebensraum.* While Jews, Poles, and other *fremdvölkische* (alien) elements were deemed racially unsuitable by the Nazis to share the same living space with Germans, the Nazis had considerably fewer problems with these people serving as forced laborers in German industry and agriculture. By 1944, about eight million civilian workers and prisoners of war, more than half of them from Poland and the Soviet Union, were condemned to contribute to the German war effort. As many of them were literally worked to death, the use of slave labor fit well into the Nazis' extermination strategy.

German war crimes in occupied countries across Europe have been well documented and analyzed elsewhere. However, it is necessary to point out that ethnic Germans in many parts, especially of Central and Eastern Europe, played important roles in aiding German forces against resistance movements. Invaluable for their local knowledge, many of them were recruited to assist the Wehrmacht, SS, and Gestapo in their attempts to root out partisan movements in Slovakia, Romania, Yugoslavia, and Italy. In addition, many ethnic Germans also volunteered for the SS, such as the approximately twenty thousand Banat Swabians who made up the SS Prinz Eugen Division.

THE SHAPING OF ALLIED PLANS FOR A RESOLUTION OF THE GERMAN QUESTION AFTER THE WAR

The beginning of the Second World War was the most obvious indication that the order established by the Paris peace treaties after the First World War had not been a durable one. However, its failure had become clear much earlier and had manifested itself primarily in two interdependent processes: Germany did not accept, or only partially accepted, what had been imposed in Versailles, and the Western Allies either bowed to German demands or did nothing, or not enough, to counter them prior to Germany's attack on Poland in 1939. However one chooses to distribute the blame for the failure of the interwar system, the bottom line remains the same, that the settlement in 1919 had not resolved the German question.

This was widely acknowledged by the Allied powers of the Second World War and was one of the factors that shaped their war aims and their postwar plans for Germany. The primary goal was to prevent Germany from ever becoming a security risk again for its neighbors or for any new international order. This purpose related, first of all, to German military and political power and was expressed in the Allies' determination to achieve Germany's unconditional surrender and to occupy the country in its entirety. It also manifested itself in initially vague, but gradually more and more precise, plans for territorial readjustments and population transfers, both of which were to give Germany's neighbors greater external security and internal stability. Finally, there was also a punitive dimension to Allied plans, seeking the punishment of those responsible for the war, the Holocaust, and the numerous war crimes committed in occupied territories. However, additional war aims of individual members of the anti-Hitler coalition also played a role in shaping Allied plans. The two most significant for a discussion of the German question are Soviet plans for territorial expansion to the west and the consequently necessary compensation of Poland with German territories—the "westward shift" of Poland—and the desire by both Poland and Czechoslovakia, as well as some other states in southeastern Europe, to rid themselves of their troublesome German minorities after the war. What was agreed at Potsdam in 1945 was thus the outcome of a complex and dynamic interaction between the Allied powers and their associates. It was a compromise that bore the mark of provisionality in many respects, and it was to be short-lived, too.

Throughout the wartime deliberations of the three principal allies—the United States, United Kingdom, and Soviet Union—and other members of the anti-Hitler coalition, a number of key themes can be identified that are particularly relevant for their approach to a postwar resolution to the German question. The first is the unconditional surrender of Germany and its occupation by Allied troops. The demand for unconditional surrender was agreed upon between Roosevelt and Churchill at their meeting in Casablanca in January 1943 and was subsequently also accepted by Stalin. It took almost another year for the Allies to decide on the military occupation of Germany as part of their postwar strategy of dealing with the German question—that is, to secure complete disarmament, denazification, decentralization, and eventual democratization of the former German Reich as well as to exercise ultimate control over political, economic, and social development for the foreseeable future. When, at the end of 1943, the first meeting of all three heads of state took place in the Iranian capital of Tehran, the "Big Three" strongly tended toward an even more radical solution—the territorial dismemberment of Germany into several independent entities. Yet in the end advocates of a joint occupation of Germany prevailed, and plans for dismemberment were abandoned, at least for the time being.

The discussion of territorial arrangements was not confined to whether Germany should continue to exist as a single entity under supreme Allied control. As early as the end of 1941, when the German advance had been stopped outside Moscow and Leningrad, Stalin had embarked on the road of arguing for territorial revisions that went beyond the undoing of all German acquisitions after 1937. That is, apart from demanding the restoration of an independent Austria and

Czechoslovakia in their 1937 borders, Stalin had his own vision for territorial rearrangements to benefit the Soviet Union. Over the years and with the increasing strength and importance of the Soviet Union as a vital member of the anti-Hitler coalition during the course of the war, Stalin's plans became more and more ambitious, and when the Big Three met at Tehran the westward shift of Poland was discussed for the first time explicitly. Several months before the end of the war, in Yalta in February 1945, Soviet expansion into eastern Poland was formally agreed upon; however, the extent of Poland's territorial compensation in the west remained unspecified. By then, plans for the establishment of different zones of occupation for each of the three powers had been approved, as had an Allied Control Council that was to enable the victors to exercise their powers within a joint framework for the administration of Germany as a unified entity. While dismemberment was not ruled out completely, it appeared more and more unlikely.

Yalta is also important inasmuch as the Soviet Union, the United States, and the United Kingdom decided there to allocate to France its own zone of occupation (to be carved out of the territory of the British and American zones) and to invite France to join the Allied Control Council. Reparations too were discussed in some detail, and the three Allies agreed that these should be exacted in principle in three different ways: "from the national wealth of Germany located on the territory of Germany herself as well as outside her territory . . . for the purpose of destroying the war potential of Germany," by "annual deliveries of goods from current production," and through the "use of German labor." No agreement could be reached, however, on the total sum of reparations, and the matter was referred to a reparations commission to be set up in Moscow.

Thus, by the end of the war the foundations for Germany's future had been laid: unconditional surrender, total occupation, division among the Allies into zones of occupation, and the payment of reparations. In addition it had also been made clear from early in the war that the basis for any of these policies was Germany in the borders of 1937—that is, without Austria and without the Sudetenland. Problematic in this context were two issues: territorial compensation for Poland at the expense of Germany, and the large-scale removal of German population groups from the Sudetenland and the territories to be acquired by Poland and the Soviet Union. There was not much doubt in the minds of any of the Allies or of Polish or Czech politicians that the transfer of the Germans from their countries was an essential precondition for a more peaceful postwar order. In fact, the idea of population transfers and exchanges was neither new nor confined to Germany. It had been common practice throughout the twentieth century (the Greco-Turkish exchange agreed in Lausanne in 1923 and the transfer of the Baltic Germans in 1939–40, among others, served as precedents for Allied deliberations) and was also to affect the Slovak-Hungarian and Polish-Soviet borderlands in the post-1945 period. However, while the principle of a transfer was accepted, its particularities were never formally agreed upon among the Allies. The British government, which had set up a special advisory commission on the issue, was most acutely aware of the potential problems and the limitations of population transfers. This was one of the reasons that Churchill tried to prevent too large a territorial expansion of Poland, as each square mile given to Poland potentially meant more Germans having to be accommodated in the Allied zones of occupation, quite apart from the fact that the westward shift of Poland also deprived Germany of some of its key agricultural areas. Yet the course of the war and the realities it established on the ground made such resistance futile. By the time the Big Three met again in Potsdam, the expulsions were already under way on a large scale, the partition of East Prussia between Poland and the Soviet Union had all but formally occurred, and German territories east of the rivers Oder and Neisse had been placed under "Polish administration" by Stalin. All the Allies did in Potsdam was to give formal consent to the "orderly and humane transfer" of ethnic Germans.

In many other respects too the Potsdam Agreement merely confirmed and formalized policies and plans that the Allies had agreed upon explicitly or tacitly in earlier negotiations and that they had begun implementing after Germany's unconditional surrender on 8 May 1945. For example, the Allies had already issued their "Declaration Regarding the Defeat of Germany and the Assumption of Supreme Authority by Allied Powers," on 5 June 1945. In it the commanders in chief of the United States, the United Kingdom, the Soviet Union, and the French Republic declared that they would "assume supreme authority with respect to Germany, including all the powers possessed by the German Government, the High Command and any state, municipal, or local government or authority" and that they reserved the right for themselves to "determine the boundaries of Germany or any part thereof and the status of Germany or of any area at present being part of German territory."

In terms of international law, what has become known as the Potsdam Agreement is not an international, legally binding treaty. Rather, it is a joint communiqué, published immediately after the conclusion of the meeting, summarizing the proceedings. It included the decisions, agreements, and declarations about the future of Germany of the Big Three, among whom Roosevelt had been replaced by Harry Truman, while Clement Attlee took Churchill's place halfway through the conference. The main points relevant for the future development of the German question can be summarized as follows. Supreme authority in Germany was to be exercised by the commanders in chief of the Big Three and France, individually in their own zones of occupation and jointly as members of the Control Council. Occupation policy, as far as possible, was to treat the German population uniformly throughout all zones of occupation; policy was to be guided by the principles of disarmament and demilitarization, the destruction of the National Socialist Party and all otherwise affiliated organizations, the eventual rebuilding of democratic political institutions and processes in Germany (including the reform of educational and judicial institutions), the punishment of Nazi war criminals, political and economic decentralization, and the treatment of Germany as one unit for political and economic purposes, but without the establishment of a central German government.

As far as reparation claims were concerned, each of the Allied powers was to satisfy its claims from its own zone. The Soviet Union was to satisfy Polish claims from within its zone, the British and the Americans were to do the same with claims from other countries. There were also provisions for additional Soviet compensation from the western zones.

With respect to territorial changes, it was agreed that a Soviet proposal for the partition of East Prussia would be favorably looked upon and supported by the Western Allies at a forthcoming peace conference. Provisionally, the northern part of East Prussia was to be administered by the Soviet Union. Pointing to an earlier agreement reached in Yalta, it was agreed that subject to a final peace treaty, the former German territories east of the rivers Oder and Neisse, and including the southern part of East Prussia and the Free City of Danzig and its adjacent areas, should be placed under Polish administration and not be considered part of the Soviet zone of occupation.

As for the transfer of German population groups from Poland, Czechoslovakia, and Hungary, the Allies agreed, as noted, that it should take place in an orderly and humane way. Recognizing that a large influx of Germans was to be expected and with it an increased burden on the authorities in each zone of occupation to provide food and shelter, the Allies requested a suspension of the expulsions from Poland, Czechoslovakia, and Hungary and proposed that the Allied Control Council in Germany examine the specifics of further transfers and in particular the problem of the distribution of the expellees in the different zones of occupation.

Thus, by the end of the summer of 1945 the foundations for Allied policy had been laid and with them the parameters in which the German question would henceforth develop. Such, at least, had been the plan, but events in the course of the following four years would fundamentally alter the situation in Germany, Europe, and the world, creating yet a new geopolitical framework in which the dynamics of the German question would unfold over the next four decades.

ALLIED POLICY AFTER POTSDAM: FROM COOPERATION TO CONFRONTATION

The minimal consensus that had existed among the Allies was by its very nature a wartime consensus. It consisted of three principles (see Alter 2000: 104f.): unconditional military and political surrender of Germany, total occupation of Germany by Allied forces, and prohibition on separate peace treaties by any one ally with Germany. This consensus had been forged against the background of a war that had been unleashed by Germany and that threatened the values and physical existence of all three Allied powers. Recognizing that Germany could be defeated only in a joint effort, they were willing and able to cooperate. Once the primary war aim of defeating Germany had been accomplished, differences between the Allies, as well as their secondary objectives, came to the fore, and tensions grew. The Allies were initially still forced to cooperate by necessity; the period after the Potsdam Agreement was characterized by a decreasing willingness to find compromises and by a growing resolve to pursue more vigorously individual goals with respect to Germany and the postwar international order. This was primarily an issue of an East-West split, between the United States, the United Kingdom, and France on the one side and the Soviet Union on the other. But not all was rosy among the Western Allies, either. In fact, as I show in a brief case study of the Saar at the end of this chapter, French policy had its own particular

The Occupation of Germany, 1945–1949

agenda—one that would result in a temporary "triple partition" of Germany.

According to Stalin's dictum that whoever conquers a particular territory his own system on it, developments in the four different zones of occupation in Germany became increasingly divergent and confrontational, especially if one compares the three western zones with the Soviet zone of occupation.

Politically, this manifested itself in the increasing dominance of communists in the Soviet zone of occupation. Supported by the Soviet military administration, those functionaries had spent, and survived, the years of the Third Reich in the Soviet Union and were therefore considered trustworthy by Stalin and his representatives in Germany; they assumed control in the emerging German institutions in the

Soviet zone. While they did not always occupy top positions, they normally controlled key functions of the new administrations, such as justice, internal affairs, and personnel, and they used this control to shape the direction and implementation of policies in the long run. The reestablished Communist Party of Germany had a clear advantage over all other parties in the Soviet zone in that it received substantial backing from the Soviet military administration. This manifested itself on the one hand in material support, but on the other hand, and perhaps more significantly, in the way in which the Soviet administration interfered in the internal affairs of other parties, primarily by removing functionaries who were perceived as disloyal or potentially threatening.

In this way a political system was established by the late 1940s that, formally, was a multiparty system but in reality was controlled entirely by the Communist Party. The communists had, under dubious circumstances to say the least, "united" with the Social Democrats of the Soviet zone to form a new party, the Socialist Unity Party of Germany (*Sozialistische Einheitspartei Deutschlands*, SED), which dominated the political process in the Soviet zone. Nevertheless, the SED managed to attract almost half the vote in relatively free and fair elections at local and state levels in 1947 and 1948. There clearly was a longing among many parts of the population for a new beginning, be it radical change or a means of seeking absolution for their own involvement with the Nazis. The same desire existed in the western zones of occupation, but under the different conditions here it led to the creation of a liberal-democratic party system in which the communists played a role initially, but even then only marginally. Like Stalin in his zone, the Western Allies shaped the institutions of their zones according to their own systems. Marginal differences aside, this allowed them to lay the groundwork for the future democratic political system of the West German state.

Similar differences existed in relation to the economy. From the beginning, the division of Germany into eastern and western zones had disadvantaged the East: Poor in natural resources, the area had always been dependent upon supplies and deliveries from western parts or areas that no longer belonged to Germany, such as Silesia. The southern parts of the Soviet zone were industrial areas, containing manufacturing, chemical, and textile industries that, to the extent that they were still operational after Allied bombing raids, had only limited, or no, access to the materials upon which production depended.

In addition, Soviet reparations policy took a heavy toll on the economy of the eastern zone. While the Americans and British limited their reparations claims and subsequently introduced the Marshall Plan to kick-start the West German economy, Soviet policy was to dismantle factories and ship them to the Soviet Union and Poland, to take large amounts of goods out of the ongoing production process, and to take over numerous plants and mines and let them produce directly for the needs of the occupation troops or the Soviet economy. Although this policy was gradually reversed and completely abandoned after 1953, it meant that the economic conditions under which the two future German states would develop were fundamentally different. In addition, as early as 1948 there were the beginnings of central planning structures for the economy in the Soviet zone, which among other things had been made possible and necessary by expropriations of Nazi war criminals, real and alleged, and the administration of these and otherwise "ownerless" facilities by local and state authorities across the Soviet zone. The currency reform in 1948, first in the western zones (which by now had merged into the jointly run tri-zone) and then in the Soviet zone, was the last (but significant) development that completed the economic partition of Germany before the political partition.

The unilateral currency reform in the tri-zone also prompted a severe and dangerous deterioration of relations among the former allies. With the Allied institutions for the central administration of Germany all but collapsed, the blockade of the western sectors of Berlin by the Soviet Union marked a further step toward the partition not only of Germany but also of Europe. Eventually, the Western Allies and the political elite of the western zones of occupation came to the conclusion that German unity for the time being was neither possible nor particularly desirable, given alleged and real Soviet aspirations for the dominance of Europe. Thus, plans were drawn up and implemented that led to the foundation of the Federal Republic of Germany. Beginning in the autumn of 1948, deliberations began about a West German constitution, the *Grundgesetz*, or Basic Law, which was enacted by decree of the Western Allies in May 1949. Following elections to the first West German parliament, the Bundestag, in August, a government under Konrad Adenauer was constituted on 7 September 1949—the Federal Republic of Germany had been founded. One month later, on 7 October, the Soviet Union followed suit and established the German Democratic Republic.

TERRITORIAL ISSUES IN THE WEST: FRANCE, THE SAAR, AND THE ORIGINS OF THE "TRIPLE PARTITION" OF GERMANY

Despite the fact that the main fault line among the Allies was to emerge along ideological divisions and by the late 1940s would result in the division of Germany and Europe, the Western Allies did not always pursue congruent strategies. This is most obvious in the case of French policy toward the Saar, which, it could be argued, led to a "triple partition" of Germany, overcome only in the mid-1950s. While the division into the two German states was far longer lasting and more significant for the development of the German question in subsequent decades, the French occupation of the Saar, policies meant to separate this area from Germany, and its successful reunification with the Federal Republic in 1957 established precedents that are worthy of closer examination. In the context of this chapter, I shall consider only the separation of the Saar from Germany; I will turn to their reunification in chapter 5.

France, which had suffered greatly and incurred tremendous losses during the Second World War, had three basic demands at the end of the conflict—security, reparations, and participation in the occupation of German territory. Common to all three demands was that they gave rise to territorial and border questions at Germany's western borders— questions involving, just as after the end of the First World War, the Saar, the Ruhr area, and the Rhineland. The Rhine was once again argued to be a natural border that, in its whole length, represented French and European security interests. The Saar and the Ruhr, on the other hand, were deemed equally important in security considerations, primarily because of their industrial and natural resources, which had always served as backbone of the German war industry.

French proposals concerning the special treatment of the Saar, Ruhr, and Rhineland were initially not very well received either among the Allies or even in France itself, as substantial territorial gains at the cost of Germany were seen as potentially giving rise to renewed German nationalism. Such objections, however, did not stop the French government under General Charles de Gaulle from pursuing its distinct interests, particularly with respect to the Saar. In fact, these early objections helped France to formulate a successful long-term policy with respect to the Saar. First of all, it was considered necessary to disassociate the Saar question from the Rhineland and the Ruhr. This was not difficult, as the Saar, in contrast to the other two territories,

had historically been under French influence for considerable periods
and had even belonged to the French state for some time (1681–97
and 1792–1814/15). In addition, it had already served once as compensation for French war losses, between 1919–20 and 1935 (see
chapter 2). A problem that remained, and had existed in a similar way
in 1919, was the fact that the population of the Saar, in contrast to
that of Alsace, had a very strong German identity and in the 1935 referendum had demonstrated its desire to be German and to belong to
Germany rather than to France. This argument, however, could at least
be weakened by pointing to Nazi influence at the time. A French
mission sent to the Saar in the summer of 1945, after France had formally become the Allied occupation power in the Saar, strengthened
the French argument by concluding that the Saar had been a disputed
territory between France and Germany for almost three hundred years
and that it had strategic importance for France because of its defense
value, industries, and natural resources. The solution proposed by the
mission formed the basis of French policy in the years to follow—
economic integration of the Saar into France but political autonomy
within a framework of monetary and customs union, clearly outside
German boundaries—that is, the political and economic detachment
of the Saar from Germany.

In early 1946, the French government made a proposal for the future status of the Saar that marked the abandonment of earlier annexation plans in favor of economic union (Hudemann 1995: 23ff.).
Economically, the Saar was to be incorporated into France and the
French customs area, French rights to the Saar coal mines were to be
recognized by the Allies, and the German mark was immediately to
be replaced by the French franc. Politically, France envisaged the establishment of a central administrative body for the Saar, the High
Commission; the delegation of responsibility for Saar foreign and
defense policy to France; and the permanent deployment of French
troops in the area (Pohlmann 1992: 102–104). The French decision
to press for such an arrangement had been informed by a number of
factors, not all of which were to the advantage of France. On the negative side was the situation in the Saar itself. Between thirty and thirty-
five thousand people had died during the war, more than a hundred
thousand were prisoners of war, and there was also a high percentage
of wounded and missing. More than half of the housing stock had
been destroyed. Economic and social life were completely paralyzed,
mostly as a result of the casualties but also because schools, hospitals,

factories, and bridges had been destroyed. Incorporating the Saar into France, whatever the concrete method, gave France responsibility to feed and house the population (Freymond 1960: 12). This population not only had a long-standing and strong regional sense of identification with its homeland but, as noted, was generally pro-German—that is, it regarded itself, the character of its homeland, and its identity best preserved in a German national environment. In addition, the small pro-French section was split between those who wanted to establish the Saar as at least politically an autonomous unit and those who favored complete integration with France. However, on the positive side were anticipated long-term economic gains and political advantages for France. The proposed arrangement would deprive Germany of a part of its war industry, disassociate the Saar from French reparation demands, and weaken the political ties between the Saar and Germany.

The implementation of this French proposal was possible only because a number of factors worked to France's advantage, the most important of them being that Britain and the United States had so far been in favor of a special treatment for the Saar but had not developed any concrete plans (Pohlmann 1992: 69f. and 104f.). Other factors were France's relative strength compared to Germany, its status as one of the victorious powers, and the recognition of the French entitlement to military security and material compensation. Of no less importance was the beginning of the split between the United States and Britain, on the one side, and the Soviet Union on the other. The fact that the four allies were unable to achieve agreement on the Saar issue, and the increasing emphasis that the United States and Britain placed on Western integration, made it easier for France to secure a settlement of the Saar question that met its interests. Thus, while the Soviet Union strongly resisted any plans to place the Saar under a separate regime and to remove this valuable territory from the pool of reparations, France obtained conditional approval from the other two Allies in exchange for its support for the establishment of a central (West) German administration (Freymond 1960: 17–22).

While economic integration was pursued eagerly by France and encountered hardly any resistance, any moves toward further political integration met with strong opposition from within three camps— internationally from the Allies, and within France on political grounds from the socialists and on economic grounds from Lorraine. This strong opposition to political integration of the Saar into France, however, did not mean that France would stop pursuing its policy of separating the Saar at least politically from Germany. As clearly no permanent international settlement of the issue, approved by all four Allied powers, could be achieved in the foreseeable future, a Saar constitution was required to compensate partly for the absence of an international statute. A constitutional commission was set up on 13 February 1947, and a draft constitution was published on 25 September 1947. The constitution was based on similar documents adopted for the other German states but had to observe certain French directives, most of which became part of the preamble. The key points of the constitution that represented French interests in the Saar were economic integration through monetary and customs union, independence from German sovereignty, French responsibility for representing the external and defense interests of the Saar, the application of French monetary and customs legislation, and the right of the French governor in the Saar to issue decrees to safeguard the economic union and to execute monetary and customs regulations (Cowan 1950: 221). The special rights that France could derive from the economic union with the Saar were also specified in the preamble, and their enumeration was a significant success for those who had argued for stronger autonomy of the Saar, as this enumeration meant that there would be no subsequent interpretation disputes on French rights (Sander 1995: 248).

The tacit consent of the United States and Britain to these French integration measures was put on a formal legal basis with the tripartite agreement of 20 February 1948 in Berlin. The agreement consisted of four individual treaties, specifying that all coal produced in the Saar belonged to France, that the French reparations account would be reduced by seventy million marks, and that the trade relations between the Saar and the British and American zones of occupation were henceforth regarded as foreign trade (cf. Pohlmann 1992: 212–14). This considerably strengthened the French position in the Saar and vis-à-vis Germany and the Western Allies. However, because this agreement was the only one ever concluded among the Western Allies regarding the Saar, Germany could later adopt a position claiming the Saar was still part of German territory. Yet it would be wrong to suggest that the subsequent conflict between France and Germany over the Saar emerged from this agreement. Rather, it emerged from the different interpretations of it—France took it as consent from the Western Allies to pursue its policy of economic integration of the Saar, with all its obvious political consequences, while Germany insisted on the provisional status of the settlement and saw the agreement merely as a matter of regulating technical issues.

* * *

Thus, within four and a half years of the end of the Second World War, Germany as a state no longer posed a threat to European or world security. The German question, however, once again had only partly been resolved: new dimensions had been created, and others merely reduced or suppressed in importance because of the new geopolitical situation in Europe and the world. The Cold War had begun and with it a new chapter in the development of the German question, which, nevertheless, displayed its "usual" characteristics of population and territorial dimensions. These are the focus of discussion in the following two chapters.

Chapter 4

The Challenge of Integration: Refugees, Expellees, and Aussiedler and Their Integration in Germany

We demand and request today: (1) Equal rights as citizens, not just before the law, but also in the reality of everyday life; (2) Just and equal distribution to the entire German people of the burdens of the last war . . . ; (3) Integration of all occupational groups of the expellees in the life of the German people; [and] (4) Active incorporation of the German expellees in the reconstruction of Europe.

—Charter of the German Expellees (1950)

By the time the expulsions had more or less come to an official end in 1949, approximately twelve million ethnic Germans had had to leave their homelands in Poland (including the former German territories east of the Oder-Neisse line), Czechoslovakia, Hungary, Romania, and Yugoslavia. More than 60 percent of them came from Poland, almost one-quarter from Czechoslovakia, primarily from the Sudetenland.

About two-thirds of the expellees were resettled in the western zones, the bulk of them in the American and British occupation zones; of the remaining third sent to the Soviet zone, approximately 40 percent left for West Germany before 1961. A small number of ethnic Germans, especially from Czechoslovakia, Romania, and Yugoslavia, were sent to Austria. Nevertheless, the overwhelming majority ended up in what was later to become the Federal Republic of Germany, where, despite their different geographic, cultural, religious, and ideological backgrounds, they collectively played a politically significant role during the first decade of the country's existence. Subsequently, their domestic political influence declined, but their part in the public discourse did not, or at least not to the same extent. With the further arrival of over four million so-called *Aussiedler* (ethnic Germans who emigrated to the Federal Republic after 1950), by the turn of the century the issue of their integration continued to be important politically, economically, and socially. It is therefore reasonable to focus on the situation in the Federal Republic when examining this particular dimension of the German question after 1945. Nevertheless, an initial exploration of the situation in the Soviet zone of occupation and the later German Democratic Republic provides a useful comparison in terms of the integration policies adopted and the rationales behind them.

UMSIEDLER IN THE SOVIET ZONE OF OCCUPATION AND THE GERMAN DEMOCRATIC REPUBLIC

The situation in the eastern parts of Germany under Soviet control differed in a number of ways from that in the western zones. First, for the majority of refugees and expellees in the immediate postwar period, it was a transit area on their way to their "final" destination farther west. This was particularly the case for those fleeing from the advancing Soviet troops and seeking refuge in the (future) British and American zones of occupation. To a lesser, but still significant, extent this was also true for the expellees. Once the Allies had reached an agreement on quotas, there were still several million expellees who had been designated to one of the western zones of occupation; in particularly, those from areas east of the Oder-Neisse line had had to travel through the Soviet zone of occupation. With transportation infrastructure and other facilities largely destroyed, this proved an additional burden for the authorities in the Soviet zone, which, nevertheless, put up with facilitating the passage of expellees rather than having to accommodate them permanently in addition to those that had been assigned to them.

A second difference lies in the fact that roughly 40 percent of the expellees originally sent to the later East German state left before 1961, primarily for West Germany, but also to the United States and Canada. Thus, the actual number of refugees and expellees in the former GDR was only about one-sixth of their total number in Germany after the war. This also meant that by 1961 the share of the expellees and refugees in the total of the East German population had dropped from about one-quarter to some 12 percent. The long-term challenge that they posed in terms of their economic, political, and social integration was thus far less serious than in the Federal Republic.

However, the decline in numbers took effect only several years after their arrival, primarily after 1952, when the Bundestag in the Federal Republic had passed the Burden Sharing Law (*Lastenausgleichsgesetz*) and one year later the Refugee and Expellee Law (*Bundesvertrie-benengesetz*). Until then, the challenge of refugee integration was a very real and severe one, a task that put enormous strains on the economy and social fabric of the Soviet zone and later the East German state. In response, the authorities in the Soviet zone sought to push through integration policies much more quickly than their counterparts in the western zones could or were willing to. As early as September 1945, a central office for dealing with the *Umsiedler* (resettlers) was established, several months before anything similar happened in any of the western zones. The subsequent establishment of local branches across their entire occupation zone enabled the Soviet authorities and their East German counterparts to begin coordinating integration policy. This was particularly related to two sets of policy measures aimed at the integration of refugees and expellees, policies that are in considerable contrast to those pursued by the Western Allies and subsequently by West German governments. Apart from what in today's terminology would be best described as humanitarian aid measures, which were well intended but severely limited by the economic constraints the authorities faced, expellees and refugees in eastern Germany also benefited from redistribution, particularly in terms of housing. The authorities in the Soviet zone of occupation had few qualms when it came to "reassigning" property to refugee and expellee families. In the first stage, this was possible because of the large-scale expropriation of former Nazis and the sequestration of abandoned properties. In a second stage, there were also some, albeit modest and overall not very effective, efforts to distribute housing more equally—that is, to put an end to underuse or misuse of available accommodation. While these policies did not improve relations between longtime residents and the newly arrived *Umsiedler,* they enabled the authorities to close almost all the more than 350 temporary reception camps that had been set up after 1945 and provide more or less permanent accommodation to the refugees and expellees in the Soviet zone by 1948 (Ther 2002: 60, 68).

The other unique dimension of integration policy in the Soviet zone of occupation and the later GDR was that the integration of *Umsiedler* was used as a pretext for fundamental political reforms, which in the long term contributed to the setting up in the East German state of a social, political, and economic system radically different from what would emerge in the later Federal Republic. This is most obvious in the case of the land reform instigated after 1945, which provided expellees, along with agricultural smallholders and farm laborers, with land of their own. This offered two opportunities for the Soviet-controlled authorities. First, it broke up the political and economic power of the large landowners, who had always been regarded as reactionary. The large landholders had prevented the communists from gaining influence in the countryside and were—rightly or wrongly, depending on the specific case—accused of having played a crucial role in Hitler's rise to power. Second, and this was in the long term more important, the land reform enabled the later communist government of East Germany to push from the mid-1950s onward for the collectivization of the agricultural sector in East Germany; it thus contributed to the consolidation of communist power and the establishment and solidification of socialist structures in this part of society. Quite clearly, the expellees and refugees who benefited from the land reform—and they were only about 10 percent of the total in the Soviet zone of occupation (Ther 2002: 64)—were unaware of this; given their desperate situation after flight, expulsion, and the often hostile receptions they experienced from residents, it is unlikely that many of them would have refused the opportunity to become economically self-sufficient and provide for themselves and their families by becoming farmers. The vast majority of the other *Umsiedler* were subsequently integrated in other parts of the economy, and as in the three western zones and the later Federal Republic, they provided an important part of the workforce that made the rebuilding of the state possible.

Politically, authorities in the Soviet zone took even fewer chances than those in the western sectors, maintaining throughout the existence of the East German state the ban on the formation of any organizations or lobby groups that would exclusively represent *Umsiedler* interests. This was primarily caused by fear of social destabilization and open defiance of certain aspects of policy of the emerging communist regime (especially with regard to the relationships with Poland and Czechoslovakia; see chapter 5). On the other hand, there was also one marked difference between the situation in the Soviet zone and the later East German state, and that in the West: central as well as state authorities in the East pursued a clear policy of equal rights and opportunities for *Umsiedler* rather than maintaining a distance from the expellees and refugees, as happened in some instances in the West (Ther 2002: 73). Thus there was, to some extent, less need for lobbying authorities in the Soviet zone, especially if one bears in mind that the lack of success in implementing many well-intended policies aimed at speedier integration was not caused by ill will but by a severe lack of resources. In the long run, it was this lack of resources, compared with the situation in the Federal Republic, that prompted many of the *Umsiedler,* together with longtime residents in the Soviet-controlled part of Germany, to leave for the Federal Republic.

The decline by 1961 in the number of citizens with expellee or refugee backgrounds made it much easier for authorities in the GDR to eliminate their fates from public discourse. History textbooks barely mentioned the expulsions, and subsequently even the (anyway misleading) term "*Umsiedler*" was banned from the official vocabulary. During the Cold War, expellees and their organizations in West Germany were portrayed as revisionists and warmongers. Discrediting them in many ways legitimized the expulsions and prevented not only expellees in the former GDR but the overwhelming majority of the population from coming to terms with this difficult dimension of the German question.

THE INTEGRATION OF EXPELLEES AND REFUGEES IN THE FEDERAL REPUBLIC

As in the eastern parts of occupied Germany, the integration problem in the western parts was initially one of housing, food, medical care, and employment, and the accordingly hostile reception of many refugees and expellees. Subsequently, however, their positive contribution to economic and social modernization, especially of relatively backward and underdeveloped areas in Bavaria, Lower Saxony, and Schleswig-Holstein, was both appreciated and publicly acknowledged, and it contributed to the overall successful economic and social integration of the expellees. It was also helped by an extensive apparatus of legislation passed from the late 1940s and early 1950s onward, providing expellees with equal rights in all areas of social, political, and economic life in Germany and offering compensation for losses incurred as a consequence of the collective expropriation of their former homelands. Thus, within a few years after the expulsions the foundations were laid for a lasting and successful integration of approximately ten million people, equaling about one-fifth of the total population of the West German state. This is also explicit in the fact that apart from a brief period in the 1950s, the expellees never had their own political party. Rather, their integration in the political process of West Germany helped its stabilization and consolidation into a three-party system by the early 1960s.

Against this general background of the integration process, it is useful to examine two sets of developments in greater detail, as they are remarkably different from the way in which integration was pursued, and eventually accomplished, in the Soviet-controlled part of Germany. The first of these is the legal framework of integration that was established in the early years of the Federal Republic's existence. The second set of developments comprises the more practical aspects of integration, and there I shall consider in particular the expellees' economic and political integration.

The Legal Framework of Expellee Integration

Without doubt, the most important piece of legislation passed in the context of the integration process of expellees and refugees was the Law on the Affairs of Expellees and Refugees (Federal Expellee Law) of 19 May 1953. However, before examining its provisions and impact in greater detail, it is useful to consider some earlier legislative acts that paved the way toward the expellee law.

The German Basic Law of 24 May 1949 reaffirmed the traditional notion of Germanness and eligibility for German citizenship, a notion that was based on descent rather than place of birth (*ius sanguinis* versus *ius soli*). The formulation chosen—"German in the sense of the Basic Law [*Deutsche/r im Sinne des Grundgesetzes*]"—deliberately avoided the creation of a citizenship specific to the Federal Republic, thereby retaining the idea of the unity of the German nation based on its ethnic characteristics (language, culture, traditions, customs, etc.) and their preservation among the different sections of a thus *ethnically united,* albeit *territorially divided,* national whole. According to Article 116, Paragraph 1, "German in the sense of the Basic Law is everyone who has German citizenship or who, as refugee or expellee of German ethnicity [*Flüchtling oder Vertriebener deutscher Volkszugehörigkeit*] or as spouse or descendant of such a person, has been residing on German territory in the borders of 1937." Article 6 of the Law on the Regulation of Questions of Citizenship (*Gesetz zur Regelung von Fragen der Staatsangehörigkeit*) of 22 February 1955 provided that "everyone who is German in the sense of Article 116 of the Basic Law but does not have German citizenship must be naturalized upon request." Thus, Article 116 of the Basic Law and Article 6 of the Law on the Regulation of Questions of Citizenship together established an entitlement of expellees and refugees, as well as subsequently of *Aussiedler,* to German citizenship. The Law on the Regulation of Questions of Citizenship also clarified the status of those ethnic Germans who, as a result of treaties between the German Reich and Czechoslovakia (1938) and Lithuania (1939) and on the basis of decrees concerning the citizenship of ethnic Germans in the Protectorate of Bohemia and Moravia (1939), in the territories of Poland annexed to the Third Reich (1941, 1942), in parts of Austria (1941), and in Ukraine (1943), had been collectively awarded citizenship of the German Reich as qualifying as Germans under Article 116 of the Basic Law. In this way, flight, expulsion, and emigration of ethnic Germans in Central and Eastern Europe after 1945 caused only minimal insecurity in terms of citizenship for those affected and provided one element of the foundation upon which their integration could eventually succeed.

Two further pieces of legislation were passed in 1949 specifically aimed at facilitating the integration process. The first of them was the so-called Immediate Aid Law (*Soforthilfegesetz*) of 8 August 1949, which provided emergency relief for refugees and expellees, making available monthly payments of seventy Deutschmarks per eligible person, as well as grants for housing and seed funding for new business ventures. Two days later, on 10 August 1949, the Refugee Settlement Law (*Flüchtlingssiedlungsgesetz*) was passed; it regulated the integration of expellees in the agricultural sector by, among other things, providing special loans for the purchase or lease of farmland, equipment, livestock, etc. While these two laws went some way toward addressing some of the most urgent needs of the refugees and expellees, they did not address one of their central demands, as formulated in their 1950 charter, namely, the "just and equal distribution to the entire German people of the burdens of the last war." This could be accomplished only in the far more comprehensive Law on the Equalization of Burdens (Burden Sharing Law, *Lastenausgleichsgesetz*) of 14 August 1952. In its preamble the law acknowledged that some parts of the population had suffered particularly from the war and its consequences and that there was therefore a need to balance these unequal burdens and to facilitate the integration of the more disadvantaged, bearing in mind both the principle of social justice and the economic resources available. At the same time, and politically equally significant in the long term, the preamble emphasized that "the offer and acceptance of compensation does not mean the abandonment of claims to the restitution of property left behind by the expellees." It is particularly noteworthy in this context that this formulation implies that neither the Federal Republic as a subject of international law nor individual expellees and refugees accepted, at this point in time, the permanence of the loss of homeland and property. Although there was a good deal of Cold War rhetoric in pronouncements such as these, the sense of injustice over the expulsions was much more strongly felt in the 1950s, and shared among far larger parts of the population, expellees and nonexpellees alike, than it might seem from today's perspective. The fact that in the 1950s it had already become clear that return to, or restitution of property or compensation for losses by, the states that had carried out the expulsions were unlikely (especially after the establishment of communist regimes in Poland and Czechoslovakia) had little effect on this widely shared view.

The funds necessary for the implementation of the Burden Sharing Law were to be raised by a special tax on assets, on earnings from mortgages, and on earnings from loans, taxes that were collected annually until 1979, and by contributions from the federal and state governments to make up for any shortfalls. From the thus established fund, expellees and refugees were to receive various forms of compensation in the form of grants and special-condition loans. The core demand of expellees had been the "principal compensation" (*Hauptentschädigung*), and this became part of the Burden Sharing Law by establishing an indirect proportional system of compensation for proven losses of property and other assets. Compensation was paid for losses below five thousand Reichsmarks at a level of 95 percent, going down to a level of 6.5 percent for losses above one million

Reichsmarks. By 1979, about 22 percent of the value of all prewar assets lost by expellees and refugees had been thus compensated.

The Federal Expellee Law of 19 May 1953 was the most comprehensive legislative act in relation to the Federal Republic's integration policy. Its passage by the two houses of parliament meant the partial amendment of previous laws related to integration policy. The Federal Expellee Law has retained most of its importance until the present day. For the process of integration it was significant in two ways: by making material and administrative provisions, and by clarifying the legal status of expellees and their entitlement to German citizenship. With regard to the former, the law regulated in a very generous way the modalities of the integration of expellees into the labor market; special tax regimes, loan schemes, and a whole range of federal and state subsidies were made available for those wishing to set up their own businesses or medical practices or start as farmers. A procedure was put in place for the recognition of diplomas, certificates, and other official documents relating to professional qualifications. Special training and retraining programs were put in place to help younger expellees integrate into the labor market. Expellees were also given preferred status in terms of housing, including publicly subsidized accommodation and special conditions for the acquisition of property. Of particular importance was also the very generous regulation of social insurance and, in particular, pension claims, according to which expellees were entitled to recognition of all previous contributions for the calculation of their benefits. In terms of expellees' social integration, the law provided that the federal and state governments had an obligation to contribute to the preservation of the culture, customs, and traditions of the expellees by maintaining archives and libraries and by sponsoring scholarly research into various aspects of the expulsion and integration of expellees and their consequences for the latter's identities and that of the German nation as a whole. This amounted to another formal recognition of the expellees, as well as of ethnic Germans remaining in Central and Eastern Europe, as part of the German nation.

In addition to these material provisions, the Federal Expellee Law also sought to administer a more equal distribution of expellees across the territory of the Federal Republic. For the "original" expellees, this meant at most an inducement to resettle in states where labor market conditions were more favorable for their particular types of occupation. Subsequently, however, relatively strict quota were introduced

for the "distribution" of *Aussiedler* among the federal states, cul-
minating in the 1996 Residency Assignment Act (*Wohnortzuweisungsgesetz*), which threatened loss of any integration benefits if
Aussiedler left their assigned states or districts of resettlement within
two years of arriving in the Federal Republic (see below).

Apart from these various material and administrative provisions for
integration, the Federal Expellee Law also provided a comprehensive
legal definition of the term "expellee," a definition that superseded
all previous, more limited classifications. The Federal Expellee Law established three basic categories of people who were to benefit from
special integration programs:

- Expellees (*Vertriebene*):
  - German citizens or ethnic Germans (*Deutsche Staats- oder Volks-
    zugehörige*) who had lost their homes as a consequence of flight or
    expulsion from former territories of the German Reich (i.e., those
    areas assigned to provisional Polish or Soviet administration in the
    Potsdam Agreement) or from areas outside the borders of the Reich
    as of 31 December 1937.
  - German citizens or ethnic Germans (*Deutsche Staats- oder Volks-
    zugehörige*) who had had to leave Germany after 1933 because of
    potential or actual acts of violence committed against them due to
    their political beliefs, race, or religion.
  - German citizens or ethnic Germans (*Deutsche Staats- oder Volks-
    zugehörige*) who had been affected by the *Heim-ins-Reich* resettle-
    ment program of the Nazis.
  - German citizens or ethnic Germans (*Deutsche Staats- oder Volks-
    zugehörige*) who left the Eastern Bloc, Albania, or Yugoslavia after
    the end of expulsions (designation as *Aussiedler*).
  - Non-German spouses of German citizens or ethnic Germans (*Deutsche
    Staats- oder Volkszugehörige*) who were classified as expellees.

- Homeland Expellees (*Heimatvertriebene*)
  - Any expellee who had his or her permanent residence on the terri-
    tory of the state from which he or she had been subsequently
    expelled.[1]
  - Any non-German spouse or descendant born after 31 December
    1937 of a qualifying homeland expellee.

- Refugees from the Soviet Zone of Occupation (*Sowjetzonenflüchtling*)
  - German citizens or ethnic Germans (*Deutsche Staats- oder Volks-
    zugehörige*) who had had to flee the Soviet zone of occupation be-
    cause of threats to their lives or freedom.[2]

The Federal Expellee Law also regulated that rights and privileges of expellee status could not be enjoyed by people who had either benefited from, or participated in, violations of basic principles of humanity or the rule of law, a provision that effectively should have ruled out active Nazis and supporters of the communist regime in East Germany. However, this regulation was not very strictly applied, certainly not in relation to former Nazis.

Practical Aspects of Integration

The legal framework for expellee integration, developed primarily from 1949 onward, enabled the authorities of the new West German state to make good progress with the integration process, which is generally understood to have been completed by the late 1950s. This is primarily true for economic and political aspects of integration. Although it was initially assumed that the social integration of expellees had been equally successful, later studies by social historians found that this process took longer (Schulze 2002). It goes beyond the scope of this study to examine the process of social integration and its failures in any greater detail. As the presumed failures have not resulted in political upheavals, I shall concentrate in the following on an overview of the main developments of economic and political integration of the German expellees and refugees. These two dimensions of the integration process were seen by the political elites of the time as essential conditions for the solution of the refugee problem, which, it was feared, could potentially lead to total economic collapse or political radicalization and fragmentation of the emerging structures of the future West German polity.

Despite the sense of urgency that existed among the British and American occupation authorities, they were initially more concerned with the organization and logistics of the transfer of ethnic Germans from Central and Eastern Europe to their zones than with the subsequent integration of the arrivals in the economic and political process. Formulation and implementation of appropriate policies to this effect were mostly left to German authorities in the various states and districts in the British and American zones. Although occupation authorities had to give ultimate approval to laws and directives passed by their German counterparts, the latter had a certain degree of freedom in policy making. Despite this, the overall policy framework that developed across the British and American zones was relatively similar in its key directions until 1949, and it was therefore relatively easy for the federal institutions after the constitution of the West German state to pursue a unified integration policy as exemplified in the legislative framework outlined above.

Before examining economic and political dimensions of the integration process in more detail, it is useful to gain an overall picture of the number of expellees on the territory of the future Federal Republic and their distribution to individual states. It should also be noted that the authorities in the French zone of occupation refused to take in any refugees and expellees until 1949, bar some exceptions, so that the overwhelming majority of the quota for the western zones had to be accommodated in the British and American occupation zones.

According to the 1946 census, 5.9 million expellees lived on the territory of the future West German state, their number increasing to 7.9 million by 1950. In absolute terms, the largest numbers of expellees lived in Bavaria (1.7–2 million) and Lower Saxony (1.5–1.9 million), followed by Schleswig Holstein (835,000–855,000), North Rhine Westphalia (700,000–1.3 million), Baden Wurttemberg (560,000–860,000), and Hesse (550,000–720,000). In terms of their share in the population, a different picture emerges with Schleswig Holstein (32.2–33 percent) leading Lower Saxony (23.4–27.2 percent), Bavaria (18.9–21.1 percent), Hesse (13.8–16.7 percent), Baden Wurttemberg (9.4–13.4 percent), and North Rhine Westphalia (5.8–10.1 percent). These proportions are illustrated in Figures 1 and 2.

Figure 1
Expellees in Selected West German States (in Millions)

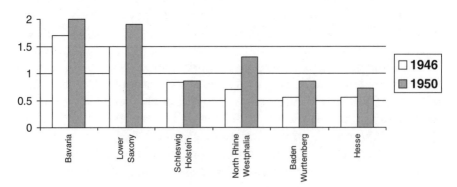

Figure 2
Expellees in Selected West German States (in % of Resident Population)

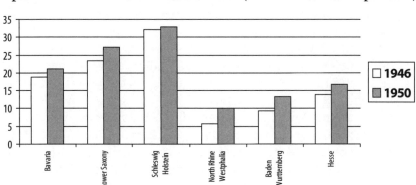

Economic Integration

The core problem of economic integration in the first years after the Second World War, in which by far the most expellees and refugees arrived in the British and American zones, was, apart from their provision with basic food and medical care, integration in the labor and housing markets. Obviously, these dimensions of integration were closely connected. After the end of the so-called wild expulsions in August 1945 and the subsequent decrease in numbers of expellees arriving in the British and American zones, the Allied Control Council approved a plan (20 November 1945) for the further transfer of ethnic Germans from Central and Eastern Europe to the territory of occupied Germany. According to this plan, a further two million people had to be accommodated in the British and American zones, which had already taken in almost six million people by the end of 1945. The magnitude of the task, therefore, lay not only in the sheer number of people who arrived but in the very short time span in which authorities had to provide for their basic needs of food, shelter, and medical care, as well as formulate policies for their long-term integration.

Once the process of reception had become more organized, by the summer of 1945, all new arrivals were initially sent to camps where they could be temporarily housed, fed, and provided with basic medical care. From these camps, designated "primary reception areas," of which several thousand existed across the states, they were transferred to private accommodation, primarily in rural areas, where, according to the authorities, there was a much greater chance for them to have access to food. Since most of the states that had been designated as reception areas, such as Bavaria, Lower Saxony, and Schleswig Holstein, were predominantly rural and agricultural areas, this did not prove too difficult. On the other hand, what these areas could generally not provide was any kind of employment other than work on farms, which in most cases did not suit the relatively skilled occupational profiles of many of the expellees. The only exception in this case was North Rhine Westphalia, a highly industrialized area with a great need for labor in the ensuing economic reconstruction process. However, urban areas had been particularly hard hit by Allied bombing raids during the war, so accommodation proved difficult. The authorities in the British and American zones struggled for a long time to overcome these and other initial problems, in particular in relation to the catering for expellees' basic needs in the transition camps and subsequently in designated resettlement areas. The key obstacle, however, in many cases remained the lack of suitable employment, which was further complicated by the return of prisoners of war and persons who had been conscripted for labor services as part of Allied reparations arrangements. Thus, the main challenge for the authorities remained until the late 1940s and early 1950s to "transform" refugees and expellees from aid-dependent into economically self-sufficient members of the population.

It became increasingly obvious that only a significant effort at economic reconstruction would enable authorities to succeed in their efforts to provide a long-term solution for the refugees and expellees. The opportunities for this improved markedly after the outbreak of the Cold War and the constitution of the two German states. First, it became clear to many expellees that a return to their homelands was unlikely and increasingly undesirable in the near future. Second, the beginning process of German integration into Western security and economic cooperation structures supplied much-needed foreign investment (above all, through the Marshall Plan), which provided the basis for the Federal Republic's "economic miracle" of the early 1950s. Third, the orientation of the federal government toward achieving social justice for the expellees and incorporating them fully in the system of social security in the emerging social market economy in West Germany matched the increasing desire of the overwhelming majority of expellees to contribute to, and benefit from, the reconstruction of Germany. That is, the state's aspiration to integrate meshed with the refugees' and expellees' aspiration to be integrated. Fourth, the expellees and refugees thus provided a willing and suitably qualified pool of labor and entrepreneurship that contributed to the economic reconstruction of the West German state as a whole, as well as to the industrialization and general development of many backward areas in Bavaria, Schleswig Holstein, and Lower Saxony. Finally, economic integration and, in particular, the contribution the expellees made to the industrialization of many underdeveloped areas of West Germany resulted in an easing of tensions with the indigenous population. If the new arrivals were initially viewed as competitors for scarce food resources and housing, their engagement for economic development was soon appreciated, as it benefited both parts of the population.

Against this background, it is not surprising that the desperate situations in which many expellees and refugees found themselves were overcome within the first decade after the foundation of the Federal Republic.

Political Integration

Not only had expellees and refugees suffered the trauma of being forced from their ancestral homeland, but they arrived to difficult conditions in underdeveloped areas of rural Bavaria, Lower Saxony, and Schleswig Holstein. They soon felt the need to organize and provide themselves with more effective means for an articulation of their distinct interests. With an official ban on expellee organizations in place in all three western occupation zones until 1949, refugees and expellees began to organize themselves in the first instance at the local level only, and often in close association with churches. Initially, there was a duality in the organizational structure. The Central Association of Expelled Germans (Zentralverband der vertriebenen Deutschen, ZvD; from 1951 on, Union of Expelled Germans [Bund vertriebener Deutscher, BvD]) concerned itself primarily with social and economic issues of integration and compensation, while regional-cultural associations (*Landsmannschaften*) focused on the preservation of the expellees' distinct geographic identities, including their traditions, customs, and culture. In August 1949 nine of them, which were already organized at the federal level or were in the process of establishing federal structures, formed the Union of Eastern German Regional-Cultural Associations (Vereinigung der ostdeutschen Landsmannschaften—VoL). Four of the *Landsmannschaften* joined the BvD in 1951 but retained their membership in the VoL. After a first attempt to overcome this dualism failed in 1951, the VoL pursued its own organizational consolidation, admitted further regional-cultural associations of expellees from southeastern Europe, changed its name to League of Regional-Cultural Associations (Verband der Landsmann-schaften—VdL) in August 1952, and began to establish its branches in each of the federal states of West Germany.

The political agenda of the various expellee organizations had been laid down in the 1950 Charter of the German Expellees. This fundamental document has guided expellee demands and policies ever since and is a vivid expression of the identity of expellees as a particular group in West German postwar society, united by collective experiences of suffering and their desire to correct the wrongs of expulsion. In the charter, the expellees proclaimed their willingness to forgo revenge and retribution, support the creation of a united and free Europe, and contribute to the reconstruction of Germany and Europe. On this basis, they demanded complete equality in West Germany, the fair sharing of the war consequences by the entire resident population, the integration of all occupational groups among them in the German economy, and the inclusion of the expellees in the European reconstruction effort. Though their demands focused on integration in West Germany, the expellees insisted on their right to their homeland and demanded that it be recognized as a fundamental human right.[3] Here lies the key to understanding what united people from the most diverse geographical, professional, social, and political backgrounds. The right to their homeland remained the focal point for all politically active expellees, even decades after it had been proclaimed in their charter, as follows: "To separate human beings with force from their homeland means to kill their spirit. We have suffered and experienced this fate. Therefore, we feel called upon to demand that the right to homeland be recognized and implemented as a God-given basic right of all humankind."

Yet their articulation of a common suffering and loss of homeland did not initially result in a common political platform. Between 1948–49 and 1952 two wings within the broad spectrum of expellee and refugee organizations fought for political leadership. One wing focused on the "national principle" and made the recovery of the lost homeland its political priority. Oriented toward the political far right, it did not manage to generate sufficient electoral support. In contrast, the Union of Expellees and Disenfranchised (Bund der Heimatvertriebenen und Entrechteten—BHE; after November 1952, Gesamtdeutscher Block [BHE]) gained its profile and spectacular electoral support by addressing the specific social and economic interests of the expellees *in* the Federal Republic. The great irony in the history of this political party is that the more successful it was in facilitating the social and economic integration of the expellees, the less this population group felt the need for a distinct political party. The BHE's failure to form a permanent and stable coalition with other smaller center parties led to its fall below the 5 percent threshold in the federal elections in 1957 and again in 1961, after it had been subsumed within the All-German Party (Gesamtdeutsche Partei), thus no longer qualifying for representation in the federal parliament. This failure of the BHE to maintain a presence at the federal and state levels of political representation opened the way for the political integration of the expellees and refugees in the mainstream German political parties, thus playing a vital role in the consolidation of the democratic party system of the Federal Republic. Thus, the expellees and refugees have been a significant and positively contributing factor to postwar (West) German history—which is, after all, characterized by the successful development of democracy and rule of law and the peaceful realization of German unification.[4]

The electoral failure of the BHE in 1957, among other things, made it clear to activists in both the BvD and the VdL that the representation of expellee interests could become more efficient if a single organization would be created within which the thus far separate entities would pool their resources. By October 1957 this process was completed, and the Union of Expellees—United Regional-Cultural Associations and State Organizations (Bund der Vertriebenen—Vereinigte Landsmannschaften und Landesverbände—BdV) formed. It consisted of twenty regional-cultural associations,[5] eleven state organizations (one in each of the federal states at the time, with five new being founded after German unification in 1990), and seven special interest groups.[6] The inaugural, 1958 issue of the organization's main publication, *German Eastern Service* (*Deutscher Ostdienst*—DOD), published a statement by the first president of the BdV, Hans Krüger (1998: 3), in which he defined the mission of his organization as being a mediator between East and West:

In the spirit of a humanist-Christian worldview, in the spirit of the best eastern German cultural traditions, in the spirit of Leibniz, Kant, Herder and Lessing, the expellees not only abandon revenge and retribution, but they seek reconciliation of the seemingly irreconcilable in order to prepare the ground for a legitimate and just peace. This noble attitude gives them the right to demand justice for themselves and for all expellees and refugees in the world.

Similar to the Charter of the German Expellees of 1950, Krüger also emphasized the right of the expellees to their homeland and to self-determination, as well as their desire to contribute to the peaceful coexistence of all peoples in freedom.

When Germany's firm commitment to integration into Western security and economic cooperation structures had been rewarded with membership in NATO in 1955, the European Coal and Steel Community (ECSC) in 1951, and the European Economic Community in 1957, the country's political elite felt confident enough to pursue a more active foreign policy toward the countries of Central and Eastern Europe as well. This obviously included a number of host states of ethnic German minorities, such as Poland, Romania, and the Soviet Union, where the largest groups of ethnic Germans lived at the time. The possibilities of direct involvement, however, were extremely limited throughout this period until 1989; the major instrument of German external minority policy was to negotiate with the host states conditions that would allow ethnic Germans to migrate to Germany.[7] A precondition for the success of this policy was the establishment of diplomatic relations with the relevant states in the Eastern Bloc, a necessity recognized by the expellee organizations as well. In his 1958 contribution to the first issue of DOD, the aforementioned Paul Krüger noted that an "isolated German *Ostpolitik* and with it the realization of the political goals of the expellees with respect to their homeland are impossible. Both depend on the correct analysis of the geopolitical situation and they have to be executed in consideration of the policy of the western bloc. . . . Geopolitically, they depend on political détente between east and west" (Krüger 1998: 4).

After the Soviet-German Treaty of 1955 and a verbal agreement in 1958, the Soviet Union permitted all persons of ethnic German origin who had been citizens of the German Reich before Hitler's attack of 21 June 1941 to emigrate. More important in the long term, however, were treaties of the early 1970s—with the Soviet Union and with Poland in 1970 and with Czechoslovakia in 1973—because they addressed an issue that was rightly thought to be of great significance for reconciliation between Germany and the countries of Central and Eastern Europe. Thus, in line with *Ostpolitik,* the sensitive issue of borders was addressed, and the German government of the day confirmed that it respected the territorial status quo. The signatory states assured respect for one another's territorial integrity and affirmed in each case that neither side had territorial claims against the other. This, however, was at least one step too far for many of the expellee activists, who sensed an acceptance of the territorial status quo as permanent, which would have implied a loss of many of their homelands. Taking the federal government to court over the so-called *Ostverträge*, they achieved rulings of the German Constitutional Court in 1973, 1975, and 1987 that rejected any suggestion that the treaties with Moscow and Warsaw violated the assertion of Germany's basic law, which defined German territory at its 1937 borders. While this interpretation pleased the BdV, it did not have any practical impact on the foreign policy of the federal government, nor did it improve the opportunity structure for the BdV to become more actively involved in foreign policy matters. On the contrary, the insistence of its leading officials on the openness of the border question led to serious discords with the federal government in the 1980s. The political impotence of the expellee organizations became strikingly obvious in 1985, when the motto for the twenty-first annual meeting of the Silesian expellees had to be changed from "Forty Years of Expulsion—Silesia Remains Ours" to "Forty Years of Expulsion—Silesia Remains Our Future in the Europe of Free Peoples" after a personal intervention by then Chancellor Helmut Kohl. By the same token, in 1987 Herbert Hupka, the chairman of the Landsmannschaft Schlesien lost his safe seat on the CDU list for the federal elections.

The expellee organizations' lack of political power, however, was partially offset by a stronger interest in social and cultural issues from the late 1980s onward, particularly at local levels. Activists, including many who had already been born in the Federal Republic, began to commit more time and funds to helping ethnic German resettlers from Central and Eastern Europe (*Aussiedler*) integrate in German society, to preserving their own cultural heritage and traditions (supported by a special government program for the promotion of eastern German culture initiated in 1988), and to developing and solidifying cross-border human contacts with Czechoslovakia and Poland and other host states of ethnic German minorities in Central and Eastern Europe.

AUSSIEDLER AND *SPÄTAUSSIEDLER* AND THEIR INTEGRATION IN THE FEDERAL REPUBLIC

Especially with its definition of *Aussiedler* as expellees and thus their eligibility for preferential treatment, the Federal Expellee Law established a legal framework that retained its relevance well beyond the integration of the expellees who arrived in the immediate aftermath of the Second World War. By specifically including *Aussiedler* in the category of expellees, the Federal Expellee Law broadened Article 116 of the Basic Law and established the subsequent entitlement of *Aussiedler* to citizenship under the 1955 Law on the Regulation of Questions of Citizenship (cf. above). In addition, their inclusion in the Federal Expellee Law gave *Aussiedler* the right to aid in the integration process and compensation for their losses and suffering.

During the period between 1950 and 1989, this policy had both humanitarian and political dimensions. From a humanitarian point of view, it is undeniable that ethnic Germans in Central and Eastern Europe continued to suffer discrimination because of their ethnicity and were additionally disadvantaged by living in illiberal communist regimes. Politically, however, the policy of accrediting *Aussiedler* as expellees also served a purpose—during the bloc confrontation of the Cold War, any *Aussiedler* who arrived in the Federal Republic was proof of the undemocratic nature of the communist bloc and its constant violation of basic human and minority rights. Ironically, the restrictive policies on emigration that constituted one feature of this undemocratic nature benefited the few ethnic Germans who were allowed to leave, as the very small numbers that came to the Federal Republic during the Cold War compared to those arriving from about 1988 onward (see Figure 3) allowed the West German state to display an extraordinary amount of generosity in the provision of aid during the integration process. *Aussiedler* were subsidized in language courses that lasted for up to twelve months, received occupational training and special education benefits, and were helped by programs set up to help them acquire or build residential properties. In addition to the low numbers of *Aussiedler* arriving, the economic situation in the Federal Republic was conducive to their smooth integration in the labor market. Furthermore, the origin of *Aussiedler* in this period, who predominantly came from Poland and Romania (see Figure 4), helped their social integration, as extensive support networks of earlier arrivals (i.e., expellees and refugees) existed who had integrated well in the Federal Republic. A final distinction between those *Aussiedler* arriving prior to the relaxation of emigration controls in the former Eastern Bloc by the end of the 1980s and those benefiting from its liberalization and eventual collapse is that the percentage of ethnic Germans among those arriving in the Federal Republic had dropped to as low as 22 percent, because family members of ethnic Germans

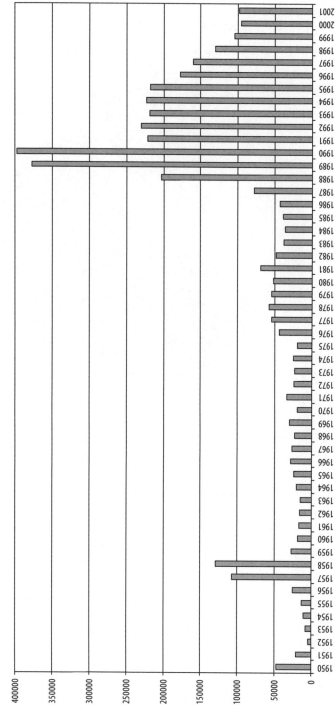

Figure 3
Aussiedler Arriving in the Federal Republic (1950–2001)

Figure 4
Origin of *Aussiedler* Arriving in the Federal Republic (1950–1987)

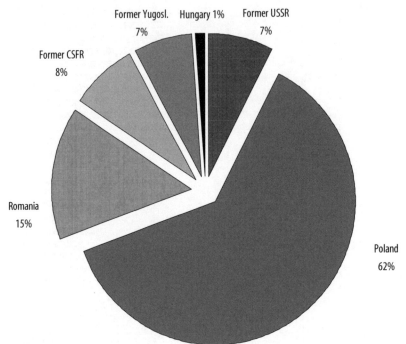

now were of predominantly non-German origin, with hardly any knowledge of German language or culture. Taken together, all these factors fundamentally changed the prospects of successful integration. Consequently, and in conjunction with improved opportunities of a more active external minority policy (see chapter 6), the federal parliament enacted a number of laws that revised the formerly very generous acceptance and integration policy; as a consequence, the status of *Aussiedler* as a privileged group of immigrants declined (Klekowski 2002).

After 1987, the overwhelming majority of *Aussiedler* came from the Soviet Union and its successor states. After an initial increase among ethnic Germans from Poland and Romania in the late 1980s and early 1990s, ethnic Germans from Russia and some of the Central Asian Republics of the former Soviet Union made up for 61 percent of all *Aussiedler* in the period between 1987 and 2001 (see Figures 5 and 6) and for a staggering 97 percent for the period between 1995 and

Figure 5
Origin of *Aussiedler* Arriving in the Federal Republic (1987–2001)

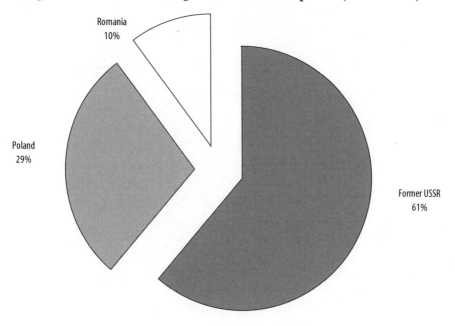

2001. The reasons for this dramatic increase of ethnic German immigrants from these areas are manifold. First of all, the majority of ethnic Germans still in Central and Eastern Europe live on the territory of the former Soviet Union. Second, they had historically the fewest opportunities to emigrate prior to the collapse of communism. Third, their living conditions remain among the worst of all German minorities in Central and Eastern Europe. Finally, specific legislative measures in the Federal Republic have limited the possibilities for ethnic Germans from other countries to gain *Aussiedler* status.

When numbers began to swell after 1988, the financial challenges posed by the sudden increase prompted the federal government to pass several laws that initially limited the benefits available to *Aussiedler* in the course of the integration process and then gradually increased the hurdles for immigration, thereby lowering the annual intake from its peak of almost four hundred thousand in 1990 to under one hundred thousand since 2000. The Law on the Modification of Integration Benefits (*Eingliederungsanpassungsgesetz*) of 22 December 1989 cut integration benefits in the area of language courses, occupational training, and housing benefits, to find a compromise between limited

Figure 6
Origin of *Aussiedler* Arriving in the Federal Republic (1995–2001)

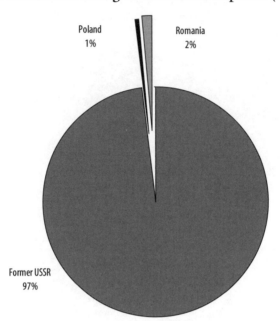

Poland
1%

Romania
2%

Former USSR
97%

resources and increased demand. On 28 June 1990 another law was passed that fundamentally altered the process of determining an applicant's *Aussiedler* status. The Law on the Acceptance of *Aussiedler* (*Aussiedleraufnahmengesetz*) determined that in principle, potential ethnic German immigrants had to apply for *Aussiedler* status from their home countries and were allowed to travel to Germany only following preliminary confirmation of this status. After their arrival in the Federal Republic, ethnic Germans are sent to one of the German states, where their status as expellees is determined; they are finally confirmed as *Aussiedler* only following successful completion of this procedure.

So far the most significant revision of the legal framework and practice of *Aussiedler* integration came with the War Consequences Conciliation Law (*Kriegsfolgenbereinigungsgesetz*) of 1 January 1993. It amended the Federal Expellee Law by creating a new legal category, that of the *"Spätaussiedler."* This particular status can only be acquired by people of ethnic German origin (*deutsche Volkszugehörige*) born before 1 January 1993. Ethnic German origin has to be proven through descent, knowledge of the German language, and preservation of German culture, customs, and traditions. In addition, the War Consequences Conciliation Law determined that except for ethnic Germans from the successor states of the Soviet Union, every applicant for *Spätaussiedler* status had to demonstrate discrimination or other suffering on the basis of their being ethnic Germans.

According to this new legal framework, only spouses and direct descendants of *Spätaussiedler* can be admitted to the Federal Republic and be granted German citizenship. Other relatives, such as spouses of children, are treated according to the much more stringent criteria of Germany's foreigner law. Another restriction was introduced, demanding that marriages must be at least three years old in order for spouses to qualify under the regulations for the acceptance of *Spätaussiedler*. A final important revision of the legal framework that occurred with the War Consequences Conciliation Law was the setting of an upper limit of 225,000 immigrants per year as *Spätaussiedler* as of 1 January 1993. This figure was revised downward to a hundred thousand people annually as of 1 January 2000.

Despite these severe restrictions and further "filters" that have been built into the system, such as a mandatory language test as a precondition for even preliminary acceptance as *Spätaussiedler*, integration problems have increased for ethnic Germans arriving in the Federal Republic. Apart from the cuts to integration benefits, persisting difficulties in the labor and housing market as well as increasing cultural problems experienced by many of the *Spätaussiedler* have meant that their dreams of a better life in Germany have not fulfilled. For many, arrival in Germany means the beginning of a long stay in transition camps in one of the German states to which they have been assigned, rather than an area that they would have chosen for themselves or where they would desire to live, primarily because of existing family ties. However, the Residency Assignment Act (*Wohnortzuweisungsgesetz*) of 1 March 1996 explicitly rules out the free choice of place of residence for *Spätaussiedler*, who otherwise have all their integration and other benefits cut for a period of up to three years. While this law makes sense from the perspective of an equal distribution of the still sizable number of ethnic German immigrants among the different states, this distribution practice often further limits the chances of *Spätaussiedler* to integrate quickly in the labor market, as they are often sent to some of the most deprived parts of the states to which they are assigned. Unemployment thus remains disproportionately high (around 50 percent among all new arrivals after 1993), and camp life is often extended to a period of well over two years before *Spätaussiedler* are able to find and afford their own private accommodation. In the 1990s, in the context of Germany's economic problems, they were also increasingly seen as unwanted competition and became targets of xenophobic attacks.

* * *

In conclusion, then, the integration of ethnic German refugees, expellees and *Aussiedler* and *Spätaussiedler* in the Federal Republic can be divided into three main periods:

- The problematic, yet eventually successful, integration of the refugees and expellees between 1945 and the late 1950s, during which about ten million ethnic Germans from Central and Eastern Europe, primarily from Poland and Czechoslovakia, were incorporated into the emerging West German state, benefiting from and contributing to its economic and political success;
- The relatively unproblematic and overall successful integration of approximately 1.4 million *Aussiedler* who arrived between 1950 and 1987 and could be relatively easily integrated in the labor and housing markets, benefiting from "suitable" occupational profiles and existing networks of other ethnic German immigrants who had arrived earlier;
- The increasingly difficult integration of the around 2.5 million *Aussiedler* and *Spätaussiedler* who arrived after 1987 and, by and large, lacked the attributes that had enabled earlier arrivals to integrate more smoothly, especially in terms of linguistic ability and occupational profile. Overwhelmed by the sheer number of people arriving, German authorities had to cut integration benefits and impose ever stricter regulations for acceptance.

Between 1990 and 2000, the federal government spent approximately 33.5 billion Deutschmarks ($16 billion) on integration measures, not counting the funds provided by individual states and local communities. While this has eased the hardship of the new arrivals and, despite the often difficult conditions and extended stays in reception camps, for many of them has meant an improvement of their standard of living over their countries of origin, there can be little doubt that integration becomes harder and harder. This is, to a considerable extent, a reflection of the premises of an integration policy that is based on standards more than half a century old. It seems time for policy makers to abandon the notion of a German nation unified by common descent and culture, regardless of where its members live. Recent changes in German legislation indicate that this is being realized. The German question, thus, at least in relation to some of its demographic dimensions, has undergone significant changes over the past half-century.

NOTES

1. This "expulsion area" (*Vertreibungsgebiet*) includes all territories which, as of 1 January 1914, were part of the German Reich, the Habsburg monarchy, or subsequently part of Poland, Estonia, Lithuania, or Latvia.

2. Flight from the Soviet zone of occupation is explicitly defined as expulsion as well.

3. The existence of such a right has recently been recognized by the UN High Commissioner for Human Rights, José Ayala Lasso (1995), who affirmed in a message to the German expellees that "the right not to be expelled from one's ancestral homeland is a fundamental human right."

4. While this may seem to be self-promotional propaganda by the BdV, it is actually an almost literal translation from a speech by the German Minister of the Interior, Otto Schily, an SPD member, delivered on the fiftieth anniversary of the BdV on 29 May 1999.

5. German Balts; Banat Swabians; Berlin—Mark Brandenburg; Bessarabia Germans; Bukowina Germans; Germans from Danzig; Dobrudscha and Bulgarian Germans; Danube Swabians; Carpathian Germns; Lithuanian Germans; Upper Silesian Germans; East Prussians; Pomerania; Russia Germans; Sathmar Swabians; Silesia, Lower and Upper Silesia; Transylvanian Saxons; Sudeten Germans; Weichsel-Warthe; and West Prussia.

6. Industrialists, youth, students, women, track athletes, the deaf, and farmers.

7. The agreements between West Germany and some of the host states for the repatriation of ethnic Germans included financial arrangements setting "per capita fees" to be paid by the federal government.

Chapter 5

From Triple Partition to Double Reunification

When the two German states were formally constituted in September and October 1949, the map of Germany looked rather different from that of the country in 1937, which, according to the pronouncements of the Allies as well as of successive West German governments, remained the point of reference prior to a final peace treaty. The former Eastern Territories (*Ostgebiete*) were under provisional Polish and Soviet administration, and the Western Allies had already indicated that they would favor a permanent settlement of the border in this way (see chapter 3). In the West, France had tightened its grip on the Saar since 1945, and although the area had not been formally annexed to France, it had at least been clearly detached from Germany and entered into an economic union with France that was all but a disguise for political control. Thus, Germany found itself partitioned in three ways in 1949. A complex set of interest and opportunity structures subsequently determined Germany's territorial fate in a way that allowed the country to overcome two of these partitions, in 1957 and in 1990, while one of them was acknowledged as permanent. Examining the dynamics of the territorial dimensions of the German question after 1945 thus entails an analysis of the Franco-German conflict

Germany, 1949–1990

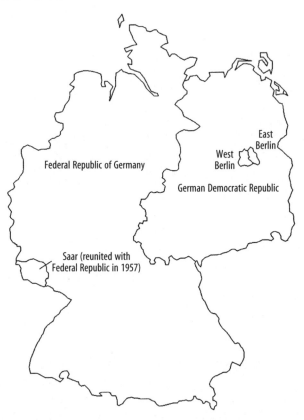

over the Saar and its resolution in the mid-1950s; of the "inter-German" question (i.e., the development of the relationship between the two German states); and of the issue of the former *Ostgebiete*. This is the content and sequence of this chapter.

THE "LITTLE" REUNIFICATION: GERMANY, FRANCE, AND THE SAAR

> Both governments regard the agreed arrangements as fulfillment of an essential precondition for the strengthening of the free world and the future of Europe. Jointly, they will continue to strive even more for the creation of a new Europe.
>
> —Joint Franco-German Declaration on the
> Signing of the Saar Treaty (1956)

Until the end of 1947, France was firmly in control of all developments relating to the Saar (see chapter 3). Germany was economically and politically weak, still governed by the Allied military governments, and in no position to exercise political influence. In the Saar itself, there was no significant opposition to French policy. This situation began to change gradually from 1948 onward. In the international arena, Germany started to recover economically and politically. With the foundation of the Federal Republic in 1949, West Germany became a political player again, yet it remained somewhat limited in its actions because the country had not yet regained full sovereignty. France, on the other hand, was weakened internally by a number of government crises, a constant lack of stable parliamentary majorities, and externally by losing ground in North Africa and Southeast Asia. In addition, European and Western integration became increasingly important aspects of the Franco-German relationship, and with it the interest and opportunity structures of both countries' political elites changed, eventually allowing for a resolution of their territorial dispute. However, it was only after an impasse of several years that the French government, in 1952 and after Anglo-American pressure, made an important concession, accepting the necessity of negotiations with Germany with the aim to achieve a permanent solution of the conflict. Prior to that, France had pursued a unilateral strategy of establishing ever closer economic and political ties with the Saar, a policy that had met with increasing resistance in the Saar and Germany. Simultaneously, however, France had denied that the dispute was of a bilateral nature at all, as the West German government had maintained from the outset. Eventually, France acknowledged Germany's role; this acknowledgement marked a major step toward more fruitful approaches to resolution.

Early Failures in Negotiating a Settlement

On 29 February 1952, Germany announced in a letter to the Council of Europe that it was determined to bring the issue of the Saar before the council during its next session. The German demands for the revision of the Saar status were that the politically, economically, and culturally independent Saar be placed under the supervision of the Council of Europe; that Saarbrücken be the seat of the organs of the European Coal and Steel Community (ECSC); that neither France nor Germany influence public opinion in the Saar; and that the Saar's population be given the opportunity to express its opinion freely in new elections to the Landtag (Freymond 1960: 110). The demands Germany raised in this memorandum were unacceptable to France, but the two governments agreed to set up a commission to analyze the situation in the Saar, a commission in which all three conflict parties—France, Germany, and the Saar—should be represented.

In Germany, the oppositional Social Democratic Party (SPD) rejected the agreement as a weakening of the German position, because it formally recognized the Saar government as an independent player in what so far had been a territorial dispute between two states. The territorial dimension was the most significant for Germany at the time, and concerns about it were shared by all major parties. If Germany agreed to a revision of its 1937 western borders, before the conclusion of a peace treaty, an unwelcome precedent might be set, weakening the German position in terms of the even more vital question of the eastern borders. This was a position that was remarkably similar to the German policy approach toward Alsace in the interwar period (see chapter 2).

The German Bundestag passed a resolution on 23 April 1952 in which the members of parliament reaffirmed their position that the Saar remained part of German territory. Chancellor Konrad Adenauer of the Christian Democratic Union (CDU) also came under pressure from within the government, particularly from the Minister of All-German Affairs, Jakob Kaiser, who opposed the compromises made by the chancellor, and from the government of one of the federal states, Rhineland-Palatine, under its minister-president Peter Altmeier. The strongest asset of this "Kaiser-Altmeier circle" was the dependence of the federal government upon the vote of Rhineland-Palatine in the upper chamber of the German parliament.

The situation of the French government was not much better. Here, the main concern was the economic loss that France would incur in case of a European settlement that did not preserve the economic union with the Saar. Although the French government made it clear that its objective was to keep the status quo, with the exception that the responsibility for the Saar's foreign affairs would be transferred to a future European organization, the French Council of the Republic insisted that no agreement be signed that implied a loosening, let alone cutting, of the existing economic ties between France and the Saar (Freymond 1960: 114).

Eventually, direct negotiations between France and Germany got under way in August 1952 in Paris after both Great Britain and the

United States and the Council of Ministers of the ECSC had again urged the two governments to seek a bilateral solution of the Saar question. Although negotiations were initially constructive, they failed nevertheless; the objectives of the two governments were too far apart. Germany directed its efforts at achieving from France concessions that would have led to the creation of a more liberal atmosphere in the Saar, suggesting such steps as permission to constitute new political parties, an end to French sequestration, and a postponement of the elections, to give new political parties an opportunity to establish themselves. The French position, in contrast, was to enter immediately into negotiations about the conditions of Europeanization of the Saar. The French government also envisaged modifying rather than abandoning the existing Franco-Saar conventions, in order to allow the continuation of the Franco-Saar economic, financial, and customs union. As no breakthrough was achieved in the negotiations and the Saar question became a more and more serious problem for European integration as a whole, the Consultative Assembly of the Council of Europe decided, on 18 September 1952, to form a subcommittee to look into the Saar conflict and make recommendations about a settlement.

On 29 October, after France and Germany had officially conceded the breakdown of their negotiations at the end of October 1952, the Saar Landtag passed an electoral law setting the date of the elections for 30 November 1952. Pro-German opposition parties were not legalized, which increased tensions within the Saar as well as between France and Germany. The election saw a victory of the Christian People's Party of the Saar (CVP) and the Social Democratic Party of the Saar (SPS), which together won about 64 percent of the vote and renewed their coalition government. However, blank and invalid votes accounted for 24.5 percent of the total vote cast, indicating significant public discontent with the situation in the Saar.

This interpretation of the election result had considerable influence on the formulation of German Saar policy until 1955. It consisted of two major strategies—legalization of opposition parties and free elections before a referendum, and the long-term orientation to regain the Saar, in a permanent peace settlement after an interim period of European government. The elections had shown that the influence of the pro-German parties was significant but not yet strong enough to have taken over government responsibilities immediately, even if they could compete in free and fair elections. Their influence, therefore, had to be strengthened. According to the reasoning of the German government, the sooner they were legalized and could begin campaigning for their cause and the later free elections to the Saar that were to take place after that legalization, the more likely it would be that a pro-German government could be established in the Saar. At the same time, however, the German government saw the danger of the creation of an independent Saar state and realized that to prevent such a development, it was necessary to diminish French influence in the Saar and to limit the extent of Saar self-government, by imposing on the territory a European status.

On 10 April 1953, the Saar government took the unprecedented initiative of launching a six-point plan for the Europeanization of the Saar, which was partly based on earlier proposals of a similar nature. The most significant points were that the Saar become a European territory and govern itself; that France hand over responsibility for the external affairs of the Saar to a "High Authority" prior to the formation of a European government; that the French embassy be replaced by a consulate holding the same rights as a German consulate; and that Franco-Saar economic union be preserved until a European economic union came into force. The final decision on the Europeanization of the Saar, however, was to be subject to the outcome of a plebiscite in the Saar.

After renewed negotiations between France and Germany in May 1953 ended without conclusion, the French government proposed a number of changes to Franco-Saar conventions in order to strengthen the legal foundations of existing ties. In response, the German Bundestag unanimously passed a resolution stressing, once again, that it considered the Saar to be German territory. At the same time, the resolution gave the government a mandate to negotiate for the restoration of democratic freedoms in the Saar and for the return of the Saar to Germany. In an attempt to raise the international profile of the Saar question, the German federal government also made its opposition to the new Franco-Saar conventions known in an official protest note to the three Western Allied High Commissioners for Germany. A more decisive course of action, however, seemed inappropriate at the time, as the German government had to strike a difficult balance between its European and Saar policies.

In the Saar itself, opposition against the conventions came in its most organized form from the trade unions. An attempt of the government to break trade-union opposition failed. The dismissal of their leader only prompted trade unionists to reelect him, and the banning of the miners' trade union led to a broadening of the opposition movement as a whole and an intensification of its contacts with Germany.

Parallel to the failed Franco-German attempt to come to a settlement in 1953, the Council of Europe's subcommittee on the Saar had begun explorations, and on 26 April 1954—the day when the fall of Dien Bien Phu marked a further decline of France as a world power— its recommendations were published. The Saar was to become a European territory as soon as the European Political Community was constituted; until then an interim solution with a European commissioner, who was neither French nor German nor from the Saar, was to be instituted. The common market between France and the Saar was to be preserved, while gradually similar relations between the Saar and Germany should be established. An agreement between France, Germany, and the Saar to preserve German culture and language in the region was to be signed. The new status of the Saar was to be guaranteed by France, Germany, Britain, and the United States until the conclusion of a peace treaty. The implementation of the new status would be subject to a plebiscite in the Saar (Schmidt 1959: 760–75). Despite remaining differences between France and Germany, the two countries reached an agreement at the end of May according to which they would seek a solution of their dispute based on the proposed plan pending the conclusion of a final settlement in a peace treaty.

Reaching a Final Settlement: The Prerogative of Consolidating the Western Alliance

Although the agreement reached in May 1954 demonstrated the considerable progress made in the negotiations, the French foreign ministry and government did not approve of what their own minister had achieved and instead renewed the demand for an immediate and permanent European status of the Saar—which, of course, was rejected by Germany. In this situation, the Council of Europe's subcommittee on the Saar worked out a new plan for the settlement of the Saar question. This plan consisted of two parts—the definition of a European status of the Saar, and regulations governing the conduct of political parties in the Saar. Although it was passed by the General Affairs Committee, the Council of Europe itself left the plan unmentioned in its resolution of 25 May 1954, in which it expressed only its hope that bilateral negotiations between France and Germany would soon come to a conclusion. However, after the proposals for the European Defence Community (EDC) and the European Political Community (EPC) were rejected in the French National Assembly on 30 August 1954, the idea to settle the conflict through the Europeanization of the Saar territory became meaningless, at least in its original version.

Four weeks after the failure of the EDC, the Western Allies reached an agreement at their London conference to admit Germany and Italy to NATO and to restore (West) German sovereignty. This meant that in terms of the Saar question the status quo ante had been restored: German integration into the Western alliance and the regaining of its sovereignty were still possible, as was a French veto, the execution of which was made dependent upon the prior settlement of the Saar question. When France played this last trump card, an agreement was reached on 23 October 1954. In fourteen articles the new statute outlined the European status of the Saar in the period until the conclusion of a peace treaty. This agreement was ratified in the French parliament on 23 December 1954 and in the Council of the Republic on 26 March 1955. The ratification of the statute agreement in the Federal Republic, in contrast, was a much more difficult process. Its critics were not only to be found among the SPD opposition but also among the CDU's partners in the government coalition, and even within the CDU itself. Yet the opposition faced a dilemma. It could prevent the ratification of the Saar statute and hope for a better deal in renegotiations, but it would have to risk, at the same time, the failure of German integration into NATO and of restoration of German sovereignty. Alternatively, to approve the Saar statute would be a de facto acknowledgment of the loss of the Saar. Eventually, a majority voted in favor of the agreement, and it was ratified in Germany in the Bundestag on 27 February 1955 and in the Bundesrat on 18 March 1955. Finally, the SPD had brought the matter before the German constitutional court; the latter ruled on 4 May 1955 that the agreement did not violate the Basic Law of the Federal Republic. At a further Franco-German meeting on 14 January 1955, both governments jointly approached the Council of the Western European Union to appoint an international commission to observe the Saar referendum, and they agreed that all future differences be settled within the framework of the Western Alliance.

The date of the plebiscite was set by the Saar Landtag for 23 October 1955. The referendum resulted in a 67 percent rejection of the statute, which was a clear sign of the desire of the Saar population to be German and to belong to Germany. As a consequence of the rejection of the proposed Saar statute, the Saar government immediately resigned. France and Germany, on the other hand, assured one another that the outcome of the referendum would not threaten their relationship. The subsequent elections in the Saar on 18 December 1955 saw an overwhelming victory of the pro-German parties and the formation of a pro-German coalition government on 2 January 1956. On 31 January 1956, the new Landtag voted in favor of a resolution that declared an end to the separation of the Saar from Germany and a wish to integrate the Saar politically and economically into the Federal Republic.

France, accepting the political consequences of the referendum, demanded compensation for the inevitable economic losses it would suffer. These matters were settled in bilateral talks between March and the end of May 1956. Eventually, on 5 June 1956, a general agreement on the Franco-German treaties—a conglomerate of five separate agreements—was reached between the two heads of government at a meeting in Luxembourg. The treaties were ratified simultaneously in the German Bundestag and the French National Assembly on 27 October 1956. The international obstacles to reunification with Germany being removed, the Saar Landtag was able to make the necessary changes to the Saar constitution and to pass a law according to which the Saar would join the Federal Republic of Germany according to Article 23 of the German Basic Law. As of 1 January 1957, the Saar became part of the Federal Republic of Germany.

THE GERMAN-GERMAN QUESTION

> We are in favor of the peaceful coexistence of two German states. However, we know that one day the peace-loving and democratic forces in West Germany will win the day and embark on the road to socialism. And with this, the essential pre-condition for the unification of our currently divided nation will be fulfilled.
> —Walter Ulbricht (1961)

> Where choice is unavoidable, the welfare of people has to have absolute priority. For, what is good for the people in the divided country is also good for the nation.
> —Willy Brandt (1989)

The reunification of West Germany with the Saar had set an important precedent, in that it had demonstrated that the territorial status quo established in 1945 was not necessarily a permanent arrangement but rather that it was possible to overcome individual aspects of German partition in peaceful and constructive negotiations. At the same time, however, it was also clear that the resolution of the Saar conflict was anything but a model for the reunification of the two German states. Not only had two different political and economic regimes been established in them, but both states belonged to antagonistic military alliances, the very border between which ran right through the middle of Germany. While German unification remained one of the constitutional imperatives for successive West German governments, the issue was for decades reserved for Cold War propaganda, with the political elites well aware of the fact that the geopolitical balance of power between East and West made it most unlikely to happen. So ingrained was this line of thought that when the opportunity for reunification finally arose in earnest in late 1989, it found political elites across Europe completely unprepared. Before then, however, several decades were characterized by a rather different state of affairs in German-German relations, which for the most part reflected the nature of relations between the two superpowers, the United States and the Soviet Union.

The development of the German-German dimension of the German question throughout its existence remained primarily a territorial issue, namely, that of overcoming this specific partition of Germany. At the same time, however, and because of its connectedness with the geopolitical situation, the German question also remained one of crucial significance for peace and stability in Europe and beyond. Even though the political elites in either of the two German states could not and did not formulate their political strategies and tactics vis-à-vis each other without the consent of the respective superpower, a closer examination of their policy agendas between 1949 and 1990 is a useful exercise for understanding the inter-German dynamics of the German question.

The *Deutschlandpolitik* of the SED: From "German Unity and Just Peace" to the "Peaceful Coexistence of Two German States"

The ruling communist party in the East German state, the SED, formulated and implemented its *Deutschlandpolitik* in complete dependence on the Soviet Union. Even at times when Soviet policy was clearly not in the interest of the East German state and its population, there was little or no room for the SED to pursue a program of its own. All policy pronouncements and initiatives of the party must therefore be judged against this background, not in order to make excuses for a totalitarian party but to understand the dynamics of policy making and implementation in East Germany in general, and in particular in relation to foreign policy and *Deutschlandpolitik*.

Up to the mid-1950s, the SED proceeded from the assumption of the continued existence of Germany as a single unit; the GDR government saw itself as the German government and refused to recognize its West German counterpart, reasoning that the creation of the Federal Republic had been an act of separatism driven by the three Western powers, clearly in breach of what the Allies had agreed upon at Potsdam. Interestingly, East Germany thus proclaimed its right to speak solely for Germany as a whole before the Federal Republic did. Upon his election as first president of the GDR, Wilhelm Pieck stated that his government would not rest before those parts of Germany that had been unlawfully separated from the whole and subjected to the rule of occupying forces were reunited with the core territory of Germany, the German Democratic Republic, in a united and democratic Germany. In contrast to later West German statements to a similar effect, the GDR's sole-representation claim thus as soon as 1949 excluded the so-called former *Ostgebiete,* which the Federal Republic, at least implicitly, included in its claims to represent Germany. Stalin too, when congratulating the East German leaders on the establishment of their state, declared that they had laid the foundation for a united, democratic, and peaceful Germany, an act that he called a "turning point in European history." Apart from the fact that Stalin's position very much reflected the general "external" view of the German question as one of peace and stability in Europe, the Soviet leader here clearly stated his desire for a united Germany. Obviously, what he and the GDR leadership had in mind was a unified German state modeled along the lines of East Germany. This manifested itself in the rejection of any demand for free and fair multiparty elections in the whole of Germany, which was the precondition set by the Federal Republic and the three Western Allies for agreement to any proposal from either the Soviet Union or the GDR. These ideological differences and, resulting from them and the geopolitical balance of power in Europe, the integration of the two German states in different military alliances rapidly diminished any slim chances for German unification that may have existed.

In East Germany, this state of affairs resulted in the proclamation of a socialist society at the second party conference of the SED in July 1952; the creation of the country's own armed forces from 1952 onward; the bloody repression of the workers' uprising in June 1953 by Soviet tanks; and the founding-membership of the GDR in the Warsaw Pact, the Eastern Bloc equivalent of NATO. Interestingly, however, the East German government, upon joining the Warsaw Pact, reserved its right to act autonomously in its international relations with respect to German reunification. The East German minister-president, Otto Grotewohl, noted in particular that "the East German government proceeds from the assumption that the reunited Germany will be free from any obligations into which one part of the country entered in the form of military treaties and agreements prior to reunification" (quoted in Fritsch-Bournazel 1990: 113). Clearly, this was not meant to pave the way to NATO membership of a reunited Germany (as it eventually happened, albeit with certain conditions imposed, in 1990) but to leave the door open for German reunification and the country's subsequent neutrality, as several Soviet and East German proposals throughout the 1950s had suggested.

The failure of the Geneva conference of 1955, when the four Allies had, more or less sincerely, once again tried to set in motion a process toward German unification, marked an important change in policy on the part of Moscow and its East German ally, the SED. If the debate had until then been dominated by finding a solution through establishing conditions for what was essentially a "reintegration" of two parts of the *same* state, an almost seismic shift occurred now, when the East accepted the existence of *two separate* German states, which had to *coexist* alongside each other prior to their (re-)unification. This must not be mistaken to mean that the SED accorded any less importance to its *Deutschlandpolitik*, at least in its public pronouncements. Yet it is important to note that the stakes under which the East German state would "accept" reunification amounted to establishing almost a mirror image of the GDR in West Germany. That this was totally unrealistic was probably clear to the political elites in East Berlin and Moscow, but it did not prevent them from pursuing this agenda in various guises. The most remarkable proposal was that by East German leader Walter Ulbricht for a confederation in 1956, which Moscow and East Berlin regarded as a suitable arrangement for approximating the economic and political systems in the two German states prior to their reunification. While this plan did not make much of an impact in 1956, it resurfaced in 1959 in the context of the Berlin Crisis. Then too, for obvious reasons, it was rejected by the Federal Republic and the Western Allies.

From the mid-1950s onward, the GDR's *Deutschlandpolitik* had another dimension apart from seeking reunification on its own terms—to gain international recognition as a sovereign state. This shift toward the *Zwei-Staaten* theory (the notion of two sovereign German states coexisting) had occurred after the failure of the 1955 Geneva conference, when Moscow and East Berlin finally had to accept that their stance that German reunification was an internal, constitutional issue was no longer realistic. It therefore became necessary to increase the international standing of the GDR as an independent state. The first step in this direction was a treaty in September 1955 between East Germany and the Soviet Union that gave the GDR sovereignty as a state, at least on paper. From then on, the East German leadership pursued a policy of achieving international recognition as a means of strengthening its position in potential German-German negotiations. However, any attempt to break free from its international isolation (only the other member states of the Eastern Bloc had diplomatically recognized the country so far) failed at this time, not least because of the so-called Hallstein Doctrine, which guided West Germany's foreign policy in relation to the GDR's sovereignty. The Hallstein Doctrine proclaimed that the diplomatic recognition by any state of East Berlin would be treated as an unfriendly act against the Federal Republic and result in severing diplomatic links with that state. Moscow and East Berlin thus found themselves in a difficult position at the end of the 1950s, with very little to show after a decade of *Deutschlandpolitik* designed to achieve German unification. As a consequence, the East's policy became more and more confrontational toward the end of the 1950s, a tendency that manifested itself in the Berlin Crisis in 1959 and some years later in the Cuban missile crisis.

The potentially most severe crisis in relation to the German-German dimension of the German question itself, however, would occur in 1961—the building of the Berlin Wall by East Germany, blocking the last escape route for East Germans. The primary causes for this final step in German partition were very much to be found in the domestic situation in East Germany. In order to understand the complex developments leading up to the building of the wall, it is necessary to go back to the early 1950s. The SED's decision in 1952 to establish the foundations of socialism in East Germany and to create standing armed forces had significant implications not only for the GDR's long-term political future but also for its immediate economic situation. Creating armed forces meant a further drain on the country's already limited economic and labor resources. Establishing the foundations of socialism, in economic terms, meant further constraints on free enterprise in industry, trade, and agriculture, as well as a policy to invest primarily in heavy industry and to limit investment in consumer industries. As a consequence, living standards not only failed to improve in the early 1950s but decreased for many people in East Germany, which was a stark contrast to the situation in West Germany, where the "economic miracle" began to produce a dramatic rise in the quality of life for the overwhelming majority of people. The situation in East Germany worsened so considerably that resulting discontent by spring 1953 had led to spontaneous strike actions, primarily among construction workers in East Berlin. When the East German government decided unilaterally to increase work norms by 10 percent without simultaneous wage increases, strikes, demonstrations, and riots occurred in all major cities in June 1953; they were brought under control only by deployment of Soviet troops.

It would be too narrow a perspective to see these events only as a manifestation of anger about the economic situation in East Germany. The demonstrators also had specifically political demands, including free and fair elections and an end to the politicization of the judicial system. After the events in June, the SED modified its domestic economic and social policy, and living conditions began to improve. However, the combined Soviet and East German response to a legitimate demonstration of dissatisfaction (strikes, according to the East German constitution at the time, were legal) had had a certain eye-opening effect for many people, and the number of those leaving the country for the Federal Republic steadily increased. As increased security along the land border made this more and more difficult, West Berlin soon became the last remaining hub of freedom for many East Germans. Even at their lowest, the number of refugees from East Germany remained well above a hundred thousand annually in the mid-1950s and increased again after 1958, when the economic situation once again began to deteriorate, reaching a monthly peak of over thirty thousand in spring 1961, partly due to the push for collectivization in the agricultural sector that left many farmers dissatisfied and simultaneously led to a deterioration in the food situation in East Germany. As the emigrants were for the most part skilled workers, engineers, teachers, doctors, and other professionals, the brain and skills drain for the East German economy was significant, leading to a further worsening of the economic situation and thus to even more decisions to leave the country. The resulting economic and potentially political destabilization posed a serious threat to peace, one that was equally recognized in the East and West and explains, in part, why no major international crisis developed out of the building of the Berlin Wall on 13 August 1961.

The East German state, now more than ever, favored the two-states theory and advocated the peaceful coexistence of East and West Germany. The tough stance on all German-German issues remained—reunification yes, but only after West Germany had become a socialist state. Until that was the case, the two German states and the "special political unit West Berlin" would have to continue to coexist peacefully alongside each other, as was made clear in official SED statements as well as in the 1968 revised constitution, which assumed the continued existence of a German nation, albeit divided into two separate states. Article 1 of the new constitution referred to East Germany as the socialist state of the German nation (*sozialistischer Staat deutscher Nation*), and Article 8 even left the door open for reunification, albeit "on the basis of democracy and socialism" (*auf der Grundlage der Demokratie und des Sozialismus*).

All this rapidly changed less than two years later. In response to the new *Ostpolitik* pursued by the incoming government coalition of Social Democrats and Liberal Democrats in the Federal Republic, the SED made another push for establishing relations between the two German states, not based on the continued existence of a unified nation but on the sovereignty of two independent states. This in many ways was a logical conclusion of events throughout the 1960s that had not only finalized the partition of Germany with the building of the Berlin Wall but also enabled the East German state to break partially its international isolation with the establishment of trade and consular missions in many countries outside the communist bloc. The consequential weakening of the West German Hallstein Doctrine (which had in a sense begun as early as 1955, with the establishment of diplomatic relations between the Federal Republic and the Soviet Union) and the change in policy by the new SPD-led government in Bonn thus opened up opportunities for a fundamental reordering of German-German relations. In this process, it was the GDR's foremost aim to receive recognition as a sovereign state. This, however, was virtually impossible, not only because of constitutional problems that would have arisen in the Federal Republic but also because of the Allied prerogatives for Germany as a whole. The Quadripartite Agreement on Berlin of 3 September 1971, the Transit Agreement between East and West Germany of 17 December 1971, and the Basic Treaty between the two German states of 21 December 1972 were all interpreted by the SED as recognizing the sovereignty of East Germany as an independent state, but in fact they all underlined Allied authority. In doing so, however, they put the relations between the two German states on a more equal footing, as they also denied that the West German state was a fully sovereign entity.

Despite the legalistic small print, both states were admitted to the United Nations, and by the end of the 1970s East Germany had established diplomatic relations with some 180 states worldwide. This was undoubtedly a success for the GDR and its communist party. The SED therefore declared the German question "solved"; the 1974 revisions to the constitution eliminated all references to the German nation and the possibility of reunification. For the following decade and a half, very little reference was made to even the existence, let alone openness, of a German question in official statements. This made it possible for the East German state to engage with its West German counterpart in a variety of negotiations at different levels and on different issues in the latter half of the 1970s and throughout the 1980s. The success of most of these undertakings was made possible also because of a greater pragmatism on the West German side that had begun in the 1960s and was relatively independent of the government in office. The principal position of the East German state remained that of the existence of two independent and sovereign German states. Not until the collapse of the communist regime in the GDR in late 1989 was that to change. Thereafter, however, in a matter of less than a year, German reunification would be achieved by peaceful means.

The *Deutschlandpolitik* of the Federal Republic: From *Westintegration* to *Ostpolitik*

The constitution of the two German states in 1949 had allowed the Soviet Union and the Western Allies to realize at least their minimum objectives with regard to Germany after the failure of the Potsdam arrangements for the joint control and administration of Germany. Each superpower had secured a loyal regime in its own zone of influence in Germany and was subsequently building up the statehood of its entity in order to consolidate its influence. Even though there were constitutional imperatives and policy pronouncements to the contrary, German unification was soon not just increasingly unlikely but also less and less in the interests of each superpower and its respective German ally. Just as East Germany integrated itself in the Eastern Bloc, the West German government pursued a firm policy of *Westintegration*—that is, of integration into the emerging structures of European and transatlantic alliances.

The policy of *Westintegration* is most closely associated with West Germany's first postwar chancellor, Konrad Adenauer, who once poignantly remarked that he was the only German chancellor who preferred the unity of Europe to the unity of his own country. While this statement reflected a certain belief in the unity of the nation, Adenauer strongly believed that West Germany's integration into Western European and transatlantic structures had to precede German unification in order to avoid any of the dangers that renewed German unity would bring with it in terms of the country's inevitable size, economic power, and political influence. Any proposals therefore that aimed at a united but neutral Germany met with Adenauer's fierce opposition, because he found it difficult to see who would be able to ensure Germany's neutrality after its reestablishment as a sovereign state. Thus, it cannot have come as a surprise that throughout his service as chancellor, Adenauer eagerly pursued all possible avenues of further integration into the Western alliance while rejecting any offers for German unification under the conditions set out by the Soviet Union, let alone the GDR. In particular, given the option in 1952 (in the "Stalin notes") between German unification under strict conditions of the country's neutrality and integration in the EDC, Adenauer's choice was clearly in favor of the EDC, even if this meant abandoning one of the few realistic opportunities, if not the only one, for achieving the unification of the two German states at the time.

Political integration went hand in hand with economic integration. The ECSC in fact preceded the EDC treaty, and economic integration was the only grand vision for European unity that was to materialize during the Cold War. The ECSC treaty was signed on 18 April 1951. It established the forerunner of today's European Union and marked the first contractual agreement in the postwar period in which the Federal Republic signed up for institutional cooperation with other countries in Western Europe. The EDC treaty, after difficult negotiations, was eventually signed in 1954, but it failed in the ratification stage in France, where old fears of German rearmament made possible a coalition of Gaullists, communists, and oppositional politicians within the government. Further plans for institutionalized political integration were not pursued. Ironically, this failure to establish a Western European defense system enabled the Federal Republic to join NATO in 1955. Adenauer's firm commitment to a pro-Western rather than a pro-German policy, which fit much better with the West's doctrine of containment throughout the 1950s, was rewarded by the Western Allies with a substantial increase in sovereignty for the Federal Republic. However, the United States, the United Kingdom, and France retained the power to negotiate a final peace treaty with Germany.

This increase in sovereignty for his country enabled Adenauer to "crown" his achievements of *Westintegration* with the successful conclusion of negotiations on the establishment of the European Economic Community (EEC). The Treaty of Rome was ratified by the German parliament in March 1957 and marked the last high point in Adenauer's foreign policy—a policy, however, that having been predicated on the division of Germany was not without its critics in the Federal Republic. These came primarily from within the SPD but to some extent also from the ranks of the Free Democratic Party (FDP). Adenauer's critics primarily took issue with his early abandonment of the idea of German unification, which they considered too high a price to pay for *Westintegration*. Yet the opportunities for either the SPD or FDP to influence foreign policy were severely limited, given the dominance of Adenauer's own party, the CDU, at the time. In addition, within the SPD there was until the late 1950s and early 1960s a split between traditionalists and reformers. While the former advocated the prerogative of national unity as a guiding principle of foreign policy, the latter took a more pragmatic approach and recognized the value of *Westintegration* as a starting point for the formulation and subsequent implementation of a *neue Ostpolitik*, a new West German policy toward Central and Eastern Europe, including the GDR.

This new policy approach is primarily connected with two SPD politicians—the later Federal chancellor Willy Brandt and his chief advisor on *Ostpolitik*, Egon Bahr. Both played leading roles in West Berlin politics until 1966 and therefore experienced firsthand the consequences of Adenauer's policy of *Westintegration*. Neither Brandt nor Bahr explicitly rejected *Westintegration*, but they belonged to a new generation of politicians within the SPD, as well as within the CDU and other political parties in West Germany, who realized that now that West Germany's integration into NATO and the EEC had become irreversible it was time to rethink the approach toward Germany's neighbors in Central and Eastern Europe. Rather than on containment, the new policy would focus on "change through rapprochement" (*Wandel durch Annäherung*). It was to become the guiding principle for the Federal Republic's foreign policy throughout the next three decades, until and beyond the accomplishment of German reunification. Egon Bahr first made this new concept public in a speech in July 1963. One month earlier, the new American president, John F. Kennedy, had proclaimed in a speech at the American University in Washington that a new peace strategy would have to pursue a policy that would eventually establish conditions in which it was in the interests of the Soviet Union and its allies to agree to a just peace. Bahr picked up on this theme of new relations between the superpowers and applied it to the situation between the two German states. In his analysis of the situation he made it clear that the German question had become intractably linked to the East-West conflict and could therefore be resolved only in this context. The key to German reunification, according to Bahr, lay in Moscow. In his view, there was no possibility of creating conditions for German reunification without the cooperation of the Soviet Union, let alone against its will. By the same token, no improvement in the humanitarian situation in East Germany would be possible without the consent and cooperation of the communist regime there. Recognition of the building of the Berlin Wall as an expression of the regime's will (and capacity) to survive meant that any realistic peace strategy would have to avoid aggravating the fears of the regime in East Germany; that meant in turn that the risks of liberalization would have to be small and thus acceptable.

Outrage in East and West and inside and outside his own party was enormous once Bahr's conception of a new *Ostpolitik* had been made public, but political reality soon proved his critics wrong. Several months later, the first agreement on cross-border travel in Berlin, the so-called *Passierscheinabkommen,* was concluded between the East German government and the Senate of West Berlin, led by Brandt as governing mayor of the city. This was one element in a much broader policy pursued by the West Berlin Senate to achieve better relations with the GDR in terms of communication, transportation, trade, and contact between people.

The policy of constructive engagement with the Eastern Bloc on the part of the Federal Republic had begun. While this was a significant turn in foreign policy, it must not be forgotten that its subsequent full implementation after the SPD's takeover of government in 1969 could have been achieved only in the context of the relaxation of superpower relations in the early and mid-1960s and on the basis of the economic and political strength grounded in the firm integration of the West German state in the structures of European and transatlantic integration and cooperation. From this perspective, *Ostpolitik* built on the success of *Westintegration*.

The period of Willy Brandt's chancellorship between 1969 and 1974 is characterized by the conclusion of treaties with the Soviet Union and Poland in 1970 and with Czechoslovakia in 1973, by the Basic Treaty with East Germany in 1972, and by the Quadripartite Agreement on Berlin of 1970. These treaties and agreements established the new framework for West Germany's foreign policy toward the countries in Central and Eastern Europe and the GDR. They were made possible by a policy shift in the Western alliance in general that aimed at complementing deterrence with increased cooperation in order to ensure the security of its member states. The so-called Harmel Report of December 1967 specifically stated that military security and a policy of détente were not only not mutually contradictory but could usefully complement one another. This reorientation of Western policy was a crucial external factor that subsequently allowed the new West German government under Willy Brandt to implement *neue Ostpolitik*.

The treaties with the Soviet Union, Poland, Czechoslovakia, and East Germany essentially acknowledged the territorial and political status quo and made it possible for *Wandel durch Annäherung* to be slowly extended beyond the inter-German relationship to other dimensions of the German question. By simultaneously ruling out the use of force and determining the parameters of cooperation, the treaties significantly decreased the tensions between Germany and all of its eastern neighbors and, in the long run, paved the way for a process of comprehensive reconciliation. Jointly and individually these treaties marked a significant achievement for the SPD's *Ostpolitik* and enabled the governments of Willy Brandt and his successor in 1974, Helmut Schmidt, to pursue a policy that, while not losing sight of the aim of German unification, bore in mind the human dimensions of any policy decisions in this respect and increased opportunities to improve the living conditions in East Germany. From this perspective, the treaties must not be seen as abandoning the aim of reunification to the conditions of *Realpolitik* but as making an immediate and positive, albeit small, impact on the human dimension of the German-German question while at the same time keeping reunification in the long run possible.

Despite earlier rhetoric to the contrary, under the conservative government coalition under Helmut Kohl, which came to power in 1982, this human dimension remained a key aspect of *Ostpolitik* and *Deutschlandpolitik*. This was the case not least because of the continuity of foreign policy dominance by the FDP, which had held the top post at the foreign ministry continuously since 1969. Throughout the 1970s and 1980s, the Federal Republic maintained this constructive approach in its relationship with the GDR, and as a result numerous agreements on trade, culture, travel and tourism, the environment, and scientific cooperation were concluded.

Following the visit of Chancellor Helmut Schmidt to East Germany in 1981 at a low point in East-West relations—due to the invasion of Afghanistan by Soviet troops in 1979, the declaration of martial law in Poland in 1981, and the beginning of a new round of the global arms race—German-German relations continued to develop remarkably well. Both countries maintained that they were willing to work toward peace and stability in Europe, and both countries' political elites realized that this was possible through the intensification of cooperation on a variety of political, economic, environmental, cultural, and humanitarian issues. For the East German leadership a further incentive existed in the fact that the country's economic situation deteriorated dramatically; the only way to reverse this potentially dangerous trend lay in greater openness toward the West. The West German government clearly recognized this as an opportunity for its own policy of *Wandel durch Annäherung*, and two multibillion-Deutschmark loans for the GDR were facilitated by Bavarian minister-president Franz-Josef Strauss, in 1983 and 1984. Preparations also began for a visit to the Federal Republic by the East German leader Erich Honecker, who had succeeded Walter Ulbricht in 1971. However, the tenuous situation in the Soviet Union following the rapid succession of leaders after Leonid Brezhnev's death in November 1982 placed things on hold until Mikhail Gorbachev finally agreed to the visit. The high point of German-German relations in the 1980s thus finally materialized in 1987. Termed an "official" rather than a "state" visit, the event nevertheless was a major turning point in the relations between the two German states, as for the first time a conservative chancellor of the Federal Republic implicitly recognized the independence and sovereignty of the GDR. This was made clear at the welcoming ceremony: both states' flags were raised, both national anthems were played, and Honecker was received with full military honors. Nevertheless, Helmut Kohl maintained throughout the visit that it remained the policy of his government to contribute to the creation of conditions in Europe under which the entire German people could fulfill its right to self-determination. Much to the astonishment of everyone, these conditions would be in place less than three years later.

German Reunification 1989–1990

The rapid collapse of communism in Central and Eastern Europe after 1989 fundamentally changed the opportunities for the *Deutschlandpolitik* of the Allies as well as the two German states. The (for the most part peaceful) regime change in Central and Eastern Europe itself, however, had been made possible by the ascent to power of Gorbachev in 1985. The new Soviet leader embarked on a course of reform in domestic as well as foreign policy, including the relationship between Moscow and its allies in Eastern Europe. Most crucially, this policy included an abandonment of the so-called Brezhnev Doctrine, according to which the Soviet Union had reserved the right to intervene in the internal affairs of its allies. This had happened on several occasions: 1953 in East Germany, 1956 in Hungary, 1968 in Czechoslovakia.

Even though Gorbachev's turn away from the old interventionist policies of his predecessors meant a significant shift in the Soviet attitude toward its Eastern European allies, the Soviet Union still remained a superpower and, in relation to the German question, one of the essential players, not just because of its status as one of the four Allies but also because of the presence of a large number of its troops on East German soil. As Egon Bahr had correctly analyzed twenty-five years earlier, the key to the German question lay in Moscow. The rapid dismantling of the communist regime in East Germany, however, was accompanied by an equally rapid change in Soviet policy toward the issue of German unification. Erich Honecker's successor as East German leader, Egon Krenz, was assured by Gorbachev on 31 October 1989 that German unification was not on the agenda, yet Krenz's successor, Hans Modrow, only three months later came back from Moscow with a plan entitled "Germany, United Fatherland" (appropriately adopting the lyrics of the East German national anthem, the singing of which had been banned under Honecker), which outlined Gorbachev's vision for achieving German unification. One day earlier, in a radio interview, Gorbachev had hinted at a change of mind on his part in relation to German unification, stating, "There are two German states, there are the Four Powers, there is the European process. . . . All of this must be brought into harmony."

Two weeks after Gorbachev's radio interview a process was begun that became known as the "two-plus-four" negotiations on German reunification. In February 1990, after some hesitation on the part of France and the United Kingdom, among other states in Western Europe, which feared they might be sidelined in the European integration process by a reunited Germany and the political and economic power it would inevitably wield, the two-plus-four formula was agreed upon at a meeting of NATO and the Warsaw Treaty in Ottawa, Canada. This marked the beginning of the final stage of the German-German question. "Two plus four" specified the participants in this negotiation process—the two German states and the four Allied powers of the Second World War, but it also referred to a certain division of labor between the two and the four, with the former hammering out the "logistical" details of the actual unification of two previously independent states, while the latter were to ensure that German unification would not threaten peace and stability in Europe and beyond.

The two German states got down to work almost immediately. Following the first free and fair East German elections for several decades in March 1990, a broad coalition government took power, led by the conservative Alliance for Germany. All the parties participating in the new government had campaigned for rapid German unification. Pressure from ordinary East Germans steadily grew, and as in the period before the building of the Berlin Wall, there was a steadily increasing number of emigrants from East to West. A first measure to stem this migration was the conclusion of a treaty on economic, social, and currency union between the two German states, introducing the Deutschmark in East Germany. This was far from actual political unification but was something that could be negotiated more quickly than the actual unification treaty, and it demonstrated to the people of East Germany that both states were serious about achieving unification. The economic, social, and currency union of the two German states took effect on 1 July 1990, three months before the actual treaty on political unification, the *Einigungsvertrag*.

The two German states were meant to take a back seat in the negotiations of the external dimensions of German unification. This is certainly true for East Germany, but in many ways the crucial negotiations that eventually allowed for the successful conclusion of the two-plus-four treaty took place between the Federal Republic and the Soviet Union, specifically between Chancellor Kohl and Gorbachev. In parallel with the two-plus-four foreign-minister meetings throughout the spring and summer of 1990, Kohl and his foreign minister, Hans-Dietrich Genscher, traveled to the Soviet Union in the middle of July in order to get Gorbachev's agreement on one particularly crucial issue—the membership of the united Germany in NATO. It had always been a Soviet demand that any reunited Germany should be neutral, but Gorbachev was well aware that insistence on this could, at best, delay German unification, not prevent it or the country's eventual membership in NATO. He therefore used this issue as a bargaining chip, extracting significant concessions from the

Germany Reunited, 3 October 1990

Federal Republic in terms of German disarmament and economic assistance for the ailing Soviet economy as well as for the withdrawal and reintegration of Soviet troops stationed in Germany. Two days after the successful conclusion of West German negotiations with Gorbachev, the two-plus-four foreign ministers agreed on a definition of the borders of a reunited Germany, confirming the territorial status quo that had been established in the immediate aftermath of the Second World War and had been consolidated through four decades of Cold War as the country's legally and internationally recognized border. On 12 September 1990 the two-plus-four treaty was signed in Moscow. German unification was formally achieved on 3 October 1990. More than four and a half decades after the end of the Second World War, Germany had regained its unity and full sovereignty.

THE UNIFICATION THAT DID NOT HAPPEN: GERMANY AND THE FORMER EASTERN TERRITORIES OF THE GERMAN REICH

After having discussed the two successful German unifications in 1957 and 1990, it remains only to examine briefly the one unification that did not happen, that of reunited Germany with the former German territories east of the rivers Oder and Neisse, the *Ostgebiete*. These had been placed under provisional Polish and Soviet administration at Potsdam, and the Western Allies had made it clear at the time that they would look favorably toward making this a permanent arrangement at a future peace conference. Therefore, while it is true that the question of Germany's borders remained somewhat open until its final settlement in 1990, one must also bear in mind that the chances of the Allies' accepting a reintegration of these territories into a reunited Germany were, from the outset, very slim at best. This was particularly the case for former East Prussia, which had been separated from the rest of Germany by the creation of the Polish Corridor in 1919 and had been divided between Poland and the Soviet Union in 1945. It was equally unlikely that the former Free City of Danzig would regain its interwar status. The main dispute therefore was over the territories immediately east of the rivers Oder and Neisse that had remained part of Germany in 1919, but, in anticipation of Poland's territorial compensation in the west for cession of land to the Soviet Union in the east, had not been allocated to the Soviet zone of occupation but had been handed over to Polish administration in 1945. On the surface, the situation in this part of the *Ostgebiete* was somewhat similar to that in the Saar. However, on closer examination, there were a number of crucial differences. First, all four Allies agreed on the need foHr Polish territorial compensation at the expense of Germany. Second, the expulsions after 1945 had effectively de-Germanized these areas, followed by the settlement of Polish expellees and refugees, primarily from the Polish-Ukrainian and Polish-Belarusian borderlands. Third, while the reunification with the Saar was achieved within about a decade after the war, the Cold War in Europe and the division of Germany prevented any credible policy on part of the West German government that could have even come close to redrawing this border. Fourth, the effective control that the Soviet Union exercised over its allies made it possible for East Germany and Poland, if in contravention of Allied arrangements in Potsdam, to conclude a treaty in 1950 that recognized the border between the two states along the Oder and Neisse. Finally, the longer Germany was divided and the longer the Cold War lasted, the more the "real" German question, or what was commonly perceived as such, became whether and how the division of Germany into two states aligned with the two antagonistic military alliances of the Cold War could be overcome. With the advent of *Ostpolitik* and the political and social marginalization of forces calling for a revision of the Oder-Neisse line—primarily the expellee organizations and their allies on the right wing of the conservative political parties in the Federal Republic—the issue became less and less salient in West German politics. The vast majority of the population accepted that German unification, insofar as it would be possible at all, meant the unification of the two German states and nothing else. It was as if the West German population overwhelmingly agreed with Willy Brandt's assessment that the recognition of the borders in Central and Eastern Europe and their inviolability now and in the future, which was part of the *Ostverträge*, "had lost nothing that had not already been lost."

Why then did the issue of the German-Polish border remain such a sensitive one in the two countries' bilateral relations after 1970? There are a number of reasons. Apart from the fact that the potential threat from Germany had an important, albeit decreasingly effective, function in the domestic stabilization of the communist regime in Poland, the German Federal Constitutional Court in 1973 and 1975, in two rulings on the *Ostverträge*, had established that the treaties did not violate Germany's Basic Law. That is, they contradicted neither the constitutional imperative of German reunification nor the assumption that Germany continued to exist in the borders of 1937. In addition, the federal government in 1972 had handed the Soviet government a "Letter on German Unity" in which it stated that neither the Moscow nor the Warsaw Treaty of 1970 prejudiced a future peace treaty with Germany or was to be taken as a *legal* basis for the existing borders and that they also did not affect the right to self-determination of the German people. This meant that there always remained, at least potentially, the threat of a sudden policy change in Germany that would seek the conclusion of new and different treaties that might lead to boundary revisions. A second reason for the wariness of Poland in particular (as the country most directly affected by any such border change), but also of other European countries in East and West that were frightened of a new hegemonial Germany, was the change of government in Germany in 1982 and the refusal by incoming chancellor Helmut Kohl to recognize formally the German-Polish border. This was primarily a domestic problem for Kohl, who was afraid that too early a recognition of what inevitably would have to occur would lose him crucial votes among the German refugees, expellees, *Aussiedler,* and their descendants. However, until 1989–90, when the possibility of German unification suddenly became real, debate on the border issue was reserved for hard-liners in East and West.

In early 1990, after the beginning of the two-plus-four negotiations, domestic and political pressure increased on the federal government under Kohl to rise to the challenge and initiate a process at the end of which would stand a formal German recognition of the existing border with Poland. Polish prime minister Tadeusz Mazowiecki made his demands clear in an interview with the German daily *Die Welt* on 5 March 1990, stating that his government had no intention to "enter into any discussions on the question of the Polish border." He echoed concerns shared in East and West, as well as in Germany itself, when he emphasized that "the stability of European borders is the *condition sine qua non* for European stability" and that "Poland would be afraid of a reunited Germany that was only insufficiently tied to Europe and did not take a clear stance on the issue of its neighbors' security." The uncertainty and unease that existed in Poland and elsewhere is understandable in the context of history, and in particular in relation to Germany's track record on territorial issues since 1919. However, it would be a mistake to assume that there was any sincere intention on the part of the federal government to revise the existing German-Polish border in the process of German unification. In fact, Chancellor Kohl himself made it finally clear at the annual Day of the Homeland (*Tag der Heimat*) celebrated by the German expellees in 1990 that the recognition of all current borders in Europe was the price that the two German states had to pay for their reunification.

In April and June 1990, first the East German parliament, and then both parliaments in parallel, issued declarations that recognized the German-Polish border. The simultaneous declaration of both parliaments in June 1990 was particularly significant as it made explicit reference to previous treaties, including the 1950 East German–Polish Treaty of Görlitz and subsequent agreements on border demarcation between the GDR and Poland of 1951 and 1989, as well as the West German–Polish treaty of 1970. These declarations, however, were just that—not international treaties. In addition, the German Basic Law still contained a number of provisions that made it legally possible, if not necessary, to seek further revisions of Germany's borders. That was the case with the preamble of the Basic Law and its insistence on the continued existence of Germany in the borders of 1937, and with Articles 23 and 146 of the Basic Law, which contained provisions on different procedures for German reunification. Even though nothing but reunification of the two German states was on the agenda of German political elites at the time, it was nevertheless in everybody's interest to achieve something more permanent and stable than parliamentary declarations.

This was acknowledged by all the negotiating parties in the two-plus-four process. At the Paris meeting of the two-plus-four foreign ministers in July 1990, just after the German-Soviet talks that had achieved Soviet consent on the NATO membership of a united Germany, five principles on the borders of the reunited Germany were agreed. These included a definition of the borders of the future Germany as those of the external borders of the two German states, with Germany abandoning any territorial claims toward any other state for all time and so amending its constitution. It was also agreed that the new German state and Poland would sign a legally binding bilateral treaty recognizing as permanent the existing border between them. When this happened within weeks after German unification in 1990, the German question ceased to have a territorial dimension.

Chapter 6

German Minorities in Europe
after 1945: From Fifth Column
to Accepted Partner?

Expellees, *Aussiedler*, German minorities in their homelands are
a bridge between Germans and their eastern neighbors; that much
is true. Yet they are also a permanent reminder against violated
human rights. This human bridge will only be stable when it is
built upon human rights, international law and minority laws.
            —Erika Steinbach (1998)

At the beginning of the twenty-first century, German minority groups
live in four countries in Western Europe and in sixteen countries in
Central and Eastern Europe.[1] Their historical origins, sizes, statuses,
and degrees of integration and assimilation differ greatly, not just between East and West but also within each of these two broadly defined geographic regions. Similarly, the degree to which Germany as
their kin state still plays a role varies as considerably as the importance
assigned to each minority group in German foreign policy. The situation of the German minorities as well as the priorities of German
external minority policy have changed significantly over the past half-
century. To explore the reasons for and dynamics of these changes is
the task of this chapter.

BETWEEN INTEGRATION AND ASSIMILATION: ETHNIC GERMANS IN DENMARK, BELGIUM, FRANCE, AND ITALY

Ethnic Germans in Western Europe (Denmark, Belgium, France, and Italy) share the same history regarding their origin. None of the German-speaking minorities there came to their present settlement areas as migrants in the modern era, as some of their ethnic kin in Central and Eastern Europe did. They have inhabited these territories for centuries, in most cases since the end of the large tribal migrations around A.D. 500. Their current status as national (or in the case of Alsace, linguistic) minorities stems from boundary revisions carried out after the First World War and confirmed in 1945 to compensate Germany's neighbors for the losses and suffering incurred as a consequence of the two wars and in order to increase their security.[2]

The democratic environment in post-1945 Western Europe, in combination with the relative economic prosperity in all four countries and their participation in the various projects of European and Western integration, has facilitated the process of political, social, and economic integration of the minorities into their host countries. None of the German-speaking populations of the four countries harbors any significant secessionist aspirations or feels discriminated against because of their different ethnic or cultural identity. In the context of ever closer European integration, the opportunities for members of all four groups to maintain contact with Germany and to travel and work there without restrictions have tremendously increased in the decades following the Second World War. Although from the perspective of the early twenty-first century all four groups appear very well integrated, the way there was different in each country, and below the surface the results of the integration processes differ as well.

With respect to Denmark, the German minority has developed a transethnic German and Danish ethnic identity, while retaining a German national identity. This *Zweiströmigkeit* (Pedersen 2000) finds its obvious expression in the self-conception of being German North Schleswigians (among the older generations) or German South Jutlanders (among the younger generations). The fact that a relatively small minority of only between ten and fifteen thousand members, or around 5 percent of the population of the administrative region in which they live, has been able to maintain such a strong sense of its German origins points to the favorable conditions that have been, and are continuing to be, provided for its members. The framework of the

Bonn-Copenhagen Declarations of 1955 secures the position of the German minority in Denmark politically, by guaranteeing its members full and equal access to the rights and liberties accorded to all Danish citizens. Increasing cross-border cooperation, which has developed subsequently, and material and other support provided from the Federal Republic of Germany have allowed the German minority to maintain its identity as a distinct national group in Denmark. Given the high level of tolerance for, not to say indifference to, the German minority's insistence on its distinctiveness, the social climate in Denmark is no less favorable than the political conditions. The social and economic integration of members of the minority has certainly also been helped by a long-standing tradition in the minority education system aiming at preparing each new generation for life in Denmark as well as Germany. In the light of ever closer integration in Europe in which the importance of historically grown rather than politically defined regions is increasing at the expense of traditional boundaries and concepts of nationhood, the opportunities for the German minority in Denmark to preserve its transethnic identity appear secure.

The total number of the German-speaking population in Belgium is estimated to be around a hundred thousand. About two-thirds of its members fall under the jurisdiction of the German-speaking community (one of the three recognized linguistic communities in the country) and enjoy special rights and protection, as the community has autonomy in all matters related to culture, education, electronic broadcasts, health, welfare, research and technology, and the use of languages. In addition, communal authority also extends to international relations in these areas and to intercommunity affairs related to matters of culture and education. Even though one-third of German speakers in Belgium fall under the jurisdiction of either the French or the Flemish community, some of them can still make use of special linguistic facilities that are available in areas with at least 25 percent German speakers. For administrative purposes, the German-speaking community is part of the Walloon (i.e., francophone) region. Despite these advantageous political conditions, the linguistic situation in which the German-speaking community finds itself is more complex. In the Eupen and St. Vith areas of eastern Belgium, German has official status and is also the language of instruction in schools, but with the exception of the Malmédy area (where it is taught as a compulsory first "foreign" language), everywhere else it has to compete with Dutch and French as the two essential languages in Belgium, and increasingly also with English. Donaldson (2000) has argued that while German still exercises a certain attraction as an "economic" language, allowing its speakers to find a job in neighboring Germany, it is, at least as far as the Walloon region is concerned, in decline. The different degree of stigmatization of German (and Germanness), the geographic dispersion of German speakers across Belgium in areas where their (linguistic) identity has different constitutional statuses, and the different levels of assimilation resulting from this make the progressive assimilation of the German-speaking community of Belgium more and more likely.

Alsace, for centuries a disputed border country between France and Germany, is today politically firmly integrated into the French state, and the cultural assimilation of its population has progressed very far. This becomes obvious from the degree to which the French language has spread in Alsace while the knowledge of German or its Alsatian dialect have declined: While there are only very few older people left who do not speak any French at all, the interest among the younger generation in the dialect is declining steadily. European integration has advantaged Alsace not only economically but also in terms of the confidence Alsatians have in their place in France and Europe. Under these conditions political integration and partial cultural assimilation have proved to be successful policies for the management of ethnocultural differences that had escalated in the interwar period (Wolff 2002: chapter 4). Nevertheless, there still exists a distinct regional identity, based on the cultural and linguistic traditions of historical Alsace but also on the development of the region after 1945. Franco-German reconciliation and the process of European integration have had a significant impact on the development in Alsace. With Germany no longer perceived as a threat, the existence of a local Alsatian culture based on Alemannic traditions is no longer interpreted as a threat to French territorial sovereignty, either. While there is only minimal institutional support for German, the decline in the number of German speakers after the Second World War suggests little demand for such support (Trouillet 1997). The local dialect, however, enjoys a significantly higher economic, social, and language status. Because it is one of the primary focal points of an Alsatian identity that distinguishes it from both Germany and France, Broadbridge (2000) has concluded that the future of the Alsatians as a distinct ethnocultural/ethnolinguistic group looks promising. Their prospects for preserving and developing their identity seem better than that of German speakers in Belgium, and in this the situation in Alsace resembles in some aspects that of the German minority in Denmark.

Despite its historically much more conflict-rich relationship with its host state and host nation, the German-speaking minority in South Tyrol is today the best protected and most empowered of all German communities in Western Europe. As a result of complex internal and external developments after 1945, Italy's German minority enjoys an extensive catalogue of rights and liberties within a regional and provincial framework of autonomy that grants the minority full self-government (Wolff 2002: chapter 6). While this political situation permits the comprehensive protection and development of the minority's ethnocultural identity, it has not been without problems in the past, creating tension between Germans and Italians in the province and resulting in an increased vote share for ethnocentric parties in the 1980s and early 1990s. Over the past decade, however, a more ethnically neutral civic identity shared by all population groups in South Tyrol has emerged, manifesting itself primarily in pride in, and loyalty to, the political institutions of autonomy in South Tyrol, which, particularly following the revisions to the autonomy statute in 2001, have become more inclusive and representative of all three ethnic groups than they have ever been before. The emergence of such an identity based on inclusive and civic values in South Tyrol resembles quite closely similar postwar developments in Denmark and France.

With regard to the German-speaking communities in Western Europe, an overall picture of great diversity thus emerges. For the most part, they find themselves in a situation at the beginning of the twenty-first century that is fundamentally different from that of the first half of the twentieth century. In all four countries, legislative and policy frameworks are in place for minority protection, and their consequences for the German-speaking (and other) minorities have been very positive, if only in the sense that they established conditions offering the members of minorities a real opportunity to determine their own futures, individually and collectively.

BETWEEN FEAR AND HOPE: ETHNIC GERMANS IN CENTRAL AND EASTERN EUROPE

For more than four decades after the end of the Second World War, the situation of German minorities in the countries of Central and Eastern Europe has been fundamentally different from that of the ethnic German communities in Western Europe. Subjected to deportation, forced labor, detention, and expulsion in the immediate aftermath of the war, their ability to preserve, let alone express or develop, their ethnocultural identity was severely limited under the communist regimes of their host countries. Members of all these minorities were subjected to various assimilation pressures ranging from the simple denial of their existence as a distinct minority group to the repression of their cultural, linguistic, and religious identities in various degrees. Apart from the intentional neglect of the conditions necessary for minorities in general to preserve their identities, ethnic Germans suffered additionally from the fact that their kin state had, very often with their active support, inflicted enormous suffering on the population of their host states (see chapter 3). Being German in Central and Eastern Europe was thus not only unpopular; it almost invited discrimination and persecution. Added to this internal pressure, the increasing opportunities over the years for emigrating to Germany and obtaining full citizenship rights there according to the provisions of Article 116 of the Federal Republic's Basic Law (see chapter 4) accelerated the process of assimilation of German minorities in Central and Eastern Europe, as many of the most consciously German members of these communities left.

The democratization process that began in Central and Eastern Europe in the late 1980s not only offered opportunities for improving conditions of minority protection but took away all barriers to emigration previously imposed by the communist regimes there. Thus, until the changes in German legislation in the early 1990s, a mass exodus of ethnic Germans, particularly from Romania, Poland, and the former Soviet Union, continued to weaken, if not partially destroy, the community structures of German minorities in Central and Eastern Europe. Parallel to raising the obstacles to immigration to Germany, the federal government has, since the late 1980s and particularly after 1990, taken many steps to support ethnic Germans in their host countries (a point to which I return in greater detail in a separate section below). German foreign policy in this respect has encompassed the conclusion of bilateral treaties with most of the Central and Eastern European states in which significant German minorities live. These treaties and a range of additional agreements now provide the basis upon which substantial material and financial aid is channeled to German minority communities across Central and Eastern Europe. Even though this has not necessarily stopped, let alone reversed, the assimilation process, it has at least slowed it down. Whether this change in the situation will be only a temporary interlude on the way to the ultimate decline of German culture in the region, or whether it will be turned into an opportunity for a fresh start, does not depend solely on the continuation of German government support for the minorities or on the persistence of democratic and tolerant environments in the host states. It also depends on the minorities themselves—whether they want to, and can, seize this opportunity, or perceive their only choice to be between emigration and assimilation.

It is not possible to predict the outcome of the current developments conclusively; nevertheless, a more detailed examination of the contextual situation in which each of the German minorities in Central and Eastern Europe lives today will permit some cautious remarks about the future of "German culture in the East."[3] With regard to the largest group of ethnic Germans in Central and Eastern Europe—those who live in the successor states of the former Soviet Union—the picture is very diverse. Apart from Russia, ethnic Germans live in the three Baltic republics, in Ukraine, in the four Central Asian successor states of the former Soviet Union, and in Georgia.[4] The numerically smallest groups live in Estonia, Latvia, and Lithuania. In terms of their origin, they come from diverse backgrounds, comprising remaining members of the historical German population in the Baltics, several thousand Memel Germans, and ethnic Germans from Russia who migrated to the Baltic Republics in the Soviet era. The latter group faces severe difficulties in obtaining citizenship rights in Estonia and Latvia. This, however, is not a specifically anti-German policy by the governments of these two countries but a consequence of discriminatory citizenship policy, primarily aimed at the sizable nonindigenous Russian population. In Georgia, a similarly small group, only some two thousand ethnic Germans, is still resident. Apart from their larger size, the single most significant difference between the German minorities in the Baltics and in Georgia, on the one hand, and those in Central Asia, on the other, is the fact that most ethnic Germans from Kazakhstan (almost seven hundred thousand), Kyrgyzstan (about sixty thousand), Tajikistan (around thirty thousand), and Uzbekistan (approximately forty thousand) have decided to leave their host states because they are denied the essential conditions to preserve their identity, because they feel discriminated against for their previously close affiliation with ethnic Russians, or because of their Christian rather than Muslim religion. Another reason, particularly in Tajikistan, was civil war in the early

1990s. The origins of Germans in these newly independent states go back to the deportations from the European parts of the Soviet Union after the beginning of the war with Germany in 1941 (see chapter 3). Only in Kyrgyzstan and Kazakhstan had there been earlier, albeit much smaller, settlements since the nineteenth century. Even though the favored destination of most émigrés remains Germany, a growing number of them settle temporarily or permanently in ethnic German settlements in Russia, especially in the two German *rayons* in western Siberia. A survey among ethnic Germans in Kyrgyzstan in 1993 found 85 percent of them determined to emigrate, their preferred destinations being Germany (80 percent), Russia (6 percent) and Ukraine (1 percent) (Eisfeld 1993: 49).

In all these countries on the territory of the former Soviet Union—with the partial exception of Ukraine, where, supported by the German federal government and within the framework of a 1996 agreement between the two countries, the forty-thousand-strong German minority is seeking to restore its traditional settlement areas—the future for the continued existence of German communities is rather bleak. Either the degree of assimilation has already progressed irreversibly or the conditions for a sustained recovery of the minority, including the rebuilding of viable community structures, are simply not there. The reasons include lack of government commitment to promote minority rights, insufficient support from Germany, popular resentment toward ethnic Germans, or the small number of the remaining members of the minority group. There is, however, a slim chance that the situation in Kazakhstan will change for the better. The minority there is much bigger, making up about 6 percent of the total population of the country. Its age structure is intact, and community structures are generally functioning. Even more important, there is an effort on the part of the Kazakh government to provide conditions that would make it possible for members of the minority to remain in the country and be able to express, preserve, and develop their distinct ethnocultural identity. The Kazakh Decree on Independence guaranteed equal rights for all citizens regardless of their ethnic or linguistic origin as one of the basic principles by which the country's future policy would be guided. This has been a remarkable departure from the often repressive and discriminating policy of the Soviet era. Since the German minority as a whole is valued for its professional and labor skills, and the mass emigration of the early 1990s had a negative impact on the economy, ethnic Germans are encouraged to stay in the country. Support from Germany has been forthcoming, and an intergovernmental conference, including minority representatives, has been in operation since 1992. By 1997, some moderate success in slowing down emigration had been achieved. Nevertheless, severe problems remain. One is the degree of Russification of the minority, a process that had already progressed very far before the collapse of the Soviet Union. This is unlikely to be changed in the near future, as part of the internal migration pattern of ethnic Germans is their increasing urbanization—that is, a move away from relatively secluded rural environments, in which the development of functioning community structures would have been somewhat easier. Another is that the economic situation in the country as a whole has been consistently bad since the early 1990s, resulting in an overall double-digit decline in industrial and agricultural output (Eisfeld 1993: 47).

The most complex situation has probably evolved in relation to ethnic Germans living in the Russian Federation (cf. Stricker 2000). Deportation and decades of repression and finally emigration have resulted in the steady decline of the minority and its increasing assimilation. This process continues despite increasing efforts by the German government to improve the living conditions of the minority in Russia. Aid programs in the areas of German-language education, economic recovery, and culture have been put in place to slow down the process of assimilation and emigration. The success of these programs, however, also depends on the will of the minority to consolidate itself and survive ultimately as a distinct ethnocultural group in Russia. Clearly, the political and economic situation in Russia also has significant bearing on whether ethnic Germans will see their futures there or in Germany.

The future prospects of the minorities in other Central and Eastern European countries are again very diverse. Leaving aside the political uncertainties of the former Yugoslavia, where the minority numbers only a few thousand, the conditions for the minorities in Hungary, Poland, Romania, and the Czech and Slovak Republics are very different. They are probably best in Hungary, where more than two hundred thousand ethnic Germans find advantageous political conditions within a model framework of minority legislation. They are fairly well integrated into Hungarian society and have widely preserved or recently revitalized their ethnocultural identity. The political stability of Hungary and the country's success in the transformation of its economy certainly contributed to this process.

The future of the German-speaking population in Romania, while it is linguistically probably the best developed of all Eastern and Central

European German minorities, is far from certain. This is all the more astonishing given the external conditions in which ethnic Germans in Romania live. Supported by the German government and the *Landsmannschaften*, the minority is no longer subjected to any significant level of discrimination. Rather, the Romanian government has long recognized the "value" of its German population in attracting foreign investment and establishing mutually beneficial bilateral relationships with Germany, and through it with NATO and the European Union. Also, the German minority in Romania was the only one of its kind in Central and Eastern Europe that had not been subjected to aggressive assimilationist programs. Predominantly German settlements in which German was the everyday language of conversation existed throughout the post-1945 period. Thus, the reason for the limited prospects for the future must be sought within the minority. Wagner (2000) has argued that the mass exodus of the late 1980s and early 1990s has not only considerably diminished the size of the minority but rendered vital community structures dysfunctional and disrupted the formerly compact settlement pattern. In addition, it was primarily the young and well-educated members of the community who emigrated, leaving behind an overage population that is no longer represented in all strata of society. It is doubtful whether this process can be reversed and the community reconstructed, even on a smaller scale.

Stevenson (2000) characterizes the situation of ethnic Germans in the Czech Republic as similarly difficult. Despite wide-ranging constitutional guarantees for the protection of national minorities, historical developments have complicated the relationship between the Czechs and their German minority. The part the minority played in the dismemberment and subsequent destruction of Czechoslovakia in 1938–39 has poisoned the relationships with the host nation ever since and prepared the ground for the postwar persecution and almost complete expulsion of the minority. This in turn has created a resentful diaspora community in Germany that has tried over the years to exert influence on the bilateral relationships between Germany and Czechoslovakia/the Czech Republic. Successive Czech governments, therefore, have been very reluctant to make concessions on issues relating to the status of the German minority or to rights demanded by the diaspora community, such as a right to return and resettle in their former homeland, let alone restitution of property or compensation for losses and suffering. Even though the German and Czech governments managed in 1997 to find and express a consensus in a joint declaration, this did not prove to be the beginning of hoped-for comprehensive reconciliation between the two countries. That the events between 1938 and the late 1940s still have a remarkable potential to disrupt bilateral relations and negatively impact broader international developments once more become clear in early 2002, when, following remarks by the Czech prime minister, Milos Zeman, implying a collective guilt of the Sudeten Germans for the events in 1938–39 and justifying their collective punishment by expulsion, the German chancellor, Gerhard Schroeder, called off a planned visit to the Czech Republic (see chapter 7).

As for Poland, the relationship between the German minority, territorially concentrated in the Upper Silesian region, and the majority population and authorities in the country is no longer threatened by either assimilation or repression or by irredentist or secessionist aspirations. Favorable political conditions, allowing parliamentary representation and opportunities for the minority to organize itself in political parties and cultural associations, have enabled ethnic Germans to maintain viable community structures and to preserve, develop, and express their ethnocultural identity despite the exodus of members of the minority that occurred in the late 1980s and early 1990s (Cordell 2000). Since then, the German minority has successfully striven to become a bridge between Poland and Germany. This has been possible because the German federal government has placed great emphasis on its relationship with Poland and because the Polish government has recognized the "value" of the German minority as a catalyst of reconciliation and of accession to NATO, which was accomplished in 1999, and eventually to the European Union. From this perspective, ethnic Germans in Poland can quite confidently look to the future.

The dichotomy of fear and hope, therefore, is to some extent a condensation of the past, present, and future of German minorities in Central and Eastern Europe. Deportation, expulsion, repression, persecution, and assimilation stand not only for the past. The resurgence of ethnonationalism in most countries hosting German minorities, even if they themselves are not always its target, could diminish the small hope that developed after the collapse of the communist regimes and the opening up of the societies in the region. With respect to the future, fear and hope symbolize assimilation and minority protection just as much as they exemplify the choice many members of ethnic German communities, particularly on the territory of the former Soviet

Union, have to make between remaining in their host countries and emigrating to the Federal Republic. Thus, what all German-speaking minorities in Central and Eastern Europe have in common is the fact that although the conditions under which their members live have generally improved over the last decade, their survival as distinct ethnocultural communities is by no means certain.

CHANGING PRIORITIES OR CHANGING OPPORTUNITIES? GERMAN EXTERNAL MINORITY POLICY AFTER 1945

The Cold War Period

The situation after 1945 was far less conducive to an active external minority policy than it had been after 1919. Then, the minority treaties concluded under the auspices of the League of Nations had provided both a legal framework as well as a certain degree of justification for kin states to involve themselves in this dimension of foreign policy. The alleged consequences of this situation—that minority groups, in particular those of ethnic Germans, were effectively used as fifth columns to undermine the internal stability and ultimately the external security of their host states—were taken to require a fundamentally different approach to the minority question in Europe after 1945. One part of this approach was the policy of forced population transfers; the other was the shift in focus from group-based rights (the League's approach) to individual rights. Thus, with the exception of the 1946 Paris Agreement between Austria and Italy, no "minority treaty" was concluded similar to those after 1919, so that no legal framework existed under which Germany could have legitimately concerned itself with the fate of ethnic Germans abroad.

This, however, did not mean that (West) German governments after 1949 did not care about German minorities, in particular in Central and Eastern Europe; it only meant that they were confronted with different opportunity structures to do so and thus had, to some extent, to adjust their interest structures considerably, compared to the situation after 1919.

If the major problem facing German policy makers after World War I was the territorial truncation of German territory and the reparations to be paid to the Allied powers, a new challenge presented itself after 1945. Many ethnic Germans, in particular from Central and Eastern European countries, were either expelled from their traditional settlement areas or deported to forced labor camps. Those able to remain in their host countries or to return there after deportation were subjected to systematic popular and state discrimination in response to the brutal occupation policies of those countries by Germany during the Second World War and the actual and alleged collaboration of ethnic Germans with the occupation forces (see chapter 3). Even though this wave of repression and expulsion ended by the early 1950s and the citizenship rights of ethnic Germans were gradually reinstated, their situation was still not considered satisfactory by the West German government, partly because they suffered all the "usual" disadvantages of life under communism, and partly because the experience of occupation by the titular nation of their host states made them vulnerable to continued discrimination.

However, in the early years of its existence, the Federal Republic was preoccupied with other issues, both domestically and in its international relations. Domestically, the rebuilding of society and the economy, including the integration of millions of refugees and expellees, took priority. On the international stage, Chancellor Adenauer had set a foreign policy agenda of which the foremost aim was to ensure the integration of the country into the Western alliance. This process of integration into the West, which provided a path to political security, economic recovery, and gradually also to social prosperity, was the preferred option of the overwhelming majority of the population and politicians. Yet, at the same time, the Western alliance as a symbol of postwar developments signaled, at least temporarily, an acceptance of the status quo, which, given the German borders in 1949, found significantly less support. While it was generally accepted that none of the territories inhabited by ethnic German minorities could be claimed as a rightful German territorial possession, the policy pursued toward the different minorities and their host states differed significantly. There has been virtually no engagement on behalf of the German communities in either France or Belgium. Successive postwar German governments have also recognized that the situation of the German minority in South Tyrol was a matter for Austria to deal with.

The only exception from this rule of disengagement after 1945 is Denmark, which differs from the other three in that as there is also a Danish minority in Germany, in the state of Schleswig-Holstein. What makes the German-Danish case also particularly interesting is the fact that it once more highlights the wider international dimensions of the

German question. Similar to the Franco-German conflict over the Saar (see chapters 3 and 5), Germany's integration into transatlantic alliance structures was dependent upon the resolution of all potential conflicts with other member states. In the case of Denmark, a founding member of NATO, this meant that a permanent framework for the protection of both minority groups had to be created. While the German government sought the conclusion of a bilateral minority treaty with Denmark, the Danish government was reluctant to agree to such an approach, primarily because of its expected impact on national legislation (Ipsen 1997: 335). The resolution that both governments found for this impasse was the drafting and simultaneous publication of two declarations—the so-called Bonn-Copenhagen Declarations of 1955, subsequently integrated into national legislation. Each government in its declaration granted the minority group on its territory a significant catalogue of rights and freedoms for the expression, development, and preservation of its distinct ethnocultural identity. Thus, a framework of minority protection emerged that put both minorities into secure and well-funded situations. Similar to the situation in South Tyrol, subsequently deepening European integration and the opportunities it brought for cross-border relations between minorities and their kin states and kin nations has removed issues of potential conflict from German-Danish relations.

When integration into the Western world had thus sufficiently progressed by the mid-1950s, through membership in NATO and the precursor institutions of today's European Union, Germany could more confidently turn eastward again. As a result of public pressure and political lobbying by the various expellee organizations, but also as a consequence of the *Alleinvertretungsanspruch* (the claim of the Federal Republic to be the sole representative of the German people[5]) the Federal Republic committed itself vis-à-vis the communist countries in Central and Eastern Europe to a foreign policy that contained a number of dimensions of "traditional" German external minority policy. The most controversial problem here was the permanent demarcation of the German-Polish border along the Oder-Neisse line, which was renounced in public by West German politicians of nearly all political colors, including the chancellors and cabinet ministers of successive governments right up to 1990. However, it was equally clear that the Bonn government was in no position to offer a credible political alternative as to how to revise the German-Polish border. Not only was this contrary to the interests of all four Allied powers of the

Second World War, but West Germany itself no longer had a common border with Poland. Despite *Alleinvertretungsanspruch*, it was a matter of political reality that the East German state had officially recognized the new border with Poland in the Treaty of Görlitz in July 1950. Thus, humanitarian efforts to improve the situation of ethnic Germans in countries of the Eastern Bloc once more became a more central feature of German external minority policy. The possibilities of direct involvement, however, were extremely limited throughout this period until 1989, with the result that the major instrument of German external minority policy was to negotiate with the host states conditions that would allow ethnic Germans to migrate to Germany. A precondition for this was the establishing of diplomatic relations with the relevant states in the Eastern Bloc.

A first step in this direction was the Soviet-German treaty of 1955, followed by a verbal agreement in 1958 according to which all persons of ethnic German origin who had been German citizens before 21 June 1941 were entitled to repatriation. This, however, solved only part of the problem, as it included only the Germans of the northern territories of former East Prussia, the Memel Germans, and ethnic Germans who, in the aftermath of the German-Soviet treaty of 1939, had been resettled to the then German territories from the Baltic states, Galicia, Volhynia, Bessarabia, and the northern Bukovina but found themselves again on Soviet or Soviet-controlled territory at the end of the war. Thus, it did not cover what was by far the largest group, approximately two million ethnic Germans who had migrated to the Russian empire in mostly the eighteenth and nineteenth centuries.

This policy of bilateral agreements was continued by all successive German governments, and after 1970 it began to include a variety of other states in the Soviet zone of influence. Treaties with Poland (1970) and Czechoslovakia (1973) specifically addressed the sensitive issues of borders, confirming that the German government of the day respected the territorial status quo (see chapter 5).

The priority of promoting coexistence between East and West against the background of the political realities of the Cold War did not leave the West German government any option apart from facilitating the emigration to the Federal Republic of ethnic Germans from Central and Eastern Europe, which included primarily ethnic Germans from the Soviet Union, Romania, and Poland. Some of the agreements concluded to this effect between Germany and host states of ethnic

Germans in Central and Eastern Europe included financial arrangements, "per capita fees" to be paid by the federal government for each person allowed to leave his or her host state. In the case of Romania, this proved to be a significant source of income for the communist regime, which charged between eight and twelve thousand Deutschmarks per person in the 1970s and 1980s.

Overall, German external minority policy was thus not very active between 1945 and 1989, partly because it had always been suspected of a hidden revisionist agenda, not only by the host states but also by elements within Germany itself, and partly because to remain in their host countries was not the preferred option of many ethnic Germans in Central and Eastern Europe. Thus, (controlled) emigration was seen as the preferred solution by all parties involved. As it was voluntary on part of the emigrants, who were quickly absorbed into German society and who benefited from the earlier integration experience of the expellees, it did not have the same negative connotations as the forced population transfers in the immediate aftermath of the Second World War.

"Promoting Democracy, Prosperity, and Ethnic Harmony": The New Policy Agenda after 1990

The transition to democracy in Central and Eastern Europe that began in 1989–90 provided an entirely different framework of new and enlarged opportunities for Germany's external minority policy. On the one hand, democratization meant the granting of such basic rights and liberties as the freedoms of speech, association, and political participation, allowing ethnic Germans in their host countries to form their own parties and to advocate actively the interests of their group. On the other hand, it also meant that there were no longer any restrictions on emigration, and given the experience of at least the past forty years, many ethnic Germans, particularly in Poland, Romania, and the Soviet Union and its successor states, seized this opportunity and emigrated to Germany. Both developments required a measured and responsible policy response from Germany—domestically to cope with the enormous influx of resettlers (see chapter 4), and internationally to assure the neighboring states in Central and Eastern Europe of the inviolability of the postwar borders while simultaneously continuing support for German minorities at qualitatively and quantitatively new levels and ensuring their protection as national minorities.

All this had to happen within the broader framework of such German foreign policy premises as support for the transition process to democracy and a market economy, creation of a new collective-security order embracing all states in Europe, and respect for international law and human rights.

Realizing that the changed conditions after 1990 required a fundamentally different foreign policy approach, the German government embedded its external minority policy into the wider framework of its efforts to promote democracy, prosperity, and security in Central and Eastern Europe. Given the ethnopolitical demography of the region, with its many national minorities, latent border disputes, and interethnic tensions, it was obvious that the role of minorities would be a crucial one in two ways. First, the ultimate test of successful democratization would have to include an assessment of whether or not members of national minorities, individually and collectively, were entitled to full equality and the right to preserve, express, and develop their distinct identities in their host states. Second, it would not be possible to operate a viable collective security system without settling existing ethnic and territorial conflicts and establishing frameworks within which future disputes could be resolved peacefully. Taking these assumptions as a starting point, the German government concluded that national minorities could play a crucial part in bringing about results in these two interrelated processes, by bridging cultural gaps.[6] The federal government sought to create with the Central and Eastern European host states and the German minorities living there partnerships that, on the basis of international treaties and bilateral agreements,[7] would promote the government's "overall foreign policy concept of a European peace policy of reconciliation, understanding, and cooperation" (*Bundestagsdrucksache* 13/3195). Cultural, social, and economic measures to support German minorities, although primarily "aimed at an improvement of the living conditions of ethnic Germans in their host countries," would naturally benefit whole regions and their populations independent of their ethnic origin, and thus promote interethnic harmony and economic prosperity while strengthening the emerging democratic political structures (*Bundestagsdrucksache* 13/3428 and *Bundestagsdrucksache* 13/1116). Thus, by creating favorable conditions for the integration of ethnic Germans in the societies of their host states as citizens with equal rights, the German government hoped to provide an alternative to emigration (*Bundestagsdrucksache* 13/3428). The following two brief case studies,

German policy toward Russia and Romania, exemplify this approach in its potential as well as in its limitations.

German External Minority Policy toward Russia

The legal framework of German external minority policy vis-à-vis Russia is set by a bilateral treaty between the two states. The German minority in Russia still numbers in the hundreds of thousands but is rather dispersed. Thus, German efforts, which encompass cultural, economic, and social projects, target only specific regions and do not cater to all members of the minority in the same way. The reasons the German government gives for focusing on three specific areas are based on the assumption that a significant number of ethnic Germans do not necessarily want to migrate to Germany but seek to live in areas together with other ethnic Germans. Therefore, the federal government sees it as essential to stabilize particular settlement areas, by providing housing for ethnic Germans coming to these areas from other parts of the Russian federation and from the Central Asian successor states of the former Soviet Union, and by improving the general living conditions in these areas in order to turn them into an acceptable alternative to "repatriation" and ensure peaceful interethnic relations between ethnic Germans, Russians, and other ethnic groups.[8]

The three regions on which material aid has been focused since 1990 are the two German *rayon*s of Halbstadt and Asowo in western Siberia, the Volga area, and the St. Petersburg region. Projects supported by the German government include the construction of residential areas, aid for farm businesses (e.g., management and agricultural consulting, provision of machinery), loans and consulting for small-business start-ups, and occupational training to improve qualifications. In order to achieve a general improvement in living conditions, the federal government has directly funded, or backed by guaranteed loans, measures to improve the infrastructure in some of the regions where ethnic Germans live. This has included projects in the health care sector (e.g., the Ambulance Center in Burni, Saratov area), the improvement of the local infrastructure (e.g., telecommunications network and petrol station in the Halbstadt *rayon*), and the expansion of retail and food production facilities (e.g., the dairy farm in Baskatowka, Marx area). Most of these projects are co-funded by the Russian government, but the majority of the financial support is provided by Germany (in 1996 almost ninety million Deutschmarks, i.e., 60 percent of the overall financial resources made available for German minorities in Central and Eastern Europe).

As a result of the decades of communist rule, during which ethnic Germans were denied the right to express and develop their cultural identity, a considerable amount of effort and funding is being spent on projects in relation to education and culture. Since 1990, almost ninety cultural centers have been set up throughout the Russian Federation to give ethnic Germans an opportunity to become familiar with present-day Germany and, above all, to learn the language of their ancestors. Using existing infrastructure, the German government has supplied these centers with technical equipment, books, and newspaper and magazine subscriptions. Most of the projects in the cultural sector happen in cooperation with the Russian government, which normally commits funds for the maintenance of buildings and the payment of staff.

The particular emphasis on educational efforts in the areas of language teaching and information about Germany is derived from the need to prepare ethnic Germans for their potential migration to Germany, in order to make integration into German society easier. In the medium term, the German government has planned to provide up to a hundred thousand places in language courses and to increase the number of cultural centers to 250. Language courses are offered at varying levels and lengths (from thirty-two to two hundred hours). Special programs for young ethnic Germans include language classes and summer camps, both aimed at inculcating knowledge about and awareness of their German roots among the coming generations. Despite good intentions, however, decreasing availability of funds over the past years has limited the success of this policy, if only in terms of the number of people that could be reached.

GERMAN EXTERNAL MINORITY POLICY TOWARD ROMANIA

The aim of German external minority policy vis-à-vis Romania, based on the German-Romanian treaty of April 1992, is to stabilize and improve the living conditions of the German minority in the country in order to provide its members with viable futures in their host state.

Because the Romanian constitution does not allow for positive discrimination as a means to remedy the situation of historically disadvantaged minority groups, the German-Romanian treaty, in its Article 16, states specifically that no concrete measure taken jointly by the two governments to secure the continued existence of the German minority or to support it in the reconstruction of its social, cultural, and economic life may disadvantage other Romanian citizens. As this coincides with one of the objectives of Germany's external minority policy—contributing to an environment of interethnic harmony—this has not limited the humanitarian aid efforts.

As in Russia, aid projects can be grouped into three main areas—social, economic, and cultural. About seventy cultural centers have been set up since 1990, enabling the German minority to preserve, develop, and express its cultural identity. Language teaching, again, plays an important role in the cultural sector, but it is primarily aimed at preserving the already existing relatively high level of knowledge. Part of the aid package, therefore, is infrastructural support, such as the reconstruction of the main building of the Honterus secondary school in Kronstadt. A special youth program has been operated since 1995.

Social projects have included the provision of spare parts, medication, and first aid equipment to hospitals in areas where ethnic Germans live. Because of the general situation in Romania, these projects have great importance well beyond the regions toward which they were originally aimed.

The economic aid program has focused on small businesses and the agricultural sector. Loans for start-up companies on preferential terms and the supply of technology and machinery support benefit around seventy companies founded or run by ethnic Germans in Romania every year. The initial emphasis on providing farms with modern equipment was replaced a couple of years ago by a program for the creation of networks that enable ethnic Germans (and their Romanian neighbors) to achieve greater cost-efficiency. In this context, a project to form a regional community of agricultural producers and an initiative to set up an organization for the wholesale distribution of fuel have been funded by the German government. Another source of support have been training programs for agricultural engineers and managers in, and funded by, the Federal Republic of Germany. The agricultural support program as a whole has been coordinated and administered by two German experts, paid by the German government.

The total of financial support committed to the support of the German minority in Romania between 1990 and 1997 amounted to 138 million Deutschmarks. For 1998, seven million Deutschmarks were made available, a significant decline compared to earlier years that was partly caused by the generally more difficult economic situation in Germany.

TOWARD A RESOLUTION OF THE GERMAN MINORITY QUESTION?

Even though the situations in which the German-speaking minorities in Europe live are different, the factors that determine their status at present, and thus influence their future, are essentially the same. They can be grouped into three categories—intraminority conditions, the situation in the host country, and the state of bilateral relationships between the host country and the Federal Republic of Germany (or Austria in the case of South Tyrol and, to a lesser degree, Hungary).

Among the intraminority conditions, the most important aspects are demographic in their nature or relate to the degree of assimilation. The size of the minority, whether it lives territorially concentrated or dispersed and in its traditional settlement areas or in areas to which it had been deported at some point, and its age and social structure influence its vitality as a distinct ethnocultural group and thus determine its future chances of survival or complete linguistic and cultural assimilation. The degree of political and social integration characterizes the extent to which the minority has been accepted as an equal part of its host society.

Integration is thus linked closely to the general situation in the host country. Three dimensions are essential in this respect—the degree to which minorities and their rights are explicitly protected in constitutional and simple legislation, the seriousness with which ethnocultural distinctiveness is recognized and supported, and the way in which popular and government sentiments influence the implementation of legal directives.

In terms of the bilateral aspect, historical and contemporary issues are important, as they both influence the considerations of the minority and its host and kin states in relation to each other. Historically speaking, Germany's external minority policy has undergone significant changes since it became a major part of the country's foreign policy agenda after the First World War (see chapter 2). Although there were "geographic" differences between the approach to minorities in

the East and the West, the interwar period was primarily characterized by the use of the minorities question for changing the borders
established in the Treaty of Versailles in 1919. Border alterations in
the East, facilitated by border guarantees in the West, were the foreign policy goal of the Weimar Republic as well as of Nazi Germany,
distinguished only by the intensity and means with which this aim was
pursued.

The East-West difference remained after 1945 but was, to some extent at least, externally determined. Collective victimization of ethnic
Germans, coupled with expulsions and deportations in the aftermath
of the Second World War, affected members of the German minorities in Central and Eastern Europe much more than in their settlement areas in the West. Simultaneously, the foundation of the West
German state and the importance of its integration into the emerging Western alliance set different priorities for foreign policy makers
in postwar Germany. Part of the acceptance of responsibility for the
consequences of the Second World War was the tacit recognition of
the geopolitical and territorial realities of Europe by successive German
governments, while the political engagement for German minorities
in Central and Eastern Europe, even if was not put aside completely,
was at least scaled down. In particular after 1969, when *Ostpolitik* was
elevated to qualitatively new levels of reconciliation, the Federal Republic tried to facilitate the emigration of ethnic Germans from their
host countries and their smooth integration into German society,
rather than to demand their recognition and protection as minorities
(see chapter 5).

From the end of the 1980s onward, this began to change gradually. The democratization of the formerly communist societies in Central and Eastern Europe opened new opportunities for Germany's
external minority policy. Greater possibilities to support the German
minorities in their host states, the need to do so in order to slow down
the mass exodus of ethnic Germans, and the genuine interest of the
former communist countries in improving their relationships with
Germany, which was seen as an important stepping-stone toward
accession to the European Union and NATO, complemented one
another in a remarkable way.

Germany's desire to bridge the gap between cultures and across history could be fulfilled only through reconciliation and mutual understanding. One element was the eventual unconditional recognition of
all postwar borders. Yet a common future of Germany and its eastern
neighbors could not be secured without addressing the situation of

the German minorities in these countries. On the basis of numerous treaties and within the framework set out by the 1990 Copenhagen Declaration of the Conference on Security and Cooperation in Europe, Germany and Poland, the Czech and Slovak Republics, Hungary, Romania, the Russian Federation, Ukraine, and Kazakhstan have developed relationships that allow both parties, with the participation of representatives of the German minority in each country, to tackle the issue of minority protection and external support for ethnic Germans. For historical as well as contemporary reasons, this has remained a very sensitive issue. As countries in Central and Eastern Europe have seen a resurgence of minority-related questions during the transition process to democracy, German external minority policy has always only been one part of a more comprehensive foreign policy approach toward its eastern neighbors, a policy that aims at a stabilization of democracy and the creation of a market economy in these countries as the wider social framework within which there can develop harmonious interethnic relationships that will inevitably benefit the German minorities as well.

Almost a century of external minority policy thus has seen different policy agendas pursued by different German governments. These were partly determined by domestically formulated objectives, partly also by existing opportunities and the way in which they were perceived by policy makers. Gradually since the early 1970s, however, the deliberate setting of a different foreign policy agenda in the form of the new *Ostpolitik* has also contributed to changing and eventually increasing opportunities for a successful external minority policy that does not treat minorities as objects of farther-reaching policy goals but makes them one of the beneficiaries of a cooperative rather than confrontational foreign policy.

The existence of a bilateral treaty including provisions related to the minority group, its right to engage in cross-border cooperation, and its receipt of formal support from the German government as well as the emigrant community are the three most important factors in this context affecting how a particular minority community locates itself both in relation to its host state as well as to its kin nation. This is as true for the German minorities in Denmark and Italy as it is for communities of ethnic Germans that continue to live in Central and Eastern Europe.

Despite the fact that historical legacies of the magnitude of those related to the German minority question in Europe are unlikely ever to be overcome completely, the situation at the beginning of the twenty-first century gives considerable reason for optimism that finally appropriate lessons have been learned by Germany, its neighbors, and the German minorities, lessons that will prevent the issue of German minorities from reemerging as a major problem for international security. The atmosphere of cooperation and compromise that has by and large prevailed since the end of the Cold War substantiates this optimism. However, the following, and final, chapter of this book will point out that the history of the German question is a heavy burden and that to deal with it properly requires sustained will, skills, and resources on the part of responsible political elites.

NOTES

1. Until the early 1990s, there was also a small ethnic German population in Turkmenistan. In the 1989 census it accounted for a little less than 4,500 people, who had come there during the deportation. The civil war in the early 1990s triggered an almost complete exodus of the Germans from there.

2. Security concerns were not addressed successfully by these border alterations after 1919. Not only did they not stop Germany from unleashing yet another world war, they effectively created fifth columns in countries that were most vulnerable to attack (see chapter 2). Even for the time after 1945, it is doubtful whether the confirmation of the 1919 borders would have prevented a similar development, if the policy of integration had not tied at least one part of Germany firmly to the Western alliance in Cold War Europe (see chapter 3).

3. I have borrowed this phrase from a German government program started in the mid-1980s that uses the term *deutsche Kultur des Ostens*.

4. All following figures are 1993 estimates of the German government (*Bundestagsdrucksache* 12/6162, 36f.). Although precise new figures do not exist, ethnic German emigration from the former Soviet Union over the past ten years has been on average a hundred thousand people per year. In addition, there has been significant "internal" migration during this period, primarily from German settlements in Kazakhstan to the German *rayons* in Russia, and to a smaller extent from there to the St. Petersburg region.

5. In a speech before the German Bundestag on 21 October 1949, Adenauer declared that "pending German reunification, the Federal Republic of Germany is the only legitimate state organization of the German people."

6. Cf., for example, "Vertriebene, Aussiedler und deutsche Minderheiten sind eine Brücke zwischen den Deutschen und ihren östlichen Nachbarn," *Bundestagsdrucksache* 13/10845, 27 May 1998.

7. The key international agreements in this context are the 1990 Copenhagen document of the CSCE and the Council of Europe's Frame-

work Declaration on minority rights. Bilateral treaties exist between Germany and Poland, the Czech and Slovak Republics, Hungary, Romania, and Russia. Major bilateral agreements were concluded with Ukraine and Kazakhstan. Cf. Heintze (2000).

8. On a smaller scale, similar efforts are also made in the Central Asian republics and in Ukraine.

Chapter 7

The German Question Continued?
The Politics of Homeland, Belonging, and Victimhood since 1990

European integration has always primarily been a political process. Since its very beginning, the key objective has been to overcome old divisions, enmities and prejudices, and to strengthen
peace, justice, freedom and security. We must never forget the
pain and the suffering caused by the horrors of the Second World
War. But the very essence of European integration has been to
move forward from there—not to look back in acrimony and
continue fighting old battles.
—Miloš Zeman and Günter Verheugen (2002)

The statement at the end of chapter 5, that the German question had
ceased to exist in its territorial dimension with the recognition by all
parties of Germany's existing frontiers as permanent in 1990, does not
and cannot imply the end of the German question—that it has
been answered once and for all. First of all, it has never been a one-
dimensional issue, and, as demonstrated in chapter 6, it remains on the
political agenda as a minority issue, particularly in relation to Central
and Eastern Europe, albeit no longer following the confrontational
patterns of the past. At the same time, it continues to be a matter of

migration of ethnic Germans, in particular from Russia and the other successor states of the former Soviet Union, to the Federal Republic and thus poses increasingly difficult challenges of integration (see chapter 4). What has, nevertheless, changed from this perspective is that in contrast to the twentieth century, the German question no longer seems to threaten stability in Europe and beyond or to endanger the internal or external security of its immediate neighbors to the East or West. Ironically, however, the fundamental change in the international climate since the collapse of communism and the end of the Cold War that made this significant transformation of the German question possible has given rise to conditions in which other dimensions of the German question have been "revitalized." Far from suggesting that there is a "new" German question dawning upon Europe and the world and endangering the achievements of the post–Cold War period, I want to outline in this concluding chapter how and why certain dimensions of the German question continue to have significance in the international arena.

THE POLITICS OF BELONGING (I): FROM TERRITORY TO PLACE

Territory has always been an important dimension in the development of the German question, and the very tension between territory and ethnic identity has been the major driving force behind several escalations of the German question into war. Territory has been used as a defining criterion in relation to citizenship rights and identities; it has been the basis of political entities (states, regions, communities) and a potent source of mass mobilization. All these functions it has performed in close connection with ethnic identity, and often territorial components have formed important dimensions of conflicting German and non-German identities. Nevertheless, it is important to distinguish between the two as key factors in the origin, development, and management of the German question.

For states and ethnic groups alike, territory possesses certain values in and of itself. These include ownership of natural resources, such as water, iron, coal, oil, or gas; they extend to the goods and services produced by the population living in this territory; and they can comprise military or strategic advantages in terms of natural boundaries, access to the open sea, and control over transport routes and waterways. Thus, throughout the history of the German question in the twentieth century, territories were a major source of conflict; they have changed hands as a result, and new conflicts have arisen as a consequence of that. Not all of those conflicts have led to major hostilities and war, but the two world wars are ample evidence of the dangerous potential for escalation that the German question used to have, particularly because of the explosive mix created by the linkage of state, nation, and territory.

Because of the significance of territory as symbol of individual and collective identities, its political, economic, and social importance for the constitution of states and its strategic value as a source of control and influence, states and ethnic groups alike make claims from any one of these perspectives to territories that they consider essential. The most common justifications for such claims to territory are indigenousness, historical entitlement, divine right, and (alleged) superiority of the culture of the claimant (Moore 1998: 142–50). Regardless of the reasons given in justification—and throughout the history of the German question all of these claims have been advanced by the different states and nations involved—territorial claims can be secessionist, irredentist, or autonomist in their nature. In the context of the German question, secessionism was most evident in relation to the interwar Sudetenland, which also combined with a good deal of irrendentism on the part of the Nazi state—that is, its desire to "recover" lost lands to which it deemed the German nation to have historical rights. Irredentism was also evident in the incorporation into Germany of Austria in 1938; Alsace and the German areas of Belgium in 1940; and of the Polish Corridor, the Free City of Danzig and other territories of Poland after 1939. To some extent at least, irredentism as a political strategy could also be seen in action in relation to the former *Ostgebiete* after 1945. It also manifested itself with regard to the Saar in the 1930s and 1950s, and, with some qualifications, in the Federal Republic's *Deutschlandpolitik* aimed at unification with East Germany. In contrast to secessionism and irredentism, which aim at revising international borders, territorial autonomism expresses the desire of the resident population (or a part thereof) inhabiting a particular territory to gain a measure of self-rule without seceding from its host state. This has been a less prominent dimension of the German question, but it should be mentioned that German communities in Italy (South Tyrol), Belgium, and Russia (two autonomous *rayons* in western Siberia) have benefited, to varying degrees, from their host states' preparedness to grant them certain rights of self-government.

The disputed territories that have thus, in part, shaped the development of the German question have therefore often simultaneously been a phenomenon of interstate, interethnic, and group-state relations. That the first half of the twentieth century was characterized by war, persecution, ethnic cleansing, and discrimination in this context was primarily a result of exclusive notions of identity and belonging that established absolute claims to territories, allowing for little or no compromise.

That "identity and belonging are . . . potentially divisive" is an observation made by Anthony Giddens (1998: 129) in *The Third Way*. This divisiveness is a result of another, and equally fundamental, function of identity and belonging, namely, to express bonds between certain people but not others. Furthermore, there is also a direct relationship between identity and belonging—without identity, there is no belonging. In this way, identity both as a self- and other-assigned category determines where people belong—or, to use a phrase coined by Ignatieff (1994: 7), "belonging . . . means being recognised and being understood." This fundamental sociopsychological need for recognition and understanding has been all the more important in periods of the development of the German question where the physical existence of people (of German and non-German background) and their material bonds to their homelands were threatened. The sense of belonging, not just to a particular community but also to a specific place, has more than once been brutally disrupted for Jews, Poles, Czechs, Germans, and others, and the reason for this disruption has primarily been located by the perpetrators of forced migration in the particular community's ethnic or national identity. It is the very purpose of forced migrations to destroy the physical connection of community and place. As such, forced migration is the result of the struggle between two mutually exclusive conceptions of belonging; those who are perceived not to belong to the (territorially) defined community are expelled, regardless of whether they feel they belong to the contested piece of land as much as it belongs to them. For different reasons and with different means and intentions (and it is important to bear this in mind), this was the case in the German acquisition of *Lebensraum* in the East and the ethnic cleansing of these areas from those whom the Nazis regarded as racially or otherwise undesirable, and it was the case in the postwar expulsions of ethnic Germans from Central and Eastern Europe.

Since for most communities place is a crucial component of identity, the loss of spatial attachment makes identity incomplete. Until,

therefore, a new place can fill this gap—become a new source of identification—there will always be longing for return to the homeland,
for its repossession by the community forced from it. The often problematic implication of this is perhaps best described as "the extreme
ambiguity of place as a political guide" (Dijkink 1996: 1). A lost homeland is a powerful source of political mobilization and action. The
assertion of a right to this homeland can manifest itself in policy agendas of reconquest, return, and the preservation of the homeland's
"ethnic" characteristics. Even if claims to the lost homeland are merely
"theoretical," because there is no real opportunity ever to realize them,
they play an essential role in the preservation of the community's identity and thus of the community as a distinct collective. Especially in
relation to ethnically motivated forced migrations, the preservation of
an identity that can continue to hold an expelled community together
is crucially related to territory. No political entrepreneur who depends
on the existence of an ethnically/nationally defined community will
be able to "instill in people a sense of kinship and brotherhood without attaching them to a place that they feel is theirs, a homeland that
is theirs by right of history" (Smith 1979: 3). In turn, the preservation of this bond to "the historic land, the land of past generations,
the land that saw the flowering of the nation's genius" (Smith 1979:
3) is the key condition for the continued existence of his or her specific constituency, and it is therefore in the political entrepreneur's
foremost interest to keep alive the sense of loss, but also a sense of
provisionality, a sense of the ultimate possibility of return to the lost
homeland. The development of the German question is full of examples of how the politics of belonging and homeland is as much
opportunistic calculation about power as it is an expression of primor-
dial dimensions of ethnic identity.

However, there is another aspect in all of this that deserves attention. If belonging is "first and foremost about protection from violence"—if, in other words, "where you belong is where you are safe
and where you are safe is where you belong" (Ignatieff 1994: 7)—
the forcible disruption of the physical link between a community and
its homeland can equally eliminate the (lost) homeland as a focus of
the community's identity in the sense of a desirable place to return.
Rather, successful integration into another safe place can create a new
sense of belonging. At its best, integration makes belonging irrelevant,
to the extent that it is no longer an issue, because protection (and
other state services) can be taken for granted and because the belonging of those who lost their homeland is not contested by anyone. In

the face of the creation of such a "new homeland," as happened very successfully in the case of the postwar integration of ethnic German refugees, expellees, and *Aussiedler,* the wish to return to the lost homeland becomes less and less important for the constitution of identity. It has only been over the decade since the end of the Cold War that the homeland has regained some of its former importance in the form of "homeland tourism" and in initiatives supporting members of the community who still live in the homeland, as well as in efforts to preserve the "ethnic character" of the homeland. Permanent return to the homeland, too, has become an option again, albeit a serious one for only very few people, in the context of the EU accession of Poland and the Czech Republic.

It is also important to note that a lost homeland can also retain its identity-forming capacity because not only will there always be certain historical memories of the community associated with it, but the actual loss of it—the event of the forced migration from the homeland—provides a no less powerful source of identification with, and belonging to, a community of people that has suffered a similarly traumatic experience. This was one of the reasons why refugees, expellees, and *Aussiedler,* despite their vastly different cultural, professional, geographic, and ideological backgrounds, formed a relatively homogenous political community in the Federal Republic, held together by the common experience of forced migration. Political agendas resulting from such a conception of the lost homeland are likely to include claims for compensation for material losses and suffering, but also, and equally important, claims for recognition and acknowledgment of such losses and suffering. Especially when the physical homeland has lost its attraction as a place to return to, the symbolic politics of homeland and belonging can be a similarly potent source of political mobilization, providing political entrepreneurs with the power base they seek. Yet even such more symbolic forms of the politics of homeland and belonging cannot do without reference to the continued existence of the homeland, even if it is beyond the grasp of the community in question. Thus, whether it is a question of the physical recovery of the homeland or the symbolic or compensatory recognition of its loss, the politics of belonging is always, at least partly, also the politics of homeland.

In order to maintain a sense of community among the millions of ethnic German refugees, expellees, and *Aussiedler,* their most active political entrepreneurs developed two distinct yet closely connected meanings of the notion of belonging. On the one hand, "belonging" came to signify that the expellees belonged to the (West) German state and cultural nation, establishing between them and the society to which they had come a political-legal connection that entitled them not only to full citizenship rights but also to a variety of compensation measures. With citizenship came voting rights, and with voting rights came the recognition by politicians that expellees were an important constituency whose votes made a difference in local, state, and federal elections, giving the expellee organizations important leverage over a number of domestic and foreign policy issues, the latter particularly as connected to their former homelands. These issues have featured prominently in the discussion in earlier chapters, and I will therefore not return to them now in any great detail.

The other meaning that belonging acquired in this specific context is best described in terms of "ethnic ownership," the belief that the lost homelands of the expellees continue to belong to them on the basis of historical, ethnic rights. This insistence on an inalienable right to their homeland has manifested itself in claims for the possibility of returning there and for compensation for losses and suffering. The public debates that addressed these issues of belonging both in Germany and in the former homelands of the refugees, expellees, and *Aussiedler* have affected the formulation and outcomes of domestic and foreign policies over the past half-century to varying degrees. The notion of belonging in its various dimensions has been used by the political representatives of the German expellees to further their own and their constituency's objectives. The opportunities to realize these objectives have been determined by political dynamics in Germany and Europe. Especially in the period after the end of the Cold War, new opportunities have arisen that have given the development of the German question an interesting new direction.

In chapter 4 I have detailed the process of political integration of expellees after 1945 and the increasing alienation between their more extremist activists and successive German governments until the early 1990s, in the course of which expellee activists acquired a public reputation for harming and actively seeking to destroy the reconciliation process with Central and Eastern Europe. This trend also resulted in a gap between the public discourse conducted by leading expellee activists and the objectives and activities of the organization's membership. The former continued to insist on the openness of the German-Polish border question, the need for an institutionalized right to return to the expellees' homelands, and entitlement to restitution of property and compensation from the states from which they had been expelled (especially from Poland and Czechoslovakia). In contrast, "ordinary" expellees and their descendants, at least since the middle of the 1980s, became engaged in the establishment of cross-border contacts with the people living in their former homelands. This included various privately funded and organized aid programs aimed at ethnic Germans who had stayed in their places of origin as well as at members of other ethnic communities, including the titular nations of these countries.

The collapse of communism in Central and Eastern Europe in 1989–90 offered new and different opportunities for the politics of belonging. To some extent history repeated itself, as belonging once again became an issue of membership in the German nation and of integration for several hundred thousand ethnic Germans from Poland and Romania who migrated to the Federal Republic. For the first time in many decades, ethnic Germans from the (former) Soviet Union were also able to emigrate to Germany in large numbers (see chapter 4). More important, however, the leaderships of the expellee organizations saw the dawn of an unprecedented opportunity to pursue a reinvigorated politics of belonging focused on the lost homeland. While it was the policy of the West German government to achieve the unification of the two German states even at the price of finally and formally abandoning all territorial claims and guaranteeing the eastern borders of East Germany like those of the united Germany, activists of the expellee organizations tried to stage a referendum in Poland under the slogan "Peace through Free Choice." Suggesting as it did that there was still a possibility for border changes, this raised completely unrealistic hopes among many members of the German minority in Poland, particularly in Upper Silesia, where the response to the signature campaign in support of the referendum was strong. Yet it proved how unrealistic these hopes were when Chancellor Kohl declared, at an event celebrating the fortieth anniversary of the Charter of the German Expellees in 1990, that the recognition of the Oder-Neisse line as Germany's eastern frontier was the price that had had to be paid for the reunification of Germany. Thereafter the BdV started two further initiatives. One was for the Europeanization of the Oder-Neisse territories, the other for the enfranchisement of members of the German minority in Poland to vote in parliamentary elections in the Federal Republic. Both of them failed as well, but this did not stop expellee activists from continuing to pursue their particular politics of belonging; it only made them rethink and adjust their agenda.

Even though, for historical reasons, no border question similar to that between Germany and Poland ever existed in the relationship between the Federal Republic and Czechoslovakia/the Czech Republic, the rhetoric of expellee activists has, if anything, been more aggressive on the Sudeten German issue in the early 1990s, demanding "unlimited sovereignty" for Sudeten Germans in their homeland (Hochfelder 1991: 58) and rejecting the "belonging of the Sudetenland to any Czechoslovak state" (Schnürch 1991: 83). Since then, the rhetoric has changed in its tone but not necessarily in its objectives. The newly elected speaker of the Sudeten Germans, Bavarian Parliament president Johann Böhm, emphasized in his address on Sudeten German Day in 2000 that demands for territorial autonomy were unlikely to succeed or, if successful, to be implemented by the Sudeten Germans in a meaningful way. Yet he added that personal autonomy[1] was an appropriate demand, both more likely to succeed and more useful for the remaining ethnic Germans in the Czech Republic "as well as for any returnees, no matter how many or how few these may be" (Böhm 2000).

Clearly, the rhetoric and policies of the BdV in the early 1990s did not strike a positive cord with the German or the Czechoslovak and Polish governments. However, from around 1993 onward, the political leadership of the expellee organizations adopted more conciliatory policies. The reason for this was partly that the German federal government had made further funding of the organizations dependent on their participation in a policy of what could be called constructive reconciliation. This development was already foreshadowed in the negotiations of the 1991 German-Polish Treaty. In return for Poland's recognition and protection of the German minority, "the German government would further reduce its support for, and would further distance itself from, those elements among the *Landsmannschaften* who demanded the right of return to their places of origin or compensation from the Polish government for material and emotional harm suffered as a result of their expulsion" (Cordell 2000: 87). The resulting policy shift in the expellee organizations also meant that they would be included in the government's various aid programs to stabilize and improve the living conditions of ethnic Germans in their homelands; it thus offered them wider opportunities to reach out to their places of origin, which was particularly welcomed by rank-and-file members, many of whom had done exactly that for many years but without anything like the resources available to them now. In 1997, the federal budget allocated 5.1 million Deutschmarks, in 1998 4.7 million, and in 1999 4.4 million for the support of measures of the expellee organizations aimed at the promotion of peaceful co-existence with the countries in Central and Eastern Europe. In addition, the BdV received an annual amount of around 3.5 million Deutschmarks in institutional funding under the budget title of "Measures Promoting the Integration of [Ethnic German] Resettlers and Expellees." Under the same title, in 1997 and 1998 more than twenty-one million Deutschmarks were spent annually on specific projects; in 1999, this was increased to more than thirty-eight million, compensating for cuts in other areas as a result of attempts to administer these funds in a more centralized way.

Overall, the relationship with Poland in particular became more relaxed, and representatives of the expellee organizations were received by the Polish prime minister and other high-ranking government officials in the mid-1990s. Remarkably, too, Herbert Hupka, the chairman of the Upper Silesian Regional-Cultural Association and a man for decades portrayed in Poland as the incarnation of German territorial revisionism, was awarded the Honorary Medal of his former hometown of Ratibor in Poland for his commitment to the economic reconstruction of the area.

Relations with the Czech Republic, in contrast, did not develop as smoothly. Despite the signing of the Treaty on Good Neighborly and Friendly Relations in 1993, a variety of issues remained unresolved and continued to complicate bilateral relations. A renewed attempt to overcome the difficulties was made with the German-Czech Declaration of 1997. Signed after years of negotiations on 21 January 1997, it highlighted the fact that the two governments could agree on very little in relation to the two most critical issues: the role of the Sudeten Germans in the breakup of Czechoslovakia in 1938 and their collective victimization and expulsion after the end of the Second World War. The German government accepted the responsibility of Germany in the developments leading up to the Munich Agreement and the destruction of Czechoslovakia, expressed deep sorrow over the suffering of Czechs during the Nazi occupation of their country, and it acknowledged that these two issues had prepared the ground for the postwar treatment and expulsion of members of the German minority in the country. The Czech government, on the other hand, regretted the postwar policy vis-à-vis ethnic Germans, which had resulted in the expulsion of a large section of the German minority and expropriation of their property. Both governments agreed that the remaining members of the German minority in the Czech Republic and the expellees and their descendants would play an important role in the future relationship of the two countries and that the support of the German minority in the Czech Republic was a matter of mutual interest. It also acknowledged and legitimized certain long-standing aspects of the politics of belonging pursued by all expellee organizations; the declaration not only recognized the fact of the expulsions but implied an acceptance of its injustice and of the victimization of innocent people. This would become a major issue in the politics of belonging in the years after 1997, when the notion of victimhood would regain its postwar prominence in a different context. However, many of the expelled Sudeten Germans and their descendants remained sceptical about the value of the declaration. A survey in Bavaria, where most of the Sudeten German expellees and their descendants live, showed that only half of all respondents who had heard of the declaration considered it to contribute to an improvement of relations with the Czech Republic. Only one-fifth felt that the interests of the Sudeten Germans were adequately reflected in the declaration. However, the same survey is also very telling from a different point of view: only a little more than half of people of Sudeten German origin, or with family members of Sudeten German origin, included in the survey had actually heard of the declaration (Köcher 1997: 53f.).

THE POLITICS OF BELONGING (II): RESHAPING VICTIMHOOD

From the perspective of the German government, the politics of belonging, as related to expellees and ethnic Germans in Central and Eastern Europe, still concerned membership and integration—expellees and their representatives were members of the political process and could, under certain circumstances, fulfill useful roles in the process of reconciliation with the country's eastern neighbors. Ethnic Germans in these countries were still considered members of the German cultural nation, which entitled them to certain benefits, even if these benefits no longer automatically included the entitlement to German citizenship. Those who were allowed into the country needed to be integrated socially, politically, and economically, just like the expellees after 1945.

In contrast, the expellee organizations pursued more vigorously a different course of action. Their leadership had for years reconceptualized belonging to include a sense of ethnic ownership and had sought to capitalize on the opportunities offered by the transition in Central and Eastern Europe and the ensuing reconciliation process. Thus, the concept of ethnic ownership became more and more clearly shaped, and with it the goals that expellee organizations sought to realize through the politics of belonging. These goals are defined by expellee activists as a right to return (permanently) to their former homelands and entitlement to compensation for their suffering and to restitution of expropriated property. In realizing this particular conception of the politics of homeland and belonging, the expellee organizations have been presented with unprecedented opportunities in the past several years that have allowed them to attach their demands to the bandwagon of mainstream (institutional) politics and win some share in the public discourse. The first of these opportunities has presented itself in the form of the ethnic cleansing in Kosovo; the second in the form of several successful class action suits in the United States, and threats thereof, aimed at compensation for forced labor during the Second World War; and the third in the form of the European Union enlargement process.

The conflict in Kosovo, with its large-scale population displacements and the subsequent international intervention to reverse them, in more than one way resembled what many expellees had experienced themselves, but it also symbolized the hopes of some of them, namely, the international recognition and enforcement of the right of people not to be expelled from their homeland, or at least to return to it if an expulsion could not be prevented. Pictures from Kosovo also brought home to many others, in Germany and elsewhere, the horrors of refugee tracks, sparking a broad public debate on an issue that had, for the most part, been deliberately ignored in the German media. By comparing, and linking, their own plight to that of Kosovo Albanians, expellee organizations managed to align themselves with a political strategy that was beyond moral reproach—that of preventing, or reversing, ethnic cleansing. By supporting the policy of Germany during the conflict, the expellee organizations sought to prepare ground upon which they could reopen the debate on their own suffering more than fifty years earlier. The expellee organizations saw their cause recognized at higher international levels as early as 1995, when the then UN High Commissioner on Human Rights, José Ayala Lasso, emphasized in a speech in the Paulskirche in Frankfurt that not to be expelled from one's homeland was a fundamental human right and noted that while the peoples in Central and Eastern Europe had suffered terribly under German occupation during the Second World War and thus had a legitimate claim to reparations, such claims "must not be realized through collective victimization on the basis of general discrimination and without the thorough investigation of individual guilt" (Ayala Lasso 1995). Even more relevant to the current political agenda of the leadership of the expellee organizations was a report of the UN Commission on Human Rights entitled *Human Rights and Population Transfer*. In its Annex II was a Draft Declaration on Population Transfer and the Implantation of Settlers, which stated in Article 8 that:

> every person has the right to return voluntarily, and in safety and dignity, to the country of origin and, within it, to the place of origin or choice. The exercise of the right to return does not preclude the victim's right to adequate remedies, including restoration of properties of which they were deprived in connection with or as a result of population transfers, compensation for any property that cannot be restored to them, and any other reparations provided for in international law.

As implied in the draft declaration, besides the right to return, forcibly displaced persons should also be entitled to the restitution of, or compensation for, property lost as a consequence of their forced displacement. This remains a very sensitive issue, particularly in German-Czech relations. In an attempt to take the heat out of bilateral relations, Chancellor Schroeder and the Czech minister-president, Miloš Zeman, issued a joint statement on 8 March 1999 declaring that neither side intended to burden their bilateral relations with "property issues" resulting from developments after the Second World War. The following day it became clear that this had backfired domestically, and Schroeder's then foreign policy adviser, Michael Steiner, had to issue another statement in which he declared that the German government did not have the right or the intention to interfere with any private claims of individual expellees.

In the eyes of the Sudeten German Regional-Cultural Association, the compensation of forced laborers during the Second World War, and also the negotiations between Germany and the representatives

of survivors from Nazi labor camps, provided expellees who had suffered particular hardship during the expulsion or in labor camps in
Czechoslovakia after 1945 with an equally legitimate claim to a symbolic gesture of compensation from the German-Czech Future Fund.
Arguing that this would be an important contribution to the reconciliation between Sudeten Germans and Czechs, the Sudeten German
Regional-Cultural Association submitted a bid to the fund's execu-
tive board, where it was promptly, and with great publicity, rejected.
At the same time, class action had also been considered as a possible
route to realize claims for the compensation of losses resulting from
collective expropriation and where possible for the restitution of properties that had been confiscated in this process. Plans for class action
in the United States, initially against insurance companies that had
profited from the collective expropriation of the Sudeten Germans,
are officially supported by the leadership of the Sudeten German
association.

The question of whether the former expellees should be entitled
to any form of compensation in general and whether this should be
used as leverage by Germany in the context of the accession negotiations is another issue that has been discussed widely in the three countries over the past several years. While official German government
policy remains firmly committed not to allow the past to threaten the
present or to allow it to poison German-Czech or German-Polish
relations, the leadership of the BdV has pursued distinct policies in
relation to this issue in Poland and the Czech Republic—with regard
to filing a class action suit in the Polish case, the BdV expressed the
view that such actions would be counterproductive and affect the
German minority still living in the country in a negative way. The reason for these different approaches, however, is not only the relative
size and influence of the German minority groups. The relations between expellees and Poland have developed more constructively since
the early 1990s, and the organizations representing expellees from the
territory of today's Poland are less well organized and do not enjoy
the same influence and backing as do those of the Sudeten Germans,
who have their power base in the state of Bavaria.

What is interesting in relation to these debates on restitution and
compensation in general is that the old left-right dichotomy in the
political process in Germany on issues concerning the expulsion of
ethnic Germans has been restored. For a period of about three years
beginning in the mid-1990s, there seemed to be a certain recogni-

tion that the expulsion had been a human tragedy and that there had been an unjust neglect by the German left of the suffering of the expellees and of their contribution to the reconciliation process with the countries of Central and Eastern Europe. In a speech at the commemoration of the fiftieth anniversary of the BdV in May 1999, the German minister of the interior noted that "contrary to frequent prejudice, the ethnic German expellees have, in their overwhelming majority, actively participated in the process of reconciliation between the European nations, and they continue to do so today." In her address on the occasion of the twenty-fifth anniversary of the Cultural Foundation of the German Expellees, the chairperson of the Culture and Media Committee of the Bundestag, Elke Leonhard of the SPD, emphasized that nobody had the right to "discredit as revisionism the legitimate interests of the expellees in the preservation of their culture and the public acknowledgement of their fate." Ironically, a dispute with the then Secretary of State for Culture, Michael Naumann, over the (under)funding of cultural institutions of the expellees prompted Leonhard to resign her post on 30 June 2000. Nevertheless, this at least partial and public recognition of the contribution of the expellees to reconciliation with Central and Eastern Europe certainly contributed to the fact that issues of and related to the expulsion have recently regained considerable discursive power. Yet with the (attempted) linking of the expulsion of the Sudeten Germans to the Czech Republic's EU accession, the politics of homeland and belonging has also acquired an unexpected international institutional dimension.

In the course of the intensifying accession negotiations between the EU and the Czech Republic and Poland, this process now has almost acquired a dynamic of its own, which is evidence of the fact that a number of issues related, in particular, to past developments of the German question have not yet been fully resolved. The issue of the return of expelled ethnic Germans or their descendants to either Poland or the Czech Republic is a real one, in the sense that one of the five fundamental freedoms of the European Union, that of the movement of people, would give a legal right to Germans (and everyone else) to acquire property and settle in the new member states. However, apart from the fact that it is highly likely that both countries will be able to negotiate a transition period in this respect—that is, to have this particular right suspended for a period of several years after their accession—fears of a return migration of ethnic Germans to their former homelands are being wildly exaggerated, primarily for domestic political purposes. A recent study conducted by the Warsaw-based Institute of Public Affairs (Dolinska and Falkowski 2001: 62f.), for example, found that as against widespread fears, especially among the rural population in Poland, only about 3 percent of all Germans included in the representative survey had the intention of buying property outside Germany, and of those again only 0.4 percent actually planned to do so in Poland. Despite the rhetoric of some hard-liners, there was, and is, no widespread desire among Sudeten German expellees or their children or grandchildren either to return to their places of origin in the Czech Republic or permanently settle there. This becomes obvious by examining various survey results on issues of national identification. In 1994, for example, only 15 percent of those seeing themselves as expellees identified more strongly in terms of their regional origin than in terms of their German citizenship. For the former East Germany, this figure is even lower, at only 7 percent (Köcher 1997: 57). Equally interesting is the fact that among the Sudeten Germans and members of their families who are generally seen as the most hard-line advocates of a right to return and the restitution of property, only 56 percent actually indicated sympathy for demands for compensation/restitution, while one-third rejected the idea. Of those sympathetic to compensation/restitution demands, almost a third declared that Sudeten Germans should, nevertheless, abandon these demands for political reasons (Köcher 1997: 57).

The most controversial and potentially most explosive issue is that of the so-called Beneš Decrees, which dealt with the confiscation of German (and Hungarian) property in Czechoslovakia and citizenship issues in relation to members of the two ethnic groups. Here too, a number of opportunities have arisen on several levels, bilaterally as well as on the European stage, for their exploitation by expellee activists.

In April 1999, a resolution was passed by the European Parliament in which its members called "on the Czech Government, in the same spirit of reconciliatory statements made by President Havel, to repeal the surviving laws and decrees from 1945 and 1946, insofar as they concern the expulsion of individual ethnic groups in the former Czechoslovakia." Prior to this resolution of the European Parliament, the U.S. House of Representatives passed a resolution (on 13 October 1998) demanding that the formerly communist countries in Central and Eastern Europe "return wrongfully expropriated properties to their rightful owners or, when actual return is not possible, to pay prompt, just and effective compensation, in accordance with principles of justice and in a manner that is just, transparent and fair." This is a highly sensitive issue not only in Czech-EU relations but also in Czech-German relations and within the political processes in both countries. The fact that there was only a small majority in favor of the European Parliament resolution must have been interpreted by the Czech government and parliament as an opportunity to intervene. Thus, Jan Zahradil, Czech parliamentarian and member of the Czech Parliament–European Parliament Mixed Commission, tried to reverse the decision. He failed after an intervention by Bernd Posselt, a member of the European Parliament but also a key political activist of the Sudeten German expellee community in the Federal Republic, who insisted on the autonomy of the European Parliament in reaching its decisions. In a new attempt to prevent a similar formulation, in a 2000 resolution of the European Parliament on the status of negotiations on the Czech Republic's membership application, Zahradil and his deputy Lastuvka wrote letters to all 626 members of the Parliament. All they achieved was an increased interest in the issue of how far the Beneš Decrees are in fact compatible with EU law and principles, resulting in a somewhat stronger formulation, stating that the European Parliament "welcomes the Czech government's willingness to scrutinize the laws and decrees of the Beneš Government dating from 1945 and 1946 and still on the statute books to ascertain whether they run counter to the EU law in force and the Copenhagen criteria."

The first European Parliament resolution was immediately seized upon by a group of members of the German Bundestag who proposed a motion, cosponsored by the CDU/CSU parliamentary party, asking the federal government "to take appropriate action in the spirit of the [resolution of the European Parliament] . . . on its own and in collaboration with the other EU member states and the institutions of the EU." A countermotion was introduced by the parliamentary parties of SPD and Alliance 90/The Greens in October 1999, asking the Bundestag to welcome a statement by Chancellor Schroeder and Minister-President Zeman of 8 March 1999 that "neither government will re-introduce property issues [into their bilateral relationship] either today or in the future." This motion received a majority vote both at committee stage and after a parliamentary debate in June 2000, while that of the CDU/CSU parliamentarians was rejected.

Also at the bilateral level, German dismemberment and occupation of Czechoslovakia, which cannot be separated from the events after

1945, and the expulsions have been dealt with in the 1992 German-Czechoslovak treaty, the 1997 German-Czech Declaration, and in a number of other official statements by both governments. In April 2002, EU Enlargement Commissioner Günter Verheugen and Prime Minister Zeman issued a joint statement in which they acknowledged that "there has been much public discussion on some of the Czechoslovak Presidential Decrees of 1945, and on some of the ensuing Czechoslovak legislation of the immediate post-war period," but also insisted that "as was the case with measures taken by other European countries at that time, some of these Acts would not pass muster today if judged by current standards—but they belong to history." This policy is widely supported by governments across Europe, in particular also because a Czech Constitutional Court ruling of March 1995 established that Presidential Decree 108/45 (on the confiscation of property) was a unique act that "for more than four decades has established no legal relations and thus no longer has a constitutive character" in the Czech legal system—that it is no longer valid or applicable. In February 1999, the Czech government stated in its Foreign Policy Concept that the decrees were "extinct," a view that was subsequently also adopted by the Czech parliament. Officials at all levels have thus managed to find ways out of the dilemma created by the EU's high aspirations in terms of human rights and by acts committed after the Second World War that contradict these norms. For obvious reasons, such a difficult balancing act is unlikely to please everyone involved, but the commitment of all governments and the EU Commission to leave the past behind and move on to a common future is in the general spirit of post-1990 developments, which has also become evident at other levels of the development of the German question, in particular in the German-Czech and German-Polish context.

Even though it was always unlikely that the admission of the Czech Republic to the EU would fail because of the country's failure to rescind the relevant decrees, the commitment of the EU to human rights in its accession policy gave advocates of a reexamination of the expulsion issue a powerful platform from which to address not only human rights violations of the Czechoslovak and Polish governments at the time but also the way in which their successors have dealt with the issue.

Yet it has also been recognized that these interests could be much more effectively pursued if the expellees received broader public recognition as victims. In order to achieve this, the leaderships of the expellee organizations have had to reshape the notion of victimhood of both victims of Nazi Germany and victims of the governments established in Central and Eastern Europe at the end of the Second World War. In doing so, expellee activists do not aim at denying that groups that have long been recognized as victims have suffered and have therefore every right to claim compensation. Rather, the objective is to achieve for their own members the same international recognition (including from countries like Poland and the Czech Republic), with all its legal consequences. To give a few examples of how the Sudeten German Regional Association has tried to capitalize on recent debates on human rights, on 8 October 1999 the Speaker of the Sudeten Germans, Franz Neubauer, declared his solidarity with a declaration by the Central Council of German Sinti and Roma accusing the Czech Republic of apartheid-style politics—plans to build a wall around a Roma residential quarter in a town in northern Bohemia had become public. On 7 April 1999, all Sudeten Germans in Germany were urged to donate money for Kosovo refugees, under the reasoning that solidarity with the people in Kosovo would sensitize the German and international public to the fate of the Sudeten Germans as well. The motto of the annual Sudeten German Day in 2000 was "For a Worldwide Ban on Expulsions" (*Vertreibung weltweit ächten*). On 24 March 2000, Neubauer welcomed the fact that Czech victims of Nazi forced-labor camps were to receive compensation, noting that this implied a recognition of the fact that crimes "of a certain dimension do not fall under the statute of limitations" and that their victims have to be compensated sooner or later. This was seen as "good news for the German expellees." Previously, there had been only one such opportunity to reshape victimhood, when the Sudeten Germans submitted a declaration to the United Nations in January 1978, in which the Sixth Federal Assembly of the Sudeten German Regional-Cultural Association justified its claims to the restitution of expropriated property with specific reference to, among other documents, UN Resolution 3236 of 22 November 1974 on the rights of the Palestinians.

However, it is important to realize that the notion of victimhood as a central part of expellee identity is by no means a new element, nor could it be one, given the very real experience of expulsion. What has changed, catapulting victimhood back to center stage in the debate about belonging, is the fact that the current national and international environments provide a wealth of opportunities for the expellee organizations to associate their constituents with a group identity that seems likely to further their key objectives.

RECKONING WITH THE PAST

The German question, as has become evident in this and all the preceding chapters, is a multidimensional issue. It has manifested itself in complex dynamics revolving around the notions of territory and nation, and the various incompatibilities between the two throughout history. While most of the individual dimensions of the German question have been resolved gradually over the past half-century, the end of the Cold War has given rise to different, and in some way new, aspects. The one that has most recently captured widespread international attention is the still ambiguous relationship that (some) refugees, expellees, and *Aussiedler* have maintained with their past and present homelands. While their relationship to the present homeland, expressed in demands for integration as citizens with equal rights and as members of the German cultural nation, has been relatively uncontested, their relationship to past homelands has not only divided the domestic public discourse in Germany but had significant implications for the Federal Republic's bilateral relations with Poland and the Czech Republic. It now also has the potential to affect the dynamics of EU enlargement.

The reason why the expulsion of the ethnic Germans more than fifty years ago still triggers heated debates and has a bearing on political processes at German and European levels can be seen not only in the magnitude of the expulsions and the suffering they inflicted on those affected by them. It has also to do with the fact that this particular aspect of the Second World War and its consequences has never been properly dealt with by means of a broad and open public debate in Germany or Poland or Czechoslovakia/the Czech Republic. It is, therefore, much easier now to take it out of the context of the Second World War or include the events that preceded the expulsions on a highly selective basis. More than thirty years after the advent of *neue Ostpolitik*, the political left and right in Germany continue to be divided over this issue, raising the political profile of, and stakes in, a debate that should essentially be about reconciliation and forgiveness. Instead, issues that are a matter of human rights become highly politicized and are presented in contexts with which they have little or nothing in common. In turn, because of ideological preconceptions, obvious links and connections between historical and current events are denied, thus creating double standards in the application and implementation of basic human rights. More often than not, radicalization and alienation inside and outside Germany have been the result.

Thus, while belonging is a concept that has, for each individual and collective, strong roots in the past and the present, it also has implications for the future. In the case of the German expellees, who themselves and in their policies today are, in many ways, the most vivid reminder of the continued existence of a German question, this has led to a complicated duality between *Heimat,* their traditional homelands in Central and Eastern Europe, and *Zuhause,* their newly found home in the Federal Republic of Germany. The majority of them have reconciled themselves with the fact that a return to their *Heimat,* in the sense of restoring a permanent homeland for an ethnically German return-migrant population anywhere in Central and Eastern Europe, is impossible (and for many of them also undesirable). Nevertheless, failure to recognize the injustice of collective victimization, and in some cases its deliberate denial inside and outside Germany, remains a potent source of mobilization around the very issues that are at the core of the German question—the extent of the compatibility of German territory and nation. This situation also enables political activists in Germany, Poland, and the Czech Republic to manipulate remotely related issues and to continue to incite debates on the expulsions and their consequences.

While it is unlikely, and to some extent also undesirable, to achieve complete closure on an issue as politically and emotionally loaded as the German question, a modus vivendi has to be sought that will allow the still-existing ambiguity of territory and nation not to polarize or threaten implications for any of those affected by it. One essential basis for that is a more comprehensive understanding of the complexity and dynamics of the political processes in the twentieth century that have become known as the German question.

NOTE

1. Personal autonomy, also referred to as nonterritorial, cultural, or segmental autonomy, is a concept that describes a particular approach to minority protection according to which membership in a particular ethnic group entitles individuals to certain, primarily cultural, rights, such as separate educational institutions, minority language publications, etc. It also assigns self-government rights in such areas to the minority group. It is thus clearly

distinguished from territorial forms of autonomy, but in practice it is often combined with them. Early practical applications are the millet system in the Ottoman Empire and certain minority rights granted in the Austro-Hungarian Empire and in Estonia and Latvia in the interwar period. More recently, the South Tyrol autonomy arrangements include aspects of personal autonomy, as does minority legislation in Estonia, Hungary, and Russia. Theoretically, the concept dates back to Adolf Frischhof's *Österreich und die Bürgerschaften seines Bestandes* (1869). It was later picked up by Austromarxists Karl Renner (e.g., *Das Selbstbestimmungsrecht der Nationen in besonderer Anwendung auf Österreich* [1918]) and Otto Bauer (e.g., *Die Nationalitätenfrage und die Sozialdemokratie* [1924]) in their studies on how to establish a viable framework within which the different ethnocultural groups of the Austro-Hungarian Empire could thrive without posing a threat to the unity of the state, and vice versa. In contemporary political science, the concept is, for example, part of Arend Lijphart's model of consociational democracy (e.g., *Democracy in Plural Societies* [1977]).

Appendix: Key Documents

THE TREATY OF VERSAILLES, 28 JUNE 1919

PART II
BOUNDARIES OF GERMANY

ARTICLE 27
The boundaries of Germany will be determined as follows:

1. With Belgium:
   From the point common to the three frontiers of Belgium, Holland, and Germany and in a southerly direction: the northeastern boundary of the former territory of neutral Moresnet, then the eastern boundary of the Kreis of Eupen, then the frontier between Belgium and the Kreis of Montjoie, then the northeastern and eastern boundary of the Kreis of Malmedy to its junction with the frontier of Luxemburg.

2. With Luxemburg:
   The frontier of August 3, 1914, to its junction with the frontier of France of 18th July, 1870.

3. With France:
   The frontier of July 18, 1870, from Luxemburg to Switzerland with the reservations made in Article 48 of Section IV (Saar Basin) of Part III.

4. With Switzerland:
   The present frontier.

5. With Austria:
   The frontier of August 3, 1914, from Switzerland to Czecho-Slovakia as hereinafter defined.

6. With Czecho-Slovakia:
   The frontier of August 3, 1914, between Germany and Austria from its junction with the old administrative boundary separating Bohemia and the province of Upper Austria to the point north of the salient of the old province of Austrian Silesia situated at about 8 kilometres east of Neustadt.

7. With Poland:
   From the point defined above to a point to be fixed on the ground about 2 kilometres east of Lorzendorf: the frontier as it will be fixed in accordance with Article 88 of the present Treaty; thence in a northerly direction to the point where the administrative boundary of Posnania crosses the river Bartsch: a line to be fixed on the ground leaving the following places in Poland: [. . .]

8. With Denmark:
   The frontier as it will be fixed in accordance with Articles 109 to III of Part III, Section XII (Schleswig).

ARTICLE 31

Germany, recognising that the Treaties of April 19, 1839, which established the status of Belgium before the war, no longer conform to the requirements of the situation, consents to the abrogation of the said Treaties and undertakes immediately to recognise and to observe whatever conventions may be entered into by the Principal Allied and Associated Powers, or by any of them, in concert with the Governments of Belgium and of the Netherlands, to replace the said Treaties of 1839. If her formal adhesions should be required to such conventions or to any of their stipulations, Germany undertakes immediately to give it.

ARTICLE 32

Germany recognises the full sovereignty of Belgium over the whole of the contested territory of Moresnet (called Moresnet neutre).

ARTICLE 33

Germany renounces in favour of Belgium all rights and title over the territory of Prussian Moresnet situated on the west of the road from Liege to Aix-la-Chapelle; the road will belong to Belgium where it bounds this territory.

ARTICLE 34

Germany renounces in favour of Belgium all rights and title over the territory comprising the whole of the Kreise of Eupen and of Malmedy. During
the six months after the coming into force of this Treaty, registers will be
opened by the Belgian authority at Eupen and Malmedy in which the inhabitants of the above territory will be entitled to record in writing a desire
to see the whole or part of it remain under German sovereignty. The results
of this public expression of opinion will be communicated by the Belgian
Government to the League of Nations, and Belgium undertakes to accept
the decision of the League.

ARTICLE 35

A Commission of seven persons, five of whom will be appointed by the Principal Allied and Associated Powers, one by Germany and one by Belgium,
will be set up fifteen days after the coming into force of the present Treaty
to settle on the spot the new frontier line between Belgium and Germany,
taking into account the economic factors and the means of communication.
Decisions will be taken by a majority and will be binding on the parties concerned.

ARTICLE 36

When the transfer of the sovereignty over the territories referred to above
has become definite, German nationals habitually resident in the territories
will definitively acquire Belgian nationality ipso facto, and will lose their
German nationality. Nevertheless, German nationals who became resident
in the territories after August 1, 1914, shall not obtain Belgian nationality
without a permit from the Belgian Government.

ARTICLE 37

Within the two years following the definitive transfer of the sovereignty over
the territories assigned to Belgium under the present Treaty, German nationals over 18 years of age habitually resident in those territories will be entitled
to opt for German nationality. Option by a husband will cover his wife, and
option by parents will cover their children under 18 years of age. Persons
who have exercised the above right to opt must within the ensuing twelve
months transfer their place of residence to Germany. They will be entitled
to retain their immovable property in the territories acquired by Belgium.
They may carry with them their movable property of every description. No
export or import duties may be imposed upon them in connection with the
removal of such property.

SECTION III
LEFT BANK OF THE RHINE

ARTICLE 42

Germany is forbidden to maintain or construct any fortifications either on the left bank of the Rhine or on the right bank to the west of a line drawn 50 kilometres to the East of the Rhine.

ARTICLE 43

In the area defined above the maintenance and the assembly of armed forces, either permanently or temporarily, and military maneuvers of any kind, as well as the upkeep of all permanent works for mobilization, are in the same way forbidden.

ARTICLE 44

In case Germany violates in any manner whatever the provisions of Articles 42 and 43, she shall be regarded as committing a hostile act against the Powers signatory of the present Treaty and as calculated to disturb the peace of the world.

SECTION IV
SAAR BASIN

ARTICLE 45

As compensation for the destruction of the coal-mines in the north of France and as part payment towards the total reparation due from Germany for the damage resulting from the war, Germany cedes to France in full and absolute possession, with exclusive rights of exploitation, unencumbered and free from all debts and charges of any kind, the coal-mines situated in the Saar Basin as defined in Article 48.

ARTICLE 49

Germany renounces in favour of the League of Nations, in the capacity of trustee, the government of the territory defined above. At the end of fifteen years from the coming into force of the present Treaty the inhabitants of the said territory shall be called upon to indicate the sovereignty under which they desire to be placed.

ANNEX
CHAPTER III
PLEBISCITE

34. At the termination of a period of fifteen years from the coming into force of the present Treaty, the population of the territory of the Saar Basin will be called upon to indicate their desires in the following manner: A vote will take place by communes or districts, on the three following alternatives: (a) maintenance of the regime established by the present Treaty and by this Annex; (b) union with France; (c) union with Germany.

All persons without distinction of sex, more than twenty years old at the date of the voting, resident in the territory at the date of the signature of the present Treaty, will have the right to vote.

The other conditions, methods, and the date of the voting shall be fixed by the Council of the League of Nations in such a way as to secure the freedom, secrecy and trustworthiness of the voting

35. The League of Nations shall decide on the sovereignty under which the territory is to be placed, taking into account the wishes of the inhabitants as expressed by the voting.

   a. If, for the whole or part of the territory, the League of Nations decides in favour of the maintenance of the regime established by the present Treaty and this Annex, Germany hereby agrees to make such renunciation of her sovereignty in favour of the League of Nations as the latter shall deem necessary. It will be the duty of the League of Nations to take appropriate steps to adapt the regime definitively adopted to the permanent welfare of the territory and the general interest;

   b. If, for the whole or part of the territory, the League of Nations decides in favour of union with France, Germany hereby agrees to cede to France in accordance with the decision of the League of Nations, all rights and title over the territory specified by the League.

   c. If, for the whole or part of the territory, the League of Nations decides in favour of union with Germany, it will be the duty of the League of Nations to cause the German Government to be re-established in the government of the territory specified by the League.

PART VIII
REPARATION
SECTION 1
GENERAL PROVISIONS

ARTICLE 231
The Allied and Associated Governments affirm and Germany accepts the responsibility of Germany and her allies for causing all the loss and damage to which the Allied and Associated Governments and their nationals have been subjected as a consequence of the war imposed upon them by the aggression of Germany and her allies.

ARTICLE 235
In order to enable the Allied and Associated Powers to proceed at once to the restoration of their industrial and economic life, pending the full determination of their claims, Germany shall pay in such installments and in such manner (whether in gold, commodities, ships, securities or otherwise) as the Reparation Commission may fix, during 1919, 1920 and the first four months of 1921, the equivalent of 20,000,000,000 gold marks. Out of this sum the expenses of the armies of occupation subsequent to the Armistice of November 11, 1918, shall first be met, and such supplies of food and raw materials as may be judged by the Governments of the Principal Allied and

Associated Powers to be essential to enable Germany to meet her obligations for reparation may also, with the approval of the said Governments, be paid for out of the above sum. The balance shall be reckoned towards liquidation of the amounts due for reparation. Germany shall further deposit bonds as prescribed in paragraph 12 (c) of Annex II hereto.

ARTICLE 236
Germany further agrees to the direct application of her economic resources to reparation as specified in Annexes III, IV, V, and VI, relating respectively to merchant shipping, to physical restoration, to coal and derivatives of coal, and to dyestuffs and other chemical products; provided always that the value of the property transferred and any services rendered by her under these Annexes, assessed in the manner therein prescribed shall be credited to her towards liquidation of her obligations under the above Articles.

ARTICLE 237
The successive installments, including the above sum, paid over by Germany in satisfaction of the above claims will be divided by the Allied and Associated Governments in proportions which have been determined upon by them in advance on a basis of general equity and of the rights of each.

AGREEMENT CONCLUDED AT MUNICH, 29 SEPTEMBER 1938, BETWEEN GERMANY, GREAT BRITAIN, FRANCE, AND ITALY

Germany, the United Kingdom, France and Italy, taking into consideration the agreement, which has been already reached in principle for the cession to Germany of the Sudeten German territory, have agreed on the following terms and conditions governing the said cession and the measures consequent thereon, and by this agreement they each hold themselves responsible for the steps necessary to secure its fulfilment:

(1) The evacuation will begin on 1st October.

(2) The United Kingdom, France and Italy agree that the evacuation of the territory shall be completed by the 10th October, without any existing installations having been destroyed, and that the Czechoslovak Government will be held responsible for carrying out the evacuation without damage to the said installations.

(3) The conditions governing the evacuation will be laid down in detail by an international commission composed of representatives of Germany, the United Kingdom, France, Italy and Czechoslovakia.

(4) The occupation by stages of the predominantly German territory by German troops will begin on 1st October. The four territories marked

on the attached map will be occupied by German troops in the following order:

The territory marked No. I on the 1st and 2nd of October; the territory marked No. II on the 2nd and 3rd of October; the territory marked No. III on the 3rd, 4th and 5th of October; the territory marked No. IV on the 6th and 7th of October. The remaining territory of preponderantly German character will be ascertained by the aforesaid international commission forthwith and be occupied by German troops by the 10th of October.

(5) The international commission referred to in paragraph 3 will determine the territories in which a plebiscite is to be held. These territories will be occupied by international bodies until the plebiscite has been completed. The same commission will fix the conditions in which the plebiscite is to be held, taking as a basis the conditions of the Saar plebiscite. The commission will also fix a date, not later than the end of November, on which the plebiscite will be held.

(6) The final determination of the frontiers will be carried out by the international commission. The commission will also be entitled to recommend to the four Powers, Germany, the United Kingdom, France and Italy, in certain exceptional cases, minor modifications in the strictly ethnographical determination of the zones which are to be transferred without plebiscite.

(7) There will be a right of option into and out of the transferred territories, the option to be exercised within six months from the date of this agreement. A German-Czechoslovak commission shall determine the details of the option, consider ways of facilitating the transfer of population and settle questions of principle arising out of the said transfer.

(8) The Czechoslovak Government will within a period of four weeks from the date of this agreement release from their military and police forces any Sudeten Germans who may wish to be released, and the Czechoslovak Government will within the same period release Sudeten German prisoners who are serving terms of imprisonment for political offences.

ANNEX

His Majesty's government in the United Kingdom and the French Government have entered into the above agreement on the basis that they stand by the offer, contained in paragraph 6 of the Anglo-French proposals of the 19th September, relating to an international guarantee of the new boundaries of the Czechoslovak State against unprovoked aggression.

When the question of the Polish and Hungarian minorities in Czechoslovakia has been settled, Germany and Italy for their part will give a guarantee to Czechoslovakia.

DECLARATION

The Heads of the Governments of the four Powers declare that the problems of the Polish and Hungarian minorities in Czechoslovakia, if not settled within three months by agreement between the respective Governments, shall form the subject of another meeting of the Heads of the Governments of the four Powers here present.

SUPPLEMENTARY DECLARATION

ALL questions which may arise out of the transfer of the territory shall be considered as coming within the terms of reference to the International Commission.

TREATY OF NONAGGRESSION BETWEEN GERMANY AND THE UNION OF SOVIET SOCIALIST REPUBLICS, 23 AUGUST 1939

The Government of the German Reich and the Government of the Union of Soviet Socialist Republics desirous of strengthening the cause of peace between Germany and the U.S.S.R and proceeding from the fundamental provisions of the Neutrality Agreement concluded in April 1926 between Germany and the U.S.S.R., have reached the following agreement:

ARTICLE I

Both High Contracting Parties obligate themselves to desist from any act of violence, any aggressive action, and any attack on each other, either individually or jointly with other powers.

ARTICLE II

Should one of the High Contracting Parties become the object of belligerent action by a third power, the other High Contracting Party shall in no manner lend its support to this third power.

ARTICLE III

The Governments of the two High Contracting Parties shall in the future maintain continual contact with one another for the purpose of consultation in order to exchange information on problems affecting their common interests.

ARTICLE IV

Neither of the two High Contracting Parties shall participate in any grouping of powers whatsoever that is directly or indirectly aimed at the other party.

ARTICLE V

Should disputes or conflicts arise between the High Contracting Parties over problems of one kind or another, both parties shall settle these disputes or conflicts exclusively through friendly exchange of opinion or, if necessary, through the establishment of arbitration commissions.

ARTICLE VI

The present treaty is concluded for a period of ten years, with the provision that, in so far as one of the High Contracting Parties does not denounce it one year prior to the expiration of this period, the validity of this treaty shall automatically be extended for another five years.

ARTICLE VII

The present treaty shall be ratified within the shortest possible time. The ratifications shall be exchanged in Berlin. The agreement shall enter into force as soon as it is signed.

SECRET ADDITIONAL PROTOCOL

On the occasion of the signature of the Nonaggression Pact between the German Reich and the Union of Socialist Soviet Republics the undersigned plenipotentiaries of each of the two parties discussed in strictly confidential conversations the question of the boundary of their respective spheres of influence in Eastern Europe. These conversations led to the following conclusions:

1. In the event of a territorial and political rearrangement in the areas belonging to the Baltic States (Finland, Estonia, Latvia, Lithuania), the northern boundary of Lithuania shall represent the boundary of the spheres of influence of Germany and the U.S.S.R. In this connection the interest of Lithuania in the Vilna area is recognized by each party.

2. In the event of a territorial and political rearrangement of the areas belonging to the Polish state the spheres of influence of Germany and the U.S.S.R. shall be bounded approximately by the line of the rivers Narew, Vistula, and San.

   The question of whether the interests of both parties make desirable the maintenance of an independent Polish state and how such a state should be bounded can only be definitely determined in the course of further political developments.

   In any event both Governments will resolve this question by means of a friendly agreement.

3. With regard to Southeastern Europe attention is called by the Soviet side to its interest in Bessarabia. The German side declares; its complete political disinterestedness in these areas.

   This protocol shall be treated by both parties as strictly secret.

ATLANTIC CHARTER, 14 AUGUST 1941

The President of the United States of America and the Prime Minister, Mr. Churchill, representing His Majesty's Government in the United Kingdom, being met together, deem it right to make known certain common principles in the national policies of their respective countries on which they base their hopes for a better future for the world.

First, their countries seek no aggrandizement, territorial or other;

Second, they desire to see no territorial changes that do not accord with the freely expressed wishes of the peoples concerned;

Third, they respect the right of all peoples to choose the form of government under which they will live; and they wish to see sovereign rights and self government restored to those who have been forcibly deprived of them;

Fourth, they will endeavor, with due respect for their existing obligations, to further the enjoyment by all States, great or small, victor or vanquished, of access, on equal terms, to the trade and to the raw materials of the world which are needed for their economic prosperity;

Fifth, they desire to bring about the fullest collaboration between all nations in the economic field with the object of securing, for all, improved labor standards, economic advancement and social security;

Sixth, after the final destruction of the Nazi tyranny, they hope to see established a peace which will afford to all nations the means of dwelling in safety within their own boundaries, and which will afford assurance that all the men in all lands may live out their lives in freedom from fear and want;

Seventh, such a peace should enable all men to traverse the high seas and oceans without hindrance;

Eighth, they believe that all of the nations of the world, for realistic as well as spiritual reasons must come to the abandonment of the use of force. Since no future peace can be maintained if land, sea or air armaments continue to be employed by nations which threaten, or may threaten, aggression outside of their frontiers, they believe, pending the establishment of a wider and permanent system of general security, that the disarmament of such nations is essential. They will likewise aid and encourage all other practicable measure which will lighten for peace-loving peoples the crushing burden of armaments.

THE YALTA CONFERENCE, 11 FEBRUARY 1945

PROTOCOL OF PROCEEDINGS OF CRIMEA CONFERENCE
The Crimea Conference of the heads of the Governments of the United States of America, the United Kingdom, and the Union of Soviet Socialist Republics, which took place from Feb. 4 to 11, came to the following conclusions:

[. . .]

III. DISMEMBERMENT OF GERMANY

It was agreed that Article 12 (a) of the Surrender terms for Germany should be amended to read as follows:

"The United Kingdom, the United States of America and the Union of Soviet Socialist Republics shall possess supreme authority with respect to Germany. In the exercise of such authority they will take such steps, including the complete dismemberment of Germany as they deem requisite for future peace and security."

The study of the procedure of the dismemberment of Germany was referred to a committee consisting of Mr. Anthony Eden, Mr. John Winant, and Mr. Fedor T. Gusev. This body would consider the desirability of associating with it a French representative.

IV. ZONE OF OCCUPATION FOR THE FRENCH AND CONTROL COUNCIL FOR GERMANY

It was agreed that a zone in Germany, to be occupied by the French forces, should be allocated France. This zone would be formed out of the British and American zones and its extent would be settled by the British and Americans in consultation with the French Provisional Government.

It was also agreed that the French Provisional Government should be invited to become a member of the Allied Control Council for Germany.

V. REPARATION

The following protocol has been approved:

Protocol

On the Talks Between the Heads of Three Governments at the Crimean Conference on the Question of the German Reparations in Kind

1. Germany must pay in kind for the losses caused by her to the Allied nations in the course of the war. Reparations are to be received in the first instance by those countries which have borne the main burden of the war, have suffered the heaviest losses and have organized victory over the enemy.

2. Reparation in kind is to be exacted from Germany in three following forms:

   (a) Removals within two years from the surrender of Germany or the cessation of organized resistance from the national wealth of Germany located on the territory of Germany herself as well as outside her territory (equipment, machine tools, ships, rolling stock, German investments abroad, shares of industrial, transport and other enterprises in Germany, etc.), these removals to be carried out chiefly for the purpose of destroying the war potential of Germany.

   (b) Annual deliveries of goods from current production for a period to be fixed.

   (c) Use of German labor.

3. For the working out on the above principles of a detailed plan for exaction of reparation from Germany an Allied reparation commission will be set up in Moscow. It will consist of three representatives—one from the Union of Soviet Socialist Republics, one from the United Kingdom and one from the United States of America.

4. With regard to the fixing of the total sum of the reparation as well as the distribution of it among the countries which suffered from the German aggression, the Soviet and American delegations agreed as follows:

   "The Moscow reparation commission should take in its initial studies as a basis for discussion the suggestion of the Soviet Government that the total sum of the reparation in accordance with the points (a) and (b) of the Paragraph 2 should be 22 billion dollars and that 50 per cent should go to the Union of Soviet Socialist Republics."

The British delegation was of the opinion that, pending consideration of the reparation question by the Moscow reparation commission, no figures of reparation should be mentioned.

The above Soviet-American proposal has been passed to the Moscow reparation commission as one of the proposals to be considered by the commission.

VI. MAJOR WAR CRIMINALS
The conference agreed that the question of the major war criminals should be the subject of inquiry by the three Foreign Secretaries for report in due course after the close of the conference.

VII. POLAND
The following declaration on Poland was agreed by the conference:

"A new situation has been created in Poland as a result of her complete liberation by the Red Army. This calls for the establishment of a Polish Provisional Government which can be more broadly based than was possible before the recent liberation of the western part of Poland. The Provisional Government which is now functioning in Poland should therefore be reorganized on a broader democratic basis with the inclusion of democratic leaders from Poland itself and from Poles abroad. This new Government should then be called the Polish Provisional Government of National Unity.

"M. Molotov, Mr. Harriman and Sir A. Clark Kerr are authorized as a commission to consult in the first instance in Moscow with members of the present Provisional Government and with other Polish democratic leaders from within Poland and from abroad, with a view to the reorganization of the present Government along the above lines. This Polish Provisional Government of National Unity shall be pledged to the holding of free and unfettered elections as soon as possible on the basis of universal suffrage and secret ballot. In these elections all democratic and anti-Nazi parties shall have the right to take part and to put forward candidates.

"When a Polish Provisional of Government National Unity has been properly formed in conformity with the above, the Government of the U.S.S.R., which now maintains diplomatic relations with the present Provisional Government of Poland, and the Government of the United Kingdom and the Government of the United States of America will establish diplomatic relations with the new Polish Provisional Government National Unity, and will exchange Ambassadors by whose reports the respective Governments will be kept informed about the situation in Poland.

"The three heads of Government consider that the eastern frontier of Poland should follow the Curzon Line with digressions from it in some regions of five to eight kilometers in favor of Poland. They recognize that Poland must receive substantial accessions in territory in the north and west. They feel that the opinion of the new Polish Provisional Government of National Unity should be sought in due course of the extent of these accessions and that the final delimitation of the western frontier of Poland should thereafter await the peace conference."

[...]

The forgoing protocol was approved and signed by the three Foreign Secretaries at the Crimean Conference Feb. 11, 1945.

THE POTSDAM CONFERENCE, 17 JULY–2 AUGUST 1945

The Berlin [Potsdam] Conference of the Three Heads of Government of the U. S. S. R., U. S. A., and U. K., which took place from July 17 to August 2, 1945, came to the following conclusions:

[...]

II. THE PRINCIPLES TO GOVERN THE TREATMENT OF GERMANY IN THE INITIAL CONTROL PERIOD

A. POLITICAL PRINCIPLES

1. In accordance with the Agreement on Control Machinery in Germany, supreme authority in Germany is exercised, on instructions from their respective Governments, by the Commanders-in-Chief of the armed forces of the United States of America, the United Kingdom, the Union of Soviet Socialist Republics, and the French Republic, each in his own zone of occupation, and also jointly, in matters affecting Germany as a whole, in their capacity as members of the Control Council.

2. So far as is practicable, there shall be uniformity of treatment of the German population throughout Germany.

3. The purposes of the occupation of Germany by which the Control Council shall be guided are:

   (i) The complete disarmament and demilitarization of Germany and the elimination or control of all German industry that could be used for military production. To these ends:

   (a) All German land, naval and air forces, the SS., SA., SD., and Gestapo, with all their organizations, staffs and institutions, including the General Staff, the Officers' Corps, Reserve Corps, military schools, war veterans' organizations and all other military and semi-military organizations, together with all clubs and associations which serve to keep alive the military tradition in Germany, shall be completely and finally abolished in such manner as permanently to prevent the revival or reorganization of German militarism and Nazism;

   (b) All arms, ammunition and implements of war and all specialized facilities for their production shall be held at the disposal of the Allies or destroyed. The maintenance and production of all aircraft and all arms. ammunition and implements of war shall be prevented.

   (ii) To convince the German people that they have suffered a total military defeat and that they cannot escape responsibility for what they have brought upon themselves, since their own ruthless warfare and the fanatical Nazi resistance have destroyed German economy and made chaos and suffering inevitable.

   (iii) To destroy the National Socialist Party and its affiliated and supervised organizations, to dissolve all Nazi institutions, to ensure that they are not revived in any form, and to prevent all Nazi and militarist activity or propaganda.

   (iv) To prepare for the eventual reconstruction of German political life on a democratic basis and for eventual peaceful cooperation in international life by Germany.

4. All Nazi laws which provided the basis of the Hitler regime or established discriminations on grounds of race, creed, or political opinion shall be abolished. No such discriminations, whether legal, administrative or otherwise, shall be tolerated.

5. War criminals and those who have participated in planning or carrying out Nazi enterprises involving or resulting in atrocities or war crimes shall be arrested and brought to judgment. Nazi leaders, influential Nazi supporters and high officials of Nazi organizations and institutions and any other persons dangerous to the occupation or its objectives shall be arrested and interned.

6. All members of the Nazi Party who have been more than nominal participants in its activities and all other persons hostile to Allied purposes shall be removed from public and semi-public office, and from positions of responsibility in important private undertakings. Such persons shall be replaced by persons who, by their political and moral qualities, are deemed capable of assisting in developing genuine democratic institutions in Germany.

7. German education shall be so controlled as completely to eliminate Nazi and militarist doctrines and to make possible the successful development of democratic ideas.

8. The judicial system will be reorganized in accordance with the principles of democracy, of justice under law, and of equal rights for all citizens without distinction of race, nationality or religion.

9. The administration in Germany should be directed towards the decentralization of the political structure and the development of local responsibility. To this end:

    (i) local self-government shall be restored throughout Germany on democratic principles and in particular through elective councils as rapidly as is consistent with military security and the purposes of military occupation;

    (ii) all democratic political parties with rights of assembly and of public discussion shall be allowed and encouraged throughout Germany;

    (iii) representative and elective principles shall be introduced into regional, provincial and state (Land) administration as rapidly as may be justified by the successful application of these principles in local self-government;

    (iv) for the time being, no central German Government shall be established. Notwithstanding this, however, certain essential central German administrative departments, headed by State Secretaries, shall be established, particularly in the fields of finance, transport, communications, foreign trade and industry. Such departments will act under the direction of the Control Council.

10. Subject to the necessity for maintaining military security, freedom of speech, press and religion shall be permitted, and religious institutions shall be respected. Subject likewise to the maintenance of military security, the formation of free trade unions shall be permitted.

B. ECONOMIC PRINCIPLES

11. In order to eliminate Germany's war potential, the production of arms, ammunition and implements of war as well as all types of aircraft and

sea-going ships shall be prohibited and prevented. Production of metals, chemicals, machinery and other items that are directly necessary to a war economy shall be rigidly controlled and restricted to Germany's approved post-war peacetime needs to meet the objectives stated in Paragraph 15. Productive capacity not needed for permitted production shall be removed in accordance with the reparations plan recommended by the Allied Commission on Reparations and approved by the Governments concerned or if not removed shall be destroyed.

12. At the earliest practicable date, the German economy shall be decentralized for the purpose of eliminating the present excessive concentration of economic power as exemplified in particular by cartels, syndicates, trusts and other monopolistic arrangements.

13. In organizing the German Economy, primary emphasis shall be given to the development of agriculture and peaceful domestic industries.

14. During the period of occupation Germany shall be treated as a single economic unit. To this end common policies shall be established in regard to:

   (a) mining and industrial production and its allocation;
   (b) agriculture, forestry and fishing;
   (c) wages, prices and rationing;
   (d) import and export programs for Germany as a whole;
   (e) currency and banking, central taxation and customs;
   (f) reparation and removal of industrial war potential;
   (g) transportation and communications.

   In applying these policies account shall be taken, where appropriate, of varying local conditions.

15. Allied controls shall be imposed upon the German economy but only to the extent necessary:

   (a) to carry out programs of industrial disarmament, demilitarization, of reparations, and of approved exports and imports.
   (b) to assure the production and maintenance of goods and services required to meet the needs of the occupying forces and displaced persons in Germany and essential to maintain in Germany average living standards not exceeding the average of the standards of living of European countries. (European countries means all European countries excluding the United Kingdom and the U. S. S. R.).
   (c) to ensure in the manner determined by the Control Council the equitable distribution of essential commodities between the several zones so as to produce a balanced economy throughout Germany and reduce the need for imports.
   (d) to control German industry and all economic and financial inter-

national transactions including exports and imports, with the aim of preventing Germany from developing a war potential and of achieving the other objectives named herein.

(e) to control all German public or private scientific bodies research and experimental institutions, laboratories, et cetera connected with economic activities.

16. In the imposition and maintenance of economic controls established by the Control Council, German administrative machinery shall be created and the German authorities shall be required to the fullest extent practicable to proclaim and assume administration of such controls. Thus it should be brought home to the German people that the responsibility for the administration of such controls and any breakdown in these controls will rest with themselves. Any German controls which may run counter to the objectives of occupation will be prohibited.

17. Measures shall be promptly taken:
    (a) to effect essential repair of transport;
    (b) to enlarge coal production;
    (c) to maximize agricultural output; and
    (d) to erect emergency repair of housing and essential utilities.

18. Appropriate steps shall be taken by the Control Council to exercise control and the power of disposition over German-owned external assets not already under the control of United Nations which have taken part in the war against Germany.

19. Payment of Reparations should leave enough resources to enable the German people to subsist without external assistance. In working out the economic balance of Germany the necessary means must be provided to pay for imports approved by the Control Council in Germany. The proceeds of exports from current production and stocks shall be available in the first place for payment for such imports.

    The above clause will not apply to the equipment and products referred to in paragraphs 4 (a) and 4 (b) of the Reparations Agreement.

III. REPARATIONS FROM GERMANY

1. Reparation claims of the U. S. S. R. shall be met by removals from the zone of Germany occupied by the U. S. S. R., and from appropriate German external assets.

2. The U. S. S. R. undertakes to settle the reparation claims of Poland from its own share of reparations.

3. The reparation claims of the United States, the United Kingdom and other countries entitled to reparations shall be met from the Western Zones and from appropriate German external assets.

4. In addition to the reparations to be taken by the U. S. S. R. from its own zone of occupation, the U. S. S. R. shall receive additionally from the Western Zones:

  (a) 15 per cent of such usable and complete industrial capital equipment, in the first place from the metallurgical, chemical and machine manufacturing industries as is unnecessary for the German peace economy and should be removed from the Western Zones of Germany, in exchange for an equivalent value of food, coal, potash, zinc, timber, clay products, petroleum products, and such other commodities as may be agreed upon.

  (b) 10 per cent of such industrial capital equipment as is unnecessary for the German peace economy and should be removed from the Western Zones, to be transferred to the Soviet Government on reparations account without payment or exchange of any kind in return.

  Removals of equipment as provided in (a) and (b) above shall be made simultaneously.

5. The amount of equipment to be removed from the Western Zones on account of reparations must be determined within six months from now at the latest.

6. Removals of industrial capital equipment shall begin as soon as possible and shall be completed within two years from the determination specified in paragraph 5. The delivery of products covered by 4 (a) above shall begin as soon as possible and shall be made by the U. S. S. R. in agreed installments within five years of the date hereof. The determination of the amount and character of the industrial capital equipment unnecessary for the German peace economy and therefore available for reparation shall be made by the Control Council under policies fixed by the Allied Commission on Reparations, with the participation of France, subject to the final approval of the Zone Commander in the Zone from which the equipment is to be removed.

7. Prior to the fixing of the total amount of equipment subject to removal, advance deliveries shall be made in respect to such equipment as will be determined to be eligible for delivery in accordance with the procedure set forth in the last sentence of paragraph 6.

8. The Soviet Government renounces all claims in respect of reparations to shares of German enterprises which are located in the Western Zones of Germany as well as to German foreign assets in all countries except those specified in paragraph 9 below.

9. The Governments of the U. K. and U. S. A. renounce all claims in respect of reparations to shares of German enterprises which are located

in the Eastern Zone of occupation in Germany, as well as to German foreign assets in Bulgaria, Finland, Hungary, Rumania and Eastern Austria.

10. The Soviet Government makes no claims to gold captured by the Allied troops in Germany.

IV. DISPOSAL OF THE GERMAN NAVY AND MERCHANT MARINE

A. The following principles for the distribution of the German Navy were agreed:

(1) The total strength of the German surface navy, excluding ships sunk and those taken over from Allied Nations, but including ships under construction or repair, shall be divided equally among the U. S. S. R., U. K., and U. S. A.

(2) Ships under construction or repair mean those ships whose construction or repair may be completed within three to six months, according to the type of ship. Whether such ships under construction or repair shall be completed or repaired shall be determined by the technical commission appointed by the Three Powers and referred to below, subject to the principle that their completion or repair must be achieved within the time limits above provided, without any increase of skilled employment in the German shipyards and without permitting the reopening of any German ship building or connected industries. Completion date means the date when a ship is able to go out on its first trip, or, under peacetime standards, would refer to the customary date of delivery by shipyard to the Government.

(3) The larger part of the German submarine fleet shall be sunk. Not more than thirty submarines shall be preserved and divided equally between the U. S. S. R., U. K., and U. S. A. for experimental and technical purposes.

(4) All stocks of armament, ammunition and supplies of the German Navy appertaining to the vessels transferred pursuant to paragraphs (1) and (3) hereof shall be handed over to the respective powers receiving such ships.

(5) The Three Governments agree to constitute a tripartite naval commission comprising two representatives for each government, accompanied by the requisite staff, to submit agreed recommendations to the Three Governments for the allocation of specific German warships and to handle other detailed matters arising out of the agreement between the Three Governments regarding the German fleet. The Commission will hold its first meeting not later

than 15th August, 1945, in Berlin, which shall be its headquarters. Each Delegation on the Commission will have the right on the basis of reciprocity to inspect German warships wherever they may be located.

(6) The Three Governments agreed that transfers, including those of ships under construction and repair, shall be completed as soon as possible, but not later than 15th February, 1946. The Commission will submit fortnightly reports, including proposals for the progressive allocation of the vessels when agreed by the Commission.

B.   The following principles for the distribution of the German Merchant Marine were agreed:

(1) The German Merchant Marine, surrendered to the Three Powers and wherever located, shall be divided equally among the U. S. S. R., the U. K., and the U. S. A. The actual transfers of the ships to the respective countries shall take place as soon as practicable after the end of the war against Japan. The United Kingdom and the United States will provide out of their shares of the surrendered German merchant ships appropriate amounts for other Allied States whose merchant marines have suffered heavy losses in the common cause against Germany, except that the Soviet Union shall provide out of its share for Poland.

(2) The allocation, manning, and operation of these ships during the Japanese War period shall fall under the cognizance and authority of the Combined Shipping Adjustment Board and the United Maritime Authority.

(3) While actual transfer of the ships shall be delayed until after the end of the war with Japan, a Tripartite Shipping Commission shall inventory and value all available ships and recommend a specific distribution in accordance with paragraph (1).

(4) German inland and coastal ships determined to be necessary to the maintenance of the basic German peace economy by the Allied Control Council of Germany shall not be included in the shipping pool thus divided among the Three Powers.

(5) The Three Governments agree to constitute a tripartite merchant marine commission comprising two representatives for each Government, accompanied by the requisite staff, to submit agreed recommendations to the Three Governments for the allocation of specific German merchant ships and to handle other detailed matters arising out of the agreement between the Three Governments regarding the German merchant ships. The Commission will hold its first meeting not later than September 1st, 1945, in Berlin, which shall be its headquarters. Each delegation on the Commis-

sion will have the right on the basis of reciprocity to inspect the German merchant ships wherever they may be located.

V. CITY OF KOENIGSBERG AND THE ADJACENT AREA

The Conference examined a proposal by the Soviet Government to the effect that pending the final determination of territorial questions at the peace settlement, the section of the western frontier of the Union of Soviet Socialist Republics which is adjacent to the Baltic Sea should pass from a point on the eastern shore of the Bay of Danzig to the east, north of Braunsberg-Goldap, to the meeting point of the frontiers of Lithuania, the Polish Republic and East Prussia.

The Conference has agreed in principle to the proposal of the Soviet Government concerning the ultimate transfer to the Soviet Union of the City of Koenigsberg and the area adjacent to it as described above subject to expert examination of the actual frontier.

The President of the United States and the British Prime Minister have declared that they will support the proposal of the Conference at the forthcoming peace settlement.

VI. WAR CRIMINALS

The Three Governments have taken note of the discussions which have been proceeding in recent weeks in London between British, United States, Soviet and French representatives with a view to reaching agreement on the methods of trial of those major war criminals whose crimes under the Moscow Declaration of October, 1943 have no particular geographical localization. The Three Governments reaffirm their intention to bring these criminals to swift and sure justice. They hope that the negotiations in London will result in speedy agreement being reached for this purpose, and they regard it as a matter of great importance that the trial of these major criminals should begin at the earliest possible date. The first list of defendants will be published before 1st September.

[. . .]

VIII. POLAND

A. DECLARATION

We have taken note with pleasure of the agreement reached among representative Poles from Poland and abroad which has made possible the formation, in accordance with the decisions reached at the Crimea Conference, of a Polish Provisional Government of National Unity recognized by the Three Powers. The establishment by the British and United States Governments of diplomatic relations with the Polish Provisional Government of National Unity has resulted in the withdrawal of their recognition from the former Polish Government in London, which no longer exists.

The British and United States Governments have taken measures to protect the interest of the Polish Provisional Government of National Unity as the recognized government of the Polish State in the property belonging to the Polish State located in their territories and under their control, whatever the form of this property may be. They have further taken measures to prevent alienation to third parties of such property. All proper facilities will be given to the Polish Provisional Government of National Unity for the exercise of the ordinary legal remedies for the recovery of any property belonging to the Polish State which may have been wrongfully alienated.

The Three Powers are anxious to assist the Polish Provisional Government of National Unity in facilitating the return to Poland as soon as practicable of all Poles abroad who wish to go, including members of the Polish Armed Forces and the Merchant Marine. They expect that those Poles who return home shall be accorded personal and property rights on the same basis as all Polish citizens.

The Three Powers note that the Polish Provisional Government of National Unity, in accordance with the decisions of the Crimea Conference, has agreed to the holding of free and unfettered elections as soon as possible on the basis of universal suffrage and secret ballot in which all democratic and anti-Nazi parties shall have the right to take part and to put forward candidates, and that representatives of the Allied press shall enjoy full freedom to report to the world upon developments in Poland before and during the elections.

B. WESTERN FRONTIER OF POLAND

In conformity with the agreement on Poland reached at the Crimea Conference the three Heads of Government have sought the opinion of the Polish Provisional Government of National Unity in regard to the accession of territory in the north 'end west which Poland should receive. The President of the National Council of Poland and members of the Polish Provisional Government of National Unity have been received at the Conference and have fully presented their views. The three Heads of Government reaffirm their opinion that the final delimitation of the western frontier of Poland should await the peace settlement.

The three Heads of Government agree that, pending the final determination of Poland's western frontier, the former German territories cast of a line running from the Baltic Sea immediately west of Swinamunde, and thence along the Oder River to the confluence of the western Neisse River and along the Western Neisse to the Czechoslovak frontier, including that portion of East Prussia not placed under the administration of the Union of Soviet Socialist Republics in accordance with the understanding reached at this conference and including the area of the former free city of Danzig, shall be under the administration of the Polish State and for such purposes should not be considered as part of the Soviet zone of occupation in Germany.

[...]

XII. ORDERLY TRANSFER OF GERMAN POPULATIONS

The Three Governments, having considered the question in all its aspects, recognize that the transfer to Germany of German populations, or elements thereof, remaining in Poland, Czechoslovakia and Hungary, will have to be undertaken. They agree that any transfers that take place should be effected in an orderly and humane manner.

Since the influx of a large number of Germans into Germany would increase the burden already resting on the occupying authorities, they consider that the Control Council in Germany should in the first instance examine the problem, with special regard to the question of the equitable distribution of these Germans among the several zones of occupation. They are accordingly instructing their respective representatives on the Control Council to report to their Governments as soon as possible the extent to which such persons have already entered Germany from Poland, Czechoslovakia and Hungary, to submit an estimate of the time and rate at which further transfers could be carried out having regard to the present situation in Germany.

The Czechoslovak Government, the Polish Provisional Government and the Control Council in Hungary are at the same time being informed of the above and are being requested meanwhile to suspend further expulsions pending an examination by the Governments concerned of the report from their representatives on the Control Council.

[...]

XIX. DIRECTIVES TO MILITARY COMMANDERS ON ALLIED CONTROL COUNCIL FOR GERMANY

The Three Governments agreed that each would send a directive to its representative on the Control Council for Germany informing him of all decisions of the Conference affecting matters within the scope of his duties.

[...]

BASIC LAW OF THE FEDERAL REPUBLIC OF GERMANY, 23 MAY 1949 (GRUNDGESETZ)

PREAMBLE

[...]
The entire German people is called upon to achieve the unity and freedom of Germany in free self-determination.

[...]

ARTICLE 23

For the time being, this Basic Law applies in the territory of the states of Baden, Bavaria, Bremen, Greater Berlin, Hamburg, Hesse, Lower Saxony, North-Rhine Westphalia, Rhineland-Palatine, Schleswig-Holstein, Württemberg-Baden and Württemberg-Hohenzollern. In other parts of Germany it will become valid upon their accession.

[. . .]

ARTICLE 116

(1) A German in the meaning of this Basic Law is, except for other legal stipulations, whoever has German citizenship or lived as a refugee or expellee of ethnic German origin or as his spouse or descendant on the territory of German empire as of 31 December 1937.

[. . .]

THE CONSTITUTION OF THE GERMAN DEMOCRATIC REPUBLIC, 7 OCTOBER 1949

ARTICLE 1

Germany is an indivisible democratic republic. . . . The republic determines all matters which are essential for the existence and development of the German people as a whole. . . . There is only one German citizenship.

THE CONSTITUTION OF THE GERMAN DEMOCRATIC REPUBLIC, 8 APRIL 1968

ARTICLE 1

The German Democratic Republic is a socialist state of the German nation.

THE CONSTITUTION OF THE GERMAN DEMOCRATIC REPUBLIC, 7 OCTOBER 1974

ARTICLE 1

The German Democratic Republic is a socialist state of the workers and farmers.

GENERAL TREATY ON GERMANY, 23 OCTOBER 1954 (GENERALVERTRAG)

ARTICLE 1

(1) Upon entering into force of this treaty, the United States of America, the United Kingdom of Great Britain and Northern Ireland and the French Republic [. . .] will end the occupation regime in the Federal

Republic, repeal the Occupation Statute and dissolve the Allied High Commission and the offices of the State Commissioners in the Federal Republic.

(2) The Federal Republic will thereby have the full powers of a sovereign state over its internal and external affairs.

[. . .]

ARTICLE 7

(1) The signatory states agree that a significant goal of their joint efforts is a settlement for the whole of Germany by means of a peace treaty freely entered into by Germany and its former opponents . . . They also agree that a final determination of Germany's borders must be postponed until such a settlement is achieved.

TREATY BETWEEN THE GERMAN DEMOCRATIC REPUBLIC AND THE UNION OF SOCIALIST SOVIET REPUBLICS, 20 SEPTEMBER 1955

The President of the German Democratic Republic and the Presidium of the Supreme Soviet of the USSR:

In view of the new situation which has arisen owing to the coming into force of the Paris Agreements of 1954; Convinced that the joint efforts of the German Democratic Republic and the Soviet Union to cooperate in the preservation and consolidation of peace and security in Europe, to restore the unity of Germany as a peace-loving and democratic state and to bring about a peace settlement with Germany are in accordance with the interest of the German and Soviet peoples and with the interests of the other European peoples; Taking into consideration the obligations of the German Democratic Republic and the Soviet Union under international agreements that concern Germany as a whole; Have resolved to conclude this treaty.

The high contracting parties solemnly confirm that the relations between them are based on complete equality of rights, mutual respect of their sovereignty and non-interference in domestic affairs.

In accordance with this, the German Democratic Republic is free to decide on questions of its internal and foreign policies, including those pertaining to its relations with the Federal Republic of Germany . . .

[. . .]

There is agreement between the high contracting parties that it is their aim to bring about a peaceful settlement for the whole of Germany by negotiation. In accordance with this, they will make the necessary efforts towards a settlement through a peace treaty and towards the restoration of the unity of Germany on a peaceful and democratic basis.

TREATY BETWEEN THE FEDERAL REPUBLIC OF GERMANY AND THE UNION OF SOCIALIST SOVIET REPUBLICS OF 12 AUGUST 1970

[...]

ARTICLE 3

... the Federal Republic of Germany and the Union of Socialist Soviet Republics share the opinion that peace in Europe can only be maintained if nobody disturbs the existing boundaries.

- They undertake to respect without restriction the territorial integrity of all states in Europe within their existing boundaries;

- they declare that they have no territorial claims against anybody, nor will they make any such claims in the future;

- they regard, now and in the future, the boundaries of all states in Europe as inviolable as they were on the day this treaty was signed, including the Oder-Neisse line, which forms the Western border of the People's Republic of Poland, and the boundary between the Federal Republic of Germany and the German Democratic Republic.

LETTER ON GERMAN UNITY OF 12 AUGUST 1970

[...]

In connection with the signature today of the Treaty between the Federal Republic of Germany and the Union of Socialist Soviet Republics, the government of the Federal Republic of Germany has the honour of declaring that this treaty does not conflict with the political goal of the Federal Republic of Germany to work for a state of peace in Europe in which the German nation will achieve its unity in free self-determination.

[...]

TREATY BETWEEN THE FEDERAL REPUBLIC OF GERMANY AND THE PEOPLE'S REPUBLIC OF POLAND CONCERNING THE BASIS FOR THE NORMALISATION OF THEIR MUTUAL RELATIONS, 7 DECEMBER 1970

The Federal Republic of Germany and the People's Republic of Poland

CONSIDERING that more than 25 years have passed since the end of the Second World War of which Poland became the first victim and which inflicted great suffering on the peoples of Europe;

CONSCIOUS that since then a new generation has grown up in both countries for which a peaceful future needs to be secured;

DESIRING to establish durable foundations for peaceful coexistence and the development of normal and good relations between them;

ANXIOUS to strengthen peace and security in Europe;

AWARE that the inviolability of frontiers and respect for the territorial integrity and sovereignty of all states in Europe within their present boundaries are a basic condition for peace;

HAVE AGREED as follows:

ARTICLE 1

(1) The Federal Republic of Germany and the People's Republic of Poland declare in mutual agreement that the existing boundary line the course of which was laid down in Article XI of the Decisions of the Potsdam Conference of 2 August 1945 . . . shall constitute the Western state border of the People's Republic of Poland.

(2) They reaffirm the inviolability of their existing frontiers now and in the future and declare to respect each other's territorial integrity without restrictions.

(3) They declare that they have no territorial claims against each other and that they will not make any such claims in the future.

[. . .]

ARTICLE IV
This treaty shall not affect any bilateral or multilateral international arrangements previously concluded by either contracting party or concerning them.

[. . .]

BASIC TREATY BETWEEN THE FEDERAL REPUBLIC OF GERMANY AND THE GERMAN DEMOCRATIC REPUBLIC, 21 DECEMBER 1972

[. . .]

ARTICLE 1
The Federal Republic of Germany and the German Democratic Republic shall develop normal good neighbourly relations with each other on the basis of equal rights.

[. . .]

ARTICLE 3
In accordance with the Charter of the United Nations, the Federal Republic

of Germany and the German Democratic Republic . . . reaffirm the inviolability now and in the future of the boundary existing between them and undertake to respect fully each other's territorial integrity.

ARTICLE 4
The Federal Republic of Germany and the German Democratic Republic proceed on the assumption that neither of the two states can the other in the international arena or act on its behalf.

[. . .]

ARTICLE 6
The Federal Republic of Germany and the German Democratic Republic proceed on the principle that the sovereign jurisdiction of each of the two states is confined to its own territory. They respect each other's independence and autonomy in their domestic and foreign affairs.

[. . .]

ARTICLE 9
The Federal Republic of Germany and the German Democratic Republic agree that the present treaty shall not affect the bilateral and multilateral international treaties already concluded by them or pertaining to them.

LETTER FROM THE GOVERNMENT OF THE FEDERAL REPUBLIC OF GERMANY TO THE GOVERNMENT OF THE GERMAN DEMOCRATIC REPUBLIC ON GERMAN UNITY, 21 DECEMBER 1972

In connection with the signing of the Treaty on the Basis of the Relations between the Federal Republic of Germany and the German Democratic Republic, the Government of the Federal Republic of Germany has the honour of declaring that this treaty does not conflict with the political aim of the Federal Republic of Germany to work towards a state of peace in Europe in which the German people will regain its unity through free self-determination.

TREATY BETWEEN THE FEDERAL REPUBLIC OF GERMANY AND THE CZECHOSLOVAK SOCIALIST REPUBLIC, 11 DECEMBER 1973

The Federal Republic of Germany and the Czechoslovak Socialist Republic;

[. . .]

ACKNOWLEDGING that that the Munich Agreement of 29 September 1938 was forced upon the Czechoslovak Republic by the national-socialist regime under threat of force;

[. . .]

ARTICLE I
The Federal Republic of Germany and the Czechoslovak Socialist Republic consider the Munich Agreement of 29 September 1938 in as much as it concerns their mutual relations . . . as null and void.

ARTICLE II
(1) This treaty shall not affect the legal effects on natural or legal persons of the law as applied between 30 September 1938 and 9 May 1945. This provision shall exclude the effects of measures which both contracting parties deem to be void owing to their incompatibility with the fundamental principles of justice.

(2) This treaty shall not affect the nationality of living or deceased persons ensuing from the legal system of either of the two contracting parties.

(3) This treaty, together with the declarations on the Munich Agreement, shall not constitute any legal basis for material claims by the Czechoslovak Socialist Republic and its natural and legal persons.

ARTICLE 4
(1) . . . the Federal Republic of Germany and the Czechoslovak Socialist Republic reaffirm the inviolability of their common border now and in the future and declare to respect each other's territorial integrity without restrictions.

(2) They declare that they have no territorial claims against each other and that they will not make any such claims in the future.

[. . .]

JOINT COMMUNIQUÉ BY ERICH HONECKER AND HELMUT KOHL, 8 SEPTEMBER 1987

[. . .]

In consideration of the existing circumstances and despite differences of opinion on fundamental issues, including the national question, it is the intention of both states, in the spirit of the Basic Treaty, to devlop normal good neighbourly relations on the basis of equal rights and to continue to take advantage of all opportunities for cooperation offered by the treaty.

[. . .]

DECLARATION BY THE VOLKSKAMMER OF THE GERMAN DEMOCRATIC REPUBLIC ON GERMAN HISTORY, 12 APRIL 1990

We, the first freely elected representatives of the GERMAN DEMOCRATIC REPUBLIC, acknowledge the responsibility of Germans in the GERMAN DEMOCRATIC REPUBLIC for their history and their future and unanimously declare to the world:

During the period of Nazi rule, Germans inflicted immeasurable suffering upon the peoples of the world. Nationalism and racial chauvinism led to genocide, particularly of Jews throughout Europe, of the peoples of the Soviet Union, of the Polish people and of Sinti and Roma.

We must not permit this guilt to be forgotten. From it we derive our responsibility for the future.

[. . .]

In this context, we happily reconfirm our unconditional recognition of the borders of Germany with all neighbouring states as they were established after the Second World War.

In particular the Polish state should know that its right to exist in secure borders will never be challenged by any territorial claims from Germany now or in the future.

We confirm the inviolability of the Oder-Neisse border with the Republic of Poland as the foundation of the peaceful coexistence of our peoples in a common European house.

This will be reaffirmed by treaty by a future all-German parliament.

(SIMULTANEOUS) DECLARATION OF THE BUNDESTAG OF THE FEDERAL REPUBLIC OF GERMANY (AND THE VOLKSKAMMER OF THE GERMAN DEMOCRATIC REPUBLIC) ON THE POLISH BORDER, 21 JUNE 1990

The German Bundestag,

[. . .]

In the expectation that the freely elected Volkskammer of the German Democratic Republic will simultaneously pass an identical resolution, expresses its resolve that the border between a united Germany and the Republic of Poland be finally confirmed as follows by means of a treaty binding under international law:

The border between the united Germany and the Republic of Poland is established under the Agreement between the German Democratic Republic and the People's Republic of Poland on the Designation of the Established Existing German-Polish State Border of 6 July 1950 as well as supplements executing and extending this agreement [. . .] as well as the Treaty between the Federal Republic of Germany and the People's Republic of Poland on the Normalization of Their Mutual Relations of 7 December 1970.

Both Sides assure the inviolability of the present border between their two states, now and in the future, and obligate themselves to mutual and unconditional respect for sovereignty and territorial integrity.

Each side declares that it has no territorial claims on the other and that no such claims will be raised in the future.

[. . .]

TREATY BETWEEN THE FEDERAL REPUBLIC OF GERMANY AND THE GERMAN DEMOCRATIC REPUBLIC ON THE ESTABLISHMENT OF THE UNITY OF GERMANY, 31 AUGUST 1990

The Federal Republic of Germany and the German Democratic Republic,

RESOLVED to achieve in free self-determination the unity of Germany in peace and freedom as an equal partner in the community of nations;

MINDFUL of the desire of the people in both parts of Germany to live together in peace and freedom in a democratic and social federal state governed by the rule of law;

[. . .]

AWARE that the inviolability of borders and of the territorial integrity sovereignty of all states in Europe within their frontiers constitutes a fundamental condition for peace;

HAVE AGREED to conclude a Treaty on the Establishment of German Unity, containing the following provisions:

CHAPTER I: Effect of Accession

ARTICLE 1: Länder

(1) Upon the accession of the German Democratic Republic to the Federal Republic of Germany in accordance with Article 23 of the Basic Law taking effect on 3 October 1990 the Länder of Brandenburg, Mecklenburg-Western Pommerania, Saxony, Saxony-Anhalt and Thuringia shall become Länder of the Federal Republic of Germany.

(2) The 23 boroughs of Berlin shall form the Land Berlin.

[...]

CHAPTER II: Basic Law

ARTICLE 3: Entry into Force of the Basic Law
Upon the accession taking effect, the Basic Law of the Federal Republic
of Germany . . . shall enter into force in the Länder of Brandenburg,
Mecklenburg-Western Pommerania, Saxony, Saxony-Anhalt and Thuringia
and in that part of the Land Berlin where it has not been valid today . . .

ARTICLE 4: Amendments to the Basic Law Resulting from Accession

[...]

(2) Article 23 shall be repealed.

TREATY ON THE FINAL SETTLEMENT WITH RESPECT TO GERMANY, 12 SEPTEMBER 1990

The Federal Republic of Germany, the German Democratic Republic, the
French Republic, the Union of Socialist Soviet Republics, the United Kingdom of Great Britain and Northern Ireland and the United States of America,

CONSCIOUS of the fact that their peoples have been living together in
peace since 1945;

MINDFUL of the recent historic changes in Europe which make it possible
to overcome the division of the continent;

HAVING REGARD to the rights and responsibilities of the Four Powers
relating to Berlin and Germany as a whole and the corresponding war-time
and post-war agreements and decisions of the Four Powers;

[...]

WELCOMING the fact that the German people, freely exercising their right
of self-determination, have expressed their will to bring about the unity of
Germany as a state so that they will be able to serve the peace of the world
as an equal and sovereign partner in a united Europe;

CONVINCED that the unification of Germany as a state with definite borders is a significant contribution to the peace and stability in Europe;

INTENDING to conclude the final settlement with respect to Germany;

RECOGNISING that thereby, and with the unification of Germany as a
democratic and peaceful state, the rights and responsibilities of the Four
Powers relating to Berlin and Germany as a whole lose their function;

[...]

HAVE AGREED as follows:

ARTICLE 1

(1) The united Germany shall comprise the territory of the Federal Republic of Germany, the German Democratic Republic and the whole of Berlin. Its external borders shall be the borders of the Federal Republic of Germany and the German Democratic Republic and shall be definitive from the date on which the present treaty enters into force.

[. . .]

(2) The united Germany and the Republic of Poland shall confirm the existing border between them in a treaty that is binding under international law.

(3) The united Germany has no territorial claims whatsoever against other states and shall not assert any in the future.

[. . .]

ARTICLE 7

(1) The French Republic, the Union of Socialist Soviet Republics, the United Kingdom of Great Britain and Northern Ireland and the United States of America hereby terminate their rights and responsibilities relating to Berlin and Germany as a whole. As a result, the corresponding quadripartite agreements, decisions and practices are terminated and all related Four Power institutions are dissolved.

(2) The united Germany shall have accordingly full sovereignty over its internal and external affairs.

[. . .]

TREATY BETWEEN THE FEDERAL REPUBLIC OF GERMANY AND THE REPUBLIC OF POLAND ON THE CONFIRMATION OF THEIR EXISTING BORDER, 14 NOVEMBER 1990

Federal Republic of Germany and the Republic of Poland—

DESIRING to develop their future relations in accordance with international law, especially the Charter of the United Nations, and with the Final Act of the Helsinki Conference on Security and Cooperation in Europe and the documents of its follow-up conferences;

RESOLVED to make a joint contribution towards the building of European peace order . . .

DEEPLY CONVINCED that the unification of Germany as a state with final borders is a significant contribution to the European peace order;

CONSIDERING the conclusion on 12 September 1990 of the Treaty on the Final Settlement with Regard to Germany;

AWARE that 45 years have passed since the end of the Second World War and that the immense suffering caused by this war, especially also including the loss of homeland by many Germans and Poles through expulsion and resettlement, remains a warning and a challenge to develop peaceful relations between the two peoples and states;

WISHING to establish though the development of their relations solid foundations for friendly coexistence and to continue the politics of permanent understanding and reconciliation between Germans and Poles—

HAVE DECIDED as follows:

ARTICLE 1
The contracting parties confirm the border between them, the demarcation of which is regulated according to the Agreement between the German Democratic Republic and the People's Republic of Poland on the Designation of the Established Existing German-Polish State Border of 6 July 1950 as well as supplements executing and extending this agreement [. . .] as well as the Treaty between the Federal Republic of Germany and the People's Republic of Poland on the Normalization of Their Mutual Relations of 7 December 1970.

ARTICLE 2
The contracting parties declare that the existing border between them is inviolable now and in the future and obligate themselves to mutual and unconditional respect for sovereignty and territorial integrity.

ARTICLE 3
The contracting parties declare that none of them has any territorial claims towards the other and that no such claims will be made in the future.

ARTICLE 4
(1) This treaty requires ratification. Ratification documents will be exchanged as soon as possible in Bonn.

(2) The Treaty enters into force upon exchange of the ratification documents.

[. . .]

TREATY BETWEEN THE FEDERAL REPUBLIC OF GERMANY AND THE REPUBLIC OF POLAND ON GOOD NEIGHBORLY RELATIONS AND FRIENDLY COOPERATION, 17 JUNE 1991

The Federal Republic of Germany and the Republic of Poland—

DESIRING to achieve closure on the painful chapters of the past and re-solved to continue the good traditions and friendly coexistence in the cen-tury-old history of Germany and Poland;

CONSIDERING the historic changes in Europe, especially the establishment of German unity and the fundamental political, economic and social changes in Poland;

[. . .]

DEEPLY CONVINCED that by realising the long-standing wish of their two peoples for understanding and reconciliation they will make a signifi-cant contribution towards the preservation of peace in Europe;

[. . .]

AWARE of the importance that the membership of the Federal Republic of Germany in the European Community and the political and economic ap-proximation of the Republic of Poland to the European Community have for the future relations of the two states;

[. . .]

HONOURING the Treaty between the Federal Republic of Germany and the Republic of Poland on the Confirmation of Their Existing Border of 14 November 1990—

HAVE AGREED as follows:

ARTICLE 1
(1) The contracting parties will develop their relations in the spirit of good neighbourhood and friendship. [. . .]
(2) The contracting parties desire the creation of a Europe in which hu-man rights and fundamental liberties are respected and in which bor-ders lose their separating character through the overcoming of economic and social disparities.

ARTICLE 2

The contracting parties acknowledge that the development of their relations . . . will be guided by the following principles:

[. . .]

They consider minorities and groups of equal standing as natural bridges between the German and the Polish people and are optimistic that these minorities and groups will make a valuable contribution to the life of their societies.

[. . .]

ARTICLE 5

(1) The contracting parties affirm that they will not resort to the threat or use of force against the territorial integrity or political independence of the respective other contracting party . . .

ARTICLE 8

(1) The contracting parties consider the aim of European unity on the basis of human rights, democracy and the rule of law to be of highest importance and will work towards the achievement of such unity.

[. . .]

(3) The Federal Republic of Germany is favourably disposed towards the perspective of the Republic of Poland's accession to the European Community once the necessary conditions have been met.

ARTICLE 20

(1) The members of the German minority in Poland, that is, individuals holding Polish citizenship and of German descent or practising German language, culture and traditions, as well as individuals holding German citizenship and of Polish descent or practising Polish language, culture and traditions have the right, individually or jointly with other members of their group, to express, preserve and develop further their ethnic, cultural, linguistic and religious identity, free of any attempts to be assimilated against their will. They have the right to exercise effectively and in full their human rights and fundamental liberties without discrimination and in full equality before the law.

(2) The contracting parties implement the rights and obligations of the international standard for minorities, especially according to the general United Nations Declaration on Human Rights of 10 December 1948, the European Convention on Human Rights and Fundamental Liberties of 4 November 1950, the International Covenant on the Elimination of All Forms of Racial Discrimination of 7 March 1966, the International Covenant on the Civil and Political Rights of 16 December 1966, the Final Act of the Helsinki Conference on 1 August 1975, the Document of the Copenhagen Meeting on the Human Dimensions of the Conference on Security and Cooperation in Europe of 29 June 1990 and the Charter of Paris for a New Europe of 21 November 1990.

(3) The contracting parties declare that the individuals mentioned in Paragraph 1 in particular have the right, individually or jointly with other members of their group

- to use their mother tongue freely in public and in private and to disseminate, exchange and receive information in it;

- to establish and maintain their own educational, cultural and religious institutions, organisations and associations, which may seek voluntary donations of a financial or other kind in accordance with national law and which must have equal opportunity to access the media of their region,
- to express and practise their religion, including the acquisition and possession of religious material, and to conduct religious classes in their mother tongue,
- to establish and maintain unhindered contacts within the country and across borders with citizens of other states with whom they share a common ethnic or national origin, a common cultural heritage or religious conviction,
- to keep their first and family names in their mother tongue,
- to establish and maintain organisations and associations in their country and to join international non-governmental organisations,
- to seek, as everyone else, effective legal means to realise their rights in accordance with national law.

(4) The contracting parties affirm that the membership in groups mentioned in Paragraph 1 is an individual decision of a person which must not be used to his or her disadvantage.

ARTICLE 21

(1) The contracting parties will protect the ethnic, cultural, linguistic and religious identity of the groups mentioned in Article 20.1 and create conditions for the promotion of this identity.

[. . .]

ARTICLE 22

(1) None of the obligations entered into in Articles 20 and 21 must be interpreted in a way that it would create the right to engage in any activity or commit any act in contravention of the aims and principles of the Charter of the United Nations, or other obligations of international law of the provisions of the Final Act of the Helsinki Conference, including the principle of the territorial integrity of states.

(2) Every member of a group mentioned in Article 20.1 in the Republic of Poland or the Federal Republic of Germany is, according to the above provisions, required to be loyal to its respective state as any other citizen by complying with the obligations derived from the laws of this state.

[. . .]

GERMAN-CZECH DECLARATION ON MUTUAL RELATIONS AND THEIR FUTURE DEVELOPMENT

The Governments of the Federal Republic of Germany and the Czech Republic, Recalling the Treaty of 27 February 1992 on Good-neighbourliness and Friendly Cooperation between the Federal Republic of Germany and the Czech and Slovak Federal Republic with which Germans and Czechs reached out to each other, Mindful of the long history of fruitful and peaceful, good-neighborly relations between Germans and Czechs during which a rich and continuing cultural heritage was created, Convinced that injustice inflicted in the past cannot be undone but at best alleviated, and that in doing so no new injustice must arise, Aware that the Federal Republic of Germany strongly supports the Czech Republic's accession to the European Union and the North Atlantic Alliance because it is convinced that this is in their common interest, Affirming that trust and openness in their mutual relations is the prerequisite for lasting and future-oriented reconciliation, jointly declare the following:

I
Both sides are aware of their obligation and responsibility to further develop German-Czech relations in a spirit of good-neighborliness and partnership, thus helping to shape the integrating Europe.

The Federal Republic of Germany and Czech Republic today share common democratic values, respect human rights, fundamental freedoms and the norms of international law, and are committed to the principles of the rule of law and to a policy of peace. On this basis they are determined to cooperate closely and in a spirit of friendship in all fields of importance for their mutual relations.

At the same time both sides are aware that their common path to the future requires a clear statement regarding their past which must not fail to recognize cause and effect in the sequence of events.

II
The German side acknowledges Germany's responsibility for its role in a historical development which led to the 1938 Munich Agreement, the flight and forcible expulsion of people from the Czech border area and the forcible breakup and occupation of the Czechoslovak Republic.

It regrets the suffering and injustice inflicted upon the Czech people through National Socialist crimes committed by Germans. The German side pays tribute to the victims of National Socialist tyranny and to those who resisted it.

The German side is also conscious of the fact that the National Socialist policy of violence towards the Czech people helped to prepare the ground for post-war flight, forcible expulsion and forced resettlement.

III

The Czech side regrets that, by the forcible expulsion and forced resettlement of Sudeten Germans from the former Czechoslovakia after the war as well as by the expropriation and deprivation of citizenship, much suffering and injustice was inflicted upon innocent people, also in view of the fact that guilt was attributed collectively. It particularly regrets the excesses which were contrary to elementary humanitarian principles as well as legal norms existing at that time, and it furthermore regrets that Law No. 115 of 8 May 1946 made it possible to regard these excesses as not being illegal and that in consequence these acts were not punished.

IV

Both sides agree that injustice inflicted in the past belongs in the past, and will therefore orient their relations towards the future. Precisely because they remain conscious of the tragic chapters of their history, they are determined to continue to give priority to understanding and mutual agreement in the development of their relations, while each side remains committed to its legal system and respects the fact that the other side has a different legal position. Both sides therefore declare that they will not burden their relations with political and legal issues which stem from the past.

V

Both sides reaffirm their obligations arising from Articles 20 and 21 of the Treaty of 27 February 1992 on Good-neighborliness and Friendly Cooperation, in which the rights of the members of the German minority in the Czech Republic and of persons of Czech descent in the Federal Republic of Germany are set out in detail.

Both sides are aware that this minority and these persons play an important role in mutual relations and state that their promotion continues to be in their common interest.

VI

Both sides are convinced that the Czech Republic's accession to the European Union and freedom of movement in this area will further facilitate the good-neighbourly relations of Germans and Czechs.

In this connection they express their satisfaction that, due to the Europe Agreement on Association between the Czech Republic and the European Communities and their Member States, substantial progress has been achieved in the field of economic cooperation, including the possibilities of self-employment and business undertakings in accordance with Article 45 of that Agreement.

Both sides are prepared, within the scope of their applicable laws and regulations, to pay special consideration to humanitarian and other concerns, especially family relationships and ties as well as other bonds, in examining applications for residence and access to the labour market.

VII

Both sides will set up a German-Czech Future Fund. The German side declares its willingness to make available the sum of DM 140 million for this Fund. The Czech side, for its part, declares its willingness to make available the sum of Kc 440 million for this Fund. Both sides will conclude a separate arrangement on the joint administration of this Fund.

This Joint Fund will be used to finance projects of mutual interest (such as youth encounter, care for the elderly, the building and operation of sanatoria, the preservation and restoration of monuments and cemeteries, the promotion of minorities, partnership projects, German-Czech discussion fora, joint scientific and environmental projects, language teaching, cross-border cooperation).

The German side acknowledges its obligation and responsibility towards all those who fell victim to National Socialist violence. Therefore the projects in question are to especially benefit victims of National Socialist violence.

VIII

Both sides agree that the historical development of relations between Germans and Czechs, particularly during the first half of the 20th century, requires joint research, and therefore endorse the continuation of the successful work of the German-Czech Commission of Historians.

At the same time both sides consider the preservation and fostering of the cultural heritage linking Germans and Czechs to be an important step towards building a bridge to the future.

Both sides agree to set up a German-Czech Discussion Forum, which is to be promoted in particular from the German-Czech Future Fund, and in which, under the auspices of both Governments and with the participation of all those interested in close and cordial German-Czech partnership, German-Czech dialogue is to be fostered.

THE DECREES OF THE PRESIDENT OF THE REPUBLIC FROM THE YEARS 1940–1945

(Submission by the Czech Republic to the European Parliament, 3 April 2002)

(1) LEGAL ASPECTS

The Decrees of the President of the Republic were issued in the period between the establishment of the Provisional Constitutional Order of the Czechoslovak Republic in 1940 and the constituent session of the Provisional National Assembly on 28 October 1945. A total of 143 decrees (including 43 decrees issued during the wartime occupation of Czechoslovakia) were issued to deal with numerous problems of political, economic, cultural and social nature which faced the authorities of the Provisional Constitutional Order during the existence of the exiled Government in London and in the period when the Government already had a seat in the territory of the Czechoslovak Republic, until the reestablishment of the Czechoslovak legislative body in the form of the Provisional National Assembly.

It is to be noted that, although these decrees in no case deal with the transfer of Sudeten German population, they have been the targets of attacks connecting them with the transfer based on Article XIII of the Protocol of the Proceedings of the Potsdam Conference. At present, the decrees cannot constitute any new legal relations—they have either been replaced by new regulations and ceased to apply, or have fulfilled their original purpose and it is thus unnecessary and even impossible to apply them; however, the validity of legal relations based upon them remains intact.

The criticism of the Sudeten Germans is focused on post-war decrees, i.e. Decree No. 16/1945 of 19 June 1945 on the Punishment of Nazi Criminals and their Accomplices and concerning Extraordinary People's Courts (know as the "Great Retributions Decree") and Decree No. 138/1945 of 27 October 1945 on the Punishment of Certain Offences against the National Honour (known as the "Small Retributions Decree"), Decree No. 33/1945 of 2 August 1945 on the Citizenship of Persons of German and Hungarian nationality and the decrees that regulated the confiscation and nationalization of the properties of persons of German nationality, including:

- Decree No. 5/1945 of 19 May 1945 on the Invalidity of Certain Property-related Acts Effected in the Period of "Non-freedom" and concerning the National Administration of the Properties of Germans, Hungarians, Traitors and Collaborators and Certain Organizations and Institutes,

This Decree was followed by:

- Decree No. 12/1945 of 21 June 1945 on the Confiscation and Expedited Distribution of Agricultural Properties of Germans, Hungarians, as well as Traitors and Enemies of the Czech and Slovak Nations,

- Decree No. 108/1945 of 25 October 1945 on the Confiscation of Enemy Property and the National Renewal Funds,

- Decree No. 50/1945 of 11 August 1945 on Measures concerning Film Industry, and

- Decrees No. 100-103/1945 of 24 October 1945 on the Nationalization of Mines and Certain Industrial Enterprises; on the Nationalization of Certain Food Industry Enterprises; on the Nationalization of Joint-stock Banks; and on the Nationalization of Private Insurance Companies.

An act determinative for the post-war legal order was Constitutional Decree No. 11 of 3 August 1944 on the Restoration of Legal Order which expresses the continuity of Czechoslovak legislation.

A study of the decrees requires a differentiated approach; some of them are no more valid and thus have no legal effect, others have retained legal effect but no longer establish new legal relations, i.e., no longer have a constitutive character. A factor determinative for their legal qualification is the opinion of the Constitutional Court of the Czech Republic stated in Finding No. 55/1995 of 8 March 1995 which is binding on all authorities and persons.

An objection against the validity of the Decrees is that they violated the legal principles of civilized European societies and therefore must be considered not as acts of law but acts of violence inconsistent with the present state of human rights.

In response to this objection, the Constitutional Court concluded that ". . . although what emerges from the past must in terms of values in principle stand up face to face to the present times, this assessment of the history cannot be a judgement of the past by the present. In other words, the order of the past cannot be put before the court ruling according to the present order, which being enlightened by subsequent experiences, draws on these experiences and looks upon and judges many events with the hindsight."Accordingly, the post-war events, such as the confiscation of enemy property without compensation, cannot be judged in the light of the constitution and the Human Rights Conventions adopted at a later stage and valid in the present.

The vast majority of the decrees dealt with issues limited in time and at present is from the political or legal point of view of little interest.

The legislation adopted in exile, just as the immediate post-war legislation of the liberated Czechoslovak state, at the present concern what is in essence an already closed circle of problems and issues intimately connected with the wartime events and the economic renewal of the country. In addition, the normative acts from this period accomplished their purposes in the immediate post-war period (they were "consumed"), so that from a contemporary perspective they no longer have any current significance and already lack any further constitutive character. That is why, in the given situation, its inconsistency with constitutional acts or international treaties cannot be reviewed today.

Any references to the decrees in the present decisions of Czech courts and other authorities are purely declaratory and cannot establish new legal relations.

(2) COMPATIBILITY WITH THE ACQUIS COMMUNAUTAIRE

The Treaty establishing the European Community (EC Treaty) does not regulate expropriations, the duration of property rights established by annulled laws, nor issues related to restitution and privatization. These problems fall within the sovereign jurisdiction of each Member State. The Community law "in no way prejudices the rules governing the system of property ownership in the Member States" (Article 295 of the EC Treaty) because, in principle, these rules are perceived as a significant element of their economic and social systems and national identity, as evidenced by the case-law of the European Court of Justice. The decision whether the State should reserve the ownership of certain assets, restrict the property rights of individuals or even deprive individuals of such rights remains at the discretion of the national authorities, insofar as it does not affect the matters regulated by the Community law to such a degree that it could jeopardize the attainment of the objectives of the EC Treaty. For example, industry-wide nationalization of manufacturing and commercial enterprises resulting in a State monopoly would be deemed incompatible with the principle of an open market economy with free competition (Article 4 I of the EC Treaty) and would jeopardize the promotion of competitiveness in the internal market which is one of the objectives of the EC Treaty.

Similarly, the method of expropriation falls within the sovereign jurisdiction of each Member State, insofar as it does not jeopardize the attainment of the objectives of the EC Treaty. For example, a national law explicitly or implicitly, effectively or potentially preventing or impeding the acquisition of immovable property by EU citizens or their groups would conflict with the prohibition of any discrimination on grounds of nationality (Article 12), ethnic origin or other grounds (Article 14 I of the EC Treaty), insofar as acquisition of immovable property is strictly necessary for the pursuit of economic activities by EU citizens as self-employed persons in the Czech Republic. In such case, the national law would jeopardize the freedom of establishment safeguarded by the EC Treaty (the "special treatment for foreign nationals on grounds of public order, public security or public health" under Article 46 I of the EC Treaty is to be applied individually, not collectively). On the other hand, its application to EU citizens who are not entrepreneurs would not conflict with the Community law because the free movement of workers (including their families) safeguarded by the EC Treaty is not necessarily tied to the acquisition of immovable property.

The Community law does not concern national citizenship laws. Citizenship of the Union (Articles 17–22 of the EC Treaty) complements and does not replace national citizenship. The right to "move and reside freely within the territory of the Member States" safeguarded by this institute is broader than the freedom of movement in the internal market; however, its exercise is not necessarily tied to the acquisition of immovable property.

The presidential decrees on the confiscation of enemy property applied to properties which were owned by certain persons on a certain date in the year 1945. From a contemporary perspective they no longer have any current significance and lack any further constitutive character, which means that they are not applicable and thus cannot establish new legal relations. The prohibition of discrimination will have no bearing on these decrees.*

This is also the case of the restitution laws introduced in the 1990's which tied the restitution entitlement to citizenship of the Czech Republic, insofar as these laws can be deemed inapplicable (the time-limits for the filing of restitution claims will have expired prior to the Czech Republic's accession to the Union). From the viewpoint of the Community law, the starting date for restitution claims (25 February 1948) is irrelevant because the setting of such time-limits falls within the discretion of each Member State (see above).

According to the agreement reached during accession negotiations with the EU, the statutory ban on acquisition of certain immovable properties (agricultural and forest land and holiday houses) by foreign nationals in the Czech Republic will be subject to transitional arrangements incorporated in the Treaty on the Czech Republic's accession to the European Union. Accordingly, it will be outside the scope of the principle of non-discrimination. After the expiry of the transitional arrangements, the acquisition of immovable property will be fully liberalized.

In the event of a conflict between a national law and a Community law, the Community law prevails irrespective of the effective date of the national law. The *lex posterior* rule thus operates only in favour of Community law. The national law does not lose its validity as part of national legislation (there is no derogation) but becomes inapplicable (at least in legal relations within the Community). This principle of course operates only in respect of national laws which are applicable, i.e. have a constitutive character, on the date of issuance of the respective Community law; it has no bearing on national laws which, although not formally annulled by the Member State, have for any reason already ceased to apply (e.g. when the prescribed obligations have been fulfilled or the legal relations which were the sole purpose of the law have ceased to exist). With regard to the principle of legal certainty which is one of the guiding principles of Community law, this primacy of Community law does not affect legal relations established or terminated prior to the introduction of the respective Community law, on the basis of a national law which is no longer applicable. The effects of this principle of primacy are declared in all treaties concerning the accession of new members to the EU.

Assumption of the obligations arising from the EC Treaty does not have a retroactive derogatory effect in respect of the presidential decrees on confiscation nor in respect of the official measures and procedures applied during the transfer of population, the validity of which is undoubtable. It does not require revision of these regulations, adoption of new ones or interference in the legal relations based on them. The EC Treaty does not provide a basis for assertion of restitution claims.

JOINT PRESS STATEMENT BY MILOŠ ZEMAN AND GÜNTER VERHEUGEN, 11 APRIL 2002

We, the Prime Minister of the Czech Republic and the Member of the European Commission in charge of Enlargement, jointly stress that European integration has always primarily been a political process. Since its very beginning, the key objective has been to overcome old divisions, enmities and prejudices, and to strengthen peace, justice, freedom and security. We must never forget the pain and the suffering caused by the horrors of the Second World War. But the very essence of European integration has been to move forward from there—not to look back in acrimony and continue fighting old battles. In Western Europe this reconciliation has been achieved decades ago. In central Europe, due to the intervening communist period, we suffered a delay but our chance is now.

As we face up to the challenges of the twenty-first century, we need to guard against awakening the demons of nationalism. Elsewhere in Europe we have seen only recently what disasters can happen otherwise.

The Czech-German Declaration of 1997 represents a decisive and historical step in the process of creating close and friendly relations and partnership between the Czech Republic and the Federal Republic of Germany.

The accession of the candidate countries to the European Union is an inseparable part of the overall process of European integration. The basic political objectives of this process can only be fully achieved when the current candidate countries become full member states. We therefore assume our common responsibility for a firm continuation of the European integration process.

Recently there has been much public discussion on some of the Czechoslovak Presidential Decrees of 1945, and on some of the ensuing Czechoslovak legislation of the immediate post-war period. As was the case with measures taken by other European countries at that time, some of these Acts would not pass muster today if judged by current standards—but they belong to history.

The EU Treaty requires Member States and EU institutions to judge applicant states on their present, not their past performance. Any part of a candidate country's legal order that is still capable of producing legal effects cannot escape the scrutiny of EU/EC law.

We are carefully assessing the above-mentioned Acts in this light. So far, the result is that those on citizenship and those on property, by their very nature and content, no longer produce legal effects. We thus maintain our position that these Czechoslovak Presidential Decrees are not part of the Accession Negotiations and should have no bearing on them. With regard to some other Acts further clarifications are being conducted.

There has also been some public discussion on the separate issue of the Czechoslovak restitution legislation and practice since the early 1990s. We are aware that within the scope of application of the EC-Treaty (which contains a concept of European citizenship) discrimination on grounds of nationality is prohibited. Respecting the date of 25 February 1948 set down as legal limit in Czechoslovak restitution legislation, the Czech authorities are conducting a review of their legislation in this light with the aim to put it in line with the EU acquis, if necessary, by the time of the Czech Republic's accession to the EU.

Bibliography

Alcock, Antony Evelyn. *The History of the South Tyrol Question*. London: Joseph, 1970.

Alter, Peter. *The German Question and Europe*. London: Arnold, 2000.

Ayala Lasso, José. "Address to the German Expellees." (Frankfurt Paulskirche, 28 May 1995).

Bauer, Otto. *Die Nationalitätenfrage und die Sozialdemokratie*. Leipzig, 1924.

Bender, Peter. *Episode oder Epoche? Zur Geschichte des geteilten Deutschland*. Munich: Deutscher Taschenbuch Verlag, 1996.

Böhm, Johann. "Address to the Sudeten German Day." (Nuremberg, 11 June 2000).

Brandt, Willy. *Erinnerungen*. Frankfurt am Main: Propyläen, 1989.

Broadbridge, Judith. "The Ethnolinguistic Vitality of Alsatian-speakers in Southern Alsace." In *German Minorities in Europe: Ethnic Identity and Cultural Belonging*, ed. Stefan Wolff. New York and Oxford: Berghahn, 2000.

Brubaker, Rogers. *Citizenship and Nationhood in France and Germany*. Cambridge, Mass.: Harvard University Press, 1992.

Bundestagsdrucksache 13/1116. *Antwort der Bundesregierung auf die kelien Anfrage der Abgeordneten Ulla Jelpke under Gruppe der PDS—Drucksache 13/893—Die Vertriebenenverbände und der angebliche 'Aufruf zum Rassenkampf' gegen Deutsche von polnischer Seite*, Deutscher Bundestag: 12 April 1995.

Bundestagsdrucksache 13/3195. *Beschlußempfehlung und Bericht des Innenaus-schusses (4. Ausschuß)zu der Unterrichtung durch die Bundesregierung— Drucksachen 12/7877, 13/725 Nr. 22—Bericht der Bundesregierung über ihre Maßnahmen zur Förderung der Kulturarbeit gemäß § 96 BVFG in den Jahren 1991 und 1992 sowie die Fortschreibung des Aktionsprogramms des Bundesministeriums des Innern zur Förderung der deutschen Kultur des Ostens in den Jahren 1994 bis 1999,* Deutscher Bundestag: 4 December 1995.

Bundestagsdrucksache 13/3428, *Antwort der Bundesregierung auf die Kleine Anfrage der Abgeordneten Annelie Buntenbach und der Fraktion BÜNDNIS 90/DIE GRÜNEN—Drucksache 13/3344—Die deutsche Minderheit in Polen in der Politik der Bundesregierung,* Deutscher Bundestag: 4 January 1996.

Calleo, David P. *Legende und Wirklichkeit der deutschen Gefahr. Neue Aspekt zur Rolle Deutschlands in der Weltgesichte von Bismarck bis heute.* Bonn: Keil, 1980.

Charter of the German Expellees (Charta der deutschen Heimatvertriebenen). Bonn: Bund der Vertriebenen—Vereinigte Landsmannschaften und Landesverbände, 1995 [1950].

Cole, John, and Wolf, Eric R. *The Hidden Frontier.* New York and London: University of California Press, 1974.

Cordell, Karl. "Poland's German Minority." In *German Minorities in Europe: Ethnic Identity and National Belonging,* ed. Stefan Wolff. Oxford: Berghahn, 2000.

Cowan, Laing Gray. *France and the Saar, 1680–1948.* New York: Columbia University Press, 1950.

Deuerlein, Ernst. *Die Einheit Deutschlands: ihre Erörterung und Behandlung auf den Kriegs- und Nachkriegskonferenzen, 1941–1949.* Frankfurt am Main: Metzner, 1957.

Dijkink, Gertjan. *National Identity and Geopolitical Vision.* London: Routledge, 1996.

Doerr, Juergen C. *The Big Powers and the German Question, 1941–1990: A Selected Bibliographic Guide.* New York: Garland, 1992.

Dolinska, Xymena, and Falkowski, Mateusz. *Polen und Deutschland: Gegenseitige Wahrnehmung vor der Osterweiterung der Europäischen Union.* Warsaw: Institute of Public Affairs, 2001.

Donaldson, Bruce. "The German-speaking Minorty of Belgium." In *German Minorities in Europe: Ethnic Identity and Cultural Belonging,* ed. Stefan Wolff. New York and Oxford: Berghahn, 2000.

Ehard, Hans. *Bayerische Politik: Ansprachen und Reden des bayerischen Ministerpräsidenten.* München: Pflaum, 1952 [1947].

Eisfeld, A. "Zwischen Bleiben und Gehen: Die Deutschen in den Nach-folgestaaten der Sowjetunion." *Aus Politik und Zeitgeschichte,* no. 48 (1993), 44–52.

Fichte, Johann Gottlieb. *Reden an die deutsche Nation.* Leipzig: 1921 [1834].

Franco-German Declaration upon the Signing of the Saar Treaty (Gemeinsame deutsch-französische Erklärung aus Anlaß der Unterzeichnung des Vertrags zur Regelung der Saarfrage in Luxemburg am 27. Oktober 1956). Bonn: Bulletin des Presse- und Informationsamtes der Bundesregierung, 1949–1956.

Freymond, Jacques. *The Saar Conflict, 1945–1955.* London: Stevens, 1960.

Frischhof, Adolf. *Österreich und die Bürgerschaften seines Bestandes.* Vienna: 1869.

Fritsch-Bournazel, Renata. *Europa und die deutsche Einheit.* Bonn: Aktuell, 1990.

———. *Confronting the German Question: Germans on the East-West Divide.* Oxford: Berg, 1988.

Geiss, Immanuel. "Die deutsche Frage im internationalen System." In *Die deutsche Frage als internationales Problem,* ed. Hans-Jürgen Schröder. Stuttgart: Steiner, 1990.

Giddens, Anthony. *The Third Way.* Cambridge: Polity, 1998.

Gruber, Alfons. *Südtirol unter dem Faschismus.* Bozen/Bolzano: Athesia, 1975.

Gruner, Wolf D. *Die deutsche Frage: ein Problem der europäischen Geschichte seit 1800.* Munich: C. H. Beck, 1985.

Grünewald, Irmgard. *Die Elsass-Lothringer im Reich 1918–1933: ihre Organisationen zwischen Integration und 'Kampf um die Seele der Heimat.'* Frankfurt am Main: Peter Lang, 1984.

Heintze, Hans-Joachim. "The Status of German Minorities in Bilateral Agreements of the Federal Republic." In *German Minorities in Europe: Ethnic Identity and National Belonging,* ed. Stefan Wolff. Oxford and New York: Berghahn, 2000.

Hill, Werner, ed. *Befreiung durch Niederlage. Die deutsche Frage: Ursprung und Perspektiven.* Frankfurt am Main: Fischer Taschenbuch Verlag, 1986.

Hirsch, Helmut. *Die Saar in Versailles: die Saarfrage auf der Friedenskonferenz von 1919.* Bonn: L. Röhrscheid, 1952.

———. *Die Saar von Genf: die Saarfrage während des Völkerbundregimes von 1920–1935.* Bonn: L. Röhrscheid, 1954.

Hochfelder, Harry. "Über die Ziele sudetendeutscher Politik." In *Die Sudetendeutschen und ihre Heimat. Erbe—Auftrag—Ziel,* ed. Rolf-Josef Eibicht. Wesseding: Gesamtdeutscher Verlag, 1991.

Hubatsch, Walther. *Die deutsche Frage.* Würzburg: A. G. Ploetz, 1961.

Hudemann, Rainer. "Die Saar zwischen Frankreich und Deutschland 1945–1947." In *Die Saar 1945–1955,* ed. Rainer Hudemann and Raymond Poidevin. Munich: Oldenbourg, 1995.

Ignatieff, Michael. *Blood and Belonging,* London: Vintage, 1994.

Ipsen, Knut. "Minderheitenschutz auf reziproker Basis: die deutsch-dänische Lösung." In *Selbsbestimmungsrecht der Völker: Herausforderung der Staatenwelt,* ed. Hans Joachim Heintze. Bonn: Dietz, 1997.

Jaworski, Rudolf. "Die Sudetendeutschen als Minderheit in der Tschechoslowakei 1918–1938." In *Die Vertreibung der Deutschen aus dem Osten. Ursachen, Ereignisse, Folgen,* ed. Wolfgang Benz. Frankfurt am Main: Fischer, 1986.

Kaiser, Karl. *Deutschlands Vereinigung: die internationalen Aspekte mit den wichtigen Dokumenten.* Bergisch Gladbach: Lübbe, 1991.

Kettenacker, Lothar. *Nationalsozialistische Volkstumspolitik im Elsaß.* Stuttgart: Deutsche Verlags-Anstalt, 1973.

Klekowski von Koppenfels, Amanda. "The Decline of Privilege: The Legal Background to the Migration of Ethnic Germans." In *Coming Home to Germany? The Integration of Ethnic Germans from Central and Eastern Europe in the Federal Republic,* ed. David Rock and Stefan Wolff. New York and Oxford: Berghahn, 2002.

Köcher, Renate. "Vertriebene der Erlebnis-und Nachfolgegeneration. Ergebnisse einer Sekundäranalyse." *Deutschland und seine Nachbarn. Forum für Kultur und Politik* (1997), 21.

Komjathy, Anthony Tihamer, and Stockwell, Rebecca. *German Minorities and the Third Reich: Ethnic Germans of East Central Europe between the Wars.* New York: Holmes and Meier, 1980.

Korte, Karl-Rudolf. Der Standort der Deutschen: Akzentverlagerungen der deutschen Frage in der Bundesrepublik Deutschland seit den siebziger Jahren. Cologne: Verlag Wissenschaft und Politik, 1990.

Kraus, Albert H. V. *Die Saarfrage (1945–1955) in der Publizistik: die Diskussion um das Saarstatut vom 23.10.1954 und sein Scheitern in der deutschen, saarländischen und französischen Presse.* Saarbrücken: Verlag Die Mitte, 1988.

Krekeler, Norbert. *Revisionsanspruch und geheime Ostpolitik der Weimarer Republik. Die Subventionierung der deutschen Minderheit in Polen 1919–1933.* Stuttgart: Deutsche Verlags-Anstalt, 1973.

Krüger, Hans. "Leitartikel in der Erstausgabe des Deutschen Ostdiensts." Originally published in 1958. Reprinted in *DoD* 40, no. 1/2, 9 January 1998.

Larres, Klaus. *Politik der Illusionen: Churchill, Eisenhower und die deutsche Frage.* Göttingen: Vandenhoeck and Ruprecht, 1995.

Lijphart, Arend. *Democracy in Plural Societies.* New Haven, Conn.: Yale University Press, 1977.

Ludwig, Michael. *Polen und die deutsche Frage.* Bonn: Forschungsinstitut der deutschen Gesellschaft für Auswärtige Politik, 1990.

Lumans, Valdis O. *Himmler's Auxiliaries: The Volksdeutsche Mittelstelle and the German National Minorities of Europe, 1933–1945.* Chapel Hill: University of North Carolina Press, 1993.

Marcus, Lucy P. "The Carpathian Germans." In *German Minorities in Europe: Ethnic Identity and National Belonging*, ed. Stefan Wolff. Oxford and New York: Berghahn, 2000.

Martin, Bernd. "Das Reich als Republik. Auf der Suche nach der verlorenen Größe." In *Deutschland in Europa. Ein historischer Rückblick*, ed. Bernd Martin. Munich: Deutscher Taschenbuch-Verlag, 1992.

Minnerup, Günter. *The German Question after the Cold War.* London: Pinter, 1992.

Moore, Margaret. "The Territorial Dimension of Self-Determination." In *National Self-Determination and Secession*, ed. Margaret Moore. Oxford: Oxford University Press, 1998.

Naimark, Norman M. *Fires of Hatred: Ethnic Cleansing in Twentieth-Century Europe.* Cambridge, Mass.: Harvard University Press, 2001.

Pedersen, Karen Margrethe. "A National Minority with a Transethnic Identity: The German Minority in Denmark." In *German Minorities in Europe: Ethnic Identity and Cultural Belonging*, ed. Stefan Wolff. New York and Oxford: Berghahn, 2000.

Pohlmann, Ulrich. *Die Saarfrage und die Alliierten 1942–1948.* Frankfurt am Main: Peter Lang, 1992.

Renner, Karl. *Das Selbstbestimmungsrecht der Nationen in besonderer Anwendung auf Österreich.* Leipzig: 1918.

Röpke, Wilhelm. *The German Question.* London: Allen and Unwin, 1946.

Rothenberger, Karl-Heinz. *Die elsass-lothringische Heimat- und Autonomiebewegung zwischen den beiden Weltkriegen.* Frankfurt am Main: Peter Lang, 1976.

Sander, Michael. "Die Verfassung des Saarlandes: Politische Planung und politischer Erfolg Frankreichs." In *Die Saar 1945–1955*, ed. Rainer Hudemann and Raymond Poidevin. Munich: Oldenbourg, 1995.

Schmidt, Robert H. *Saarpolitik 1945–57.* Berlin: Duncker and Humblot, 1959.

Schnürch, Roland. "Konsequenzen sudetendeutscher Heimatpolitik." In *Die Sudetendeutschen und ihre Heimat. Erbe—Auftrag—Ziel.* ed. Rolf-Josef Eibicht. Wesseding: Gesamtdeutscher Verlag, 1991.

Schulz, Eberhard. *Die deutsche Frage und die Nachbarn im Osten: Beiträge zu einer Politik der Verständigung.* Munich: Oldenbourg, 1989.

Schulze, Rainer. "The Struggle of Past and Present in Individual Identities: The Case of German Refugees and Expellees from the East." In *Coming Home to Germany? The Integration of Ethnic Germans from Central and Eastern Europe in the Federal Republic*, ed. David Rock and Stefan Wolff. New York and Oxford: Berghahn, 2002.

Smith, Anthony. *Nationalism in the Twentieth Century.* New York: New York University Press, 1979.

Smyser, W. R. *From Yalta to Berlin: The Cold War Struggle over Germany.* New York: St. Martin's Press, 1999.

Sowden, John Kenneth. *The German Question 1945–1973: Continuity in Change.* London: Crosby Lockwood Staples, 1975.

Steinbach, Erika. "Vertriebene, Aussiedler und deutsche Minderheiten sind eine Brücke zwischen den Deutschen und ihren östlichen Nachbarn." Contribution to Debate in the German Bundestag. 28 May 1998. Bundestagsdrucksache 13/10845.

Stevenson, Patrick. "The Ethnolinguistic Vitality of German-Speaking Communities in Central Europe." In *German Minorities in Europe: Ethnic Identity and Cultural Belonging*, ed. Stefan Wolff. New York and Oxford: Berghahn, 2000.

Stricker, Gerd. "Ethnic Germans in Russia and the Former Soviet Union." In *German Minorities in Europe: Ethnic Identity and National Belonging*, ed. Stefan Wolff. Oxford and New York: Berghahn, 2000.

Ther, Philip. "Expellee Policy in the Soviet-Occupied Zone and the GDR, 1945–1953." In *Coming Home to Germany? The Integration of Ethnic Germans from Central and Eastern Europe in the Federal Republic*, ed. David Rock and Stefan Wolff. New York and Oxford: Berghahn, 2002.

Trouillet, Bernard. *Das Elsass—Grenzland in Europa.* Weinheim: Beltz, 1997.

Ulbricht, Walter. "Die Maßnahmen unserer Regierung haben den Frieden in Europa und in der Welt gerettet." Address on East German Television. 13 August 1961. (http://www.trend.partisan.net/trd7801/t167801.html)

UN Commission on Human Rights. "Human Rights and Population Transfer. Final Report of the Special Rapporteur, Mr. Al-Khasawneh." (E/CN.4/Sub.2/1997/23).

United Nations General Assembly. *Resolution 3236 of 22 November 1974 on the Question of Palestine* (A/RES/3236 (XXIX).

Verheyen, Dirk. *The German Question: A Cultural, Historical and Geopolitical Exploration.* Boulder, Colo.: Westview Press, 1991.

Wagner, Richard. "Ethnic Germans in Romania." In *German Minorities in Europe: Ethnic Identity and Cultural Belonging*, ed. Stefan Wolff. New York and Oxford: Berghahn, 2000.

Weber, Max. *Wirtschaft und Gesellschaft.* Tübingen: Mohr, 1972 [1919].

Wolff, Stefan. *Disputed Territories: The Transnational Dynamics of Ethnic Conflict Settlement.* New York and Oxford: Berghahn, 2002.

Zeman, Miloš and Verheugen, Günter. "Joint Press Statement of Prime Minister Zeman and EU Commissioner Verheugen." Prague 11 April 2002 (http://www.czechembassy.org/wwwo/mzv/default.asp?id=11191&ido=6569&idj=2&amb=1)

Index

About the Author

STEFAN WOLFF is Reader in German Studies at the University of Bath. He is the author of *Disputed Territories: The Transnational Dynamics of Ethnic Conflict Settlement* (2002) and co-editor, with Jorg Neuheiser, of *Peace at Last? The Impact of the Good Friday Agreement on Northern Ireland* (2002).